CRIME AND SECURITY: MANAGING THE RISK TO SAFE SHOPPING

Adrian Beck
Andrew Willis

Perpetuity Press

Perpetuity Press
PO Box 376
Leicester LE2 3ZZ
First published 1995

A catalogue reference for this book is available from the British Library

ISBN 1 899287 04 3

Printed by R & G Design Ltd, Leicester

Perpetuity Press

Contents

Acknowledgements

The initial impetus for this book came from the British Retail Consortium (BRC) which has taken a lead role in investigating the costs of crime to the retail community, not least by the establishment of the Retail Crime Initiative. The initiative is building up an authoritative database on the extent of retail crime whilst at the same time signalling a determination to tackle it. The *Retail Crime Costs 1992/93 Survey* was a pioneering step in understanding the dimensions of retail crime and was followed by a similar survey in 1993–94.

The Retail Crime Initiative then commissioned further and more detailed research into the specific problems of crime and nuisance in town centres and shopping centres – two very different types of shopping environment. This project and its findings constitute the empirical dimension of this book. The research explores the types and extent of crime and nuisance problems, as well as the best ways to respond to them. It is unique in that it makes use of the views of customers in town centres and shopping centres, as well as the views of those with responsibility for managing town centres and shopping centres. The study constitutes the only comparative analysis of crime and nuisance in town centres and shopping centres; and, more importantly, it reviews the implications for crime control strategies.

The authors would like to express their thanks to the British Retail Consortium for providing the impetus and funding for the research. Particular thanks are due to Martin Speed, then of the Retail Crime Initiative, for his invaluable assistance at all stages of the project; and to John Burrows, of Morgan Harris Burrows, who acted as lead consultant for the Retail Crime Initiative, for commenting on an early draft and suggesting further lines of enquiry. Our thanks also go to the Association of Town Centre Management, especially their then Chairman, Michael Stansbury, and to the British Council of Shopping Centres, especially their President, Roger Groom, and his colleagues Ray Hoof, David McEnhill and Penrhyn Peach. Without their considerable support it would have not been possible to carry out the surveys.

We must acknowledge our indebtedness to the town-centre managers and shopping-centre managers, as well as those members of the shopping public who so readily provided answers to our questions, together with a great deal of additional unsolicited information; and to our senior research associate Robert Nathan, and to our research assistants Robert Field, Fiona Jones, Andrea Norfolk, Matthew Toye and Carolyn Young for their efforts in collecting and processing the data.

As soon as we had assembled the raw figures, it became apparent that the findings had specific security implications for both town centres and shopping centres, but that there were also broader risk management implications for the wider retail community. We are grateful to Dr Martin Gill of the University of Leicester, Centre for the Study of Public Order, for encouraging us to use the findings to explore the wider contours of 'safe shopping', as well as for his considerable editorial assistance.

We are grateful to Tina and Victoria for their forbearance in accommodating our over-long and over-involved examination of the threats to safe shopping, when they would have much preferred to have been engaged in its practice. We have been reminded that although survey methodologies have much to commend them, there are useful alternatives – such as participant observation!

Finally, we must stress that the views expressed are our own. They do not necessarily reflect those of the British Retail Consortium, the Association of Town Centre Management or the British Council of Shopping Centres, although we would hope that they will find them useful in promoting a crime-free and nuisance-free retail sector – which is in the interests of both the retailers and the shopping public. We shall be delighted if the research is used to inform 'best practice' in retail security management, but we take full responsibility for any shortcomings, errors and omissions.

1   Crime and Nuisance
       in Context

This book seeks to explore a neglected aspect of criminal victimisation –
the various threats to safe shopping – and in so doing to open a new
dimension in criminological study. Particular attention is given to a comparison between the crime and nuisance threats in two retail environments
– the traditional town centre (the high street) and the nearby shopping
centre or shopping mall. The crime prevention and risk management
implications of the findings are discussed throughout, with a particular
focus on the use and effectiveness of security measures – such as conventional policing, private security guards, closed circuit television
(CCTV) and security shutters, as well as town-centre and shopping-centre
man-agers' views about crime prevention priorities. Whenever possible,
the discussion and analysis moves beyond the bounds of town centres and
shopping centres to draw out the wider implications for 'safe shopping'.
Some readers may care to start by turning to the concluding chapter. This
can be read either as an overview of the findings and their significance or
as a preview which might direct attention to chapters of special interest.
The reader who proceeds chapter by chapter will find that the book is
structured around a number of interrelated themes.

Overview

A major component of the book is the data derived from a 1994 survey
commissioned by the Retail Crime Initiative of the British Retail
Consortium (BRC). The survey, which was the first of its kind, involved
face-to-face interviews with four sets of respondents – a systematic random sample of 334 town-centre shoppers and 288 comparable shoppers in
nearby shopping centres, drawn from six towns and cities in England; and
samples of 40 town-centre managers and 161 shopping-centre managers

throughout England, Wales and Scotland. This survey was one part of the BRC's expanding contribution to creating a comprehensive knowledge base about retail crime. The findings have not been presented elsewhere.

The specific intention was to make comparisons between perceptions of crime and nuisance in two different retail environments using the views of both shoppers and town-centre or shopping-centre managers. These can be seen as parallel indicators of the size and nature of the crime and nuisance problems in each environment. The views of the shopping public were solicited on the grounds that if they believed that the shopping environment was badly affected by crime or nuisance (whether or not this belief was correct) this could impact adversely on their shopping behaviour. They might prefer to take their custom elsewhere, to a 'safer' shopping location. Conversely, to the extent that they perceived the town centre or the shopping centre as offering a safe and secure place in which to shop, they would be inclined to continue shopping in that environment. The views of the town-centre and shopping-centre managers were sought in order to provide a rather more informed perspective on the crime and nuisance threats to safe shopping. The managers were also invited to comment on a range of existing and possible security options, such as uniformed guards or police officers on patrol and security hardware, including CCTV and security shutters. The views of both shoppers and managers were used to bring out the crime control implications.

The findings can be seen as a 'stand alone' contribution to understanding crime and nuisance in town centres and shopping centres. Major differences are identified in the nature and extent of the threats to safe shopping in the two environments, and there are similar differences in the value which town-centre and shopping-centre managers attach to, and the way they use, security measures in the two locations. At this level, there is an intriguing contrast between the crime and nuisance problems and their solutions in two retail environments. The data are of obvious interest to all those with an interest in these areas – owners, retailers and managers, as well as those with responsibilities for policing, private security, planning and commercial development. The study was undertaken at the request of the British Retail Consortium and the findings are directed particularly to the Association of Town Centre Management (ATCM) and the British Council of Shopping Centres (BCSC). The findings are timely in that they relate directly to the current debates about the future of high-street shopping, including the interest of the House of Commons Environment Committee (House of Commons, 1994).

In addition, although the data from the survey sponsored by the BRC's Retail Crime Initiative and the comparisons between the two shopping environments comprise the key findings, these cannot be divorced from the wider context of retailing and its security. Any differences in the threats to safe shopping and the approaches to security between high streets and shopping centres need to be located within the broader framework of the changing nature of retailing – especially the rise of the superstore, the increase in mall-type facilities and the move to out-of-town shopping, with all that these imply for the traditional high street. It is also important to review the studies to date of the various crime and nuisance threats to safe shopping – and to explore, with the added benefit of the current data, the ways in which shoppers' perceptions of the fear of crime can have behavioural consequences, not least in prompting them to avoid those areas which are seen to be unsafe or unsavoury. The general data suggest that the perceived threats of crime and nuisance do lead to 'avoidance behaviour'; and the specific findings highlight the fact that town centres are seen to be far more crime-prone and nuisance-prone than shopping centres, with clear consequences in terms of how the shopping public responds. The study confirms the general impact of crime and the fear of crime on shopping behaviour, but also makes clear that there are different risks, different perceived threats and different consequences for town centres and shopping centres.

Setting the findings in the wider context requires the presentation of additional information. This has been drawn from a wide variety of sources, including previous academic research such as the Home Office Crime Prevention Unit reports. More importantly, the analysis draws on a considerable amount of material which has been produced by the various agencies and organisations that exist to serve the needs of both the retailers and their shoppers – such as the British Retail Consortium and, more specifically, the Association of Town Centre Management (ATCM) and the British Council of Shopping Centres (BCSC). There is also a rich vein of information to be tapped in the various professional associations which represent the interests of the security industry, such as the British Security Industry Association (BSIA) and the International Professional Security Association (IPSA). Finally, government is taking an increasing interest in the future shape of the retail environment. This is most apparent in the work of the House of Commons Environment Committee and its recent report on the future of shopping centres (House of Commons, 1994), as well as in a parallel inquiry into the private security industry undertaken by the House of Commons Select Committee on Home Affairs (House of Commons, 1995a and 1995b).

All of these sources offer valuable data, together with interesting (and often conflicting) views about how safety and security in shopping can best be promoted, but they have not as yet been brought together into a coherent whole, let alone been subject to critical assessment. Alongside the presentation of key findings from the current town-centre and shopping-centre research, there is a parallel aim to review and analyse the limited data from previous studies in these areas, together with relevant commentaries from academic and professional sources; all of which can be used to extend the knowledge base for a systematic examination of how best to manage the risks to safe shopping.

In line with the expectations derived from previous studies, the substantive research in town centres and shopping centres confirmed that crime, nuisance and pollution operated as a disincentive to the shopping public. But the distributions of actual victimisation, fear of crime and avoidance reactions were unexpectedly very different in the two shopping environments. Town-centre managers and the shopping public in the high street were far more concerned about the threats to safe shopping than were shopping-centre managers and customers in the shopping malls. These differences were substantial.

An unexpected finding was that there were significant differences with regard to the deployment of manned security services in the two shopping environments. Town-centre security was largely predicated on conventional policing, but in the shopping centres the 'bobby on the beat' had given way to the private security guard – and the latter was seen to be both effective and acceptable. This finding has wider implications because it shows that at the same time as government is actively re-assessing the core and ancillary tasks of conventional policing – in effect, adjusting the balance between public policing and private security – in one major part of the national economy this has already been accomplished. The findings offer strong evidence for the so-called 'privatisation of policing' – and this merits an extended discussion of the implications for residual public sector policing in town centres and new-style private security in shopping centres. The discussion explores the advantages and disadvantages of both models and reviews the interest in the regulation of the private security industry shown by the House of Commons Select Committee on Home Affairs. The irony here is that where the national debate is couched mostly in terms of what could or should happen in the future, the evidence from the shopping mall is that it has already taken place, so that the shopping centre offers a case study of the privatisation of security services on a large scale.

Equally impressive data emerged on the use of closed circuit television (CCTV). In both retail environments the use of CCTV was widespread. It commanded the near-unanimous support of the shopping public as an acceptable measure and it was seen by town-centre and shopping-centre managers to be a highly effective crime prevention option. This prompted a more general exploration of the use and deployment of CCTV systems, which brought out a striking fact. There is no doubt about the huge growth in the use of CCTV in public places, especially town centres, but its seemingly exponential expansion appears to be inversely related to what is known about its actual crime control capabilities. A great deal appears to be taken on trust and there is little or no evaluation of the effectiveness of such systems. The burgeoning use of CCTV appears to be a product of its seductive appeal as a 'high-tech fix', where a strong – albeit ill-founded – belief about its value in controlling crime is all that is necessary to secure its deployment. This is seen as an example of 'security wish fulfilment'. The discussion moves beyond the immediate confines of town centres and shopping centres to examine in detail what is required to confirm or disprove the crime control potential of closed circuit television.

Finally, as regards the use of security shutters in town centres, both town-centre managers and the shopping public see them to be an effective security option and yet one which massively blights and disfigures the 'look and feel' of the town centres. Security is being purchased at the cost of aesthetic degradation. Again, this finding can be taken on its own; but the discussion proceeds to use it as a case study in attempting to reconcile legitimate demands for security against countervailing considerations for sympathetic town-centre development.

In all of these cases the source material from the Retail Crime Initiative study is used as an empirical platform from which to launch a wider discussion of major themes in retail security: the near-universal use of private security guards in one shopping environment; the mostly unchallenged and uncharted 'rise and rise' of CCTV, especially in public places; and the problem of balancing retailers' security needs and more general town-centre planning considerations.

Different readers will approach the book in different ways. Those with a professional interest in town-centre management or security in shopping centres will be most attracted to the retail environment-specific findings. Others will wish to set these data in the wider context of the changing face of retailing and the ways in which shoppers' perceptions of risk can impact on shopping behaviour. And the broader review of the very substantial increase in the use of private security guards and the installation of CCTV systems will attract those with specialised interests or responsibilities in these areas. Each of these approaches is valid, although the authors hope that the reader who approaches the text from one perspective will also gain from the associated findings; and that all readers will recognise the underlying common denominator – the safety and security of the shopping public.

Breaking boundaries

This approach seeks to broaden and deepen the boundaries of contemporary criminology, of which there are a number of well-founded criticisms. There is an unfortunate tendency for the discipline to ignore collective criminal victimisation in favour of studying crimes against the person and his or her property. There is also some reluctance to combine the study of crime with an analysis of the ways in which it might best be controlled. Finally, there is a marked disinclination to look upon the contribution of anything other than the 'official' agents of social control (the police, the courts and prisons) as either legitimate or useful in tackling the problems of crime.

Criminology is a young and incomplete discipline. Its contemporary origins can be traced to the seemingly inexorable rise in reported crime since the 1950s and the perceived need for a social policy response to it. One of the most recent and comprehensive collections of papers, *The Oxford Handbook of Criminology* (Maguire et al, 1994), indicates very clearly that after 50 years the academic study of crime in this country is overwhelmingly focused on conventional offences against property and the person – theft, burglary and interpersonal violence; and on the measurement of the incidence and prevalence of these activities, together with appropriate theoretical explanations. Victimisation is largely construed in terms of the individual and his or her personal property or personal safety.

Only a modest proportion of the literature involves the study of business-related crime and financial offences such as fraud. Although the corporate victim is beginning to be studied, the collective victim – such as the shopper – is conspicuously absent. The focus is more on the individual victim and his or her property than on the contexts in which victimisation occurs. The various sweeps of the British Crime Survey are indicative of this trend – a massive research effort to uncover the 'real' extent of crime through so-called victimisation surveys, but ones which concentrate almost exclusively on property crime and crimes against the person in and around the respondent's household (see Mayhew et al, 1993 and 1994 for the most recent examples). These studies are far from unimportant, but the perspective is too narrow, excluding as it does great swathes of victimisation. Even the prestigious 130 and more volumes of the supposedly policy-oriented *Home Office Research Study* series contain not a single contribution which addresses crime control in the retail context.

The balance is being redressed, albeit slowly. One example of the changing orientation is a recent volume *Crime at Work* (Gill, 1994), a collection of empirical studies of business, commercial and retail crime – including burglary and ram-raids on retail outlets, violence against retail staff and the terrorist threat to safe shopping. As the editor put it succinctly in the introduction, at the planning stage and during discussions with a security professional, the comment which confirmed the intention to commission contributions in a mostly unexplored field was 'What have you criminologists being doing all these years?' The present volume seeks to extend this new interest by focusing on the shopper-as-victim, and to do so in relation to different types of retail environment – the town centre and the shopping centre.

Conventional criminology also tends to focus either on the phenomenon of crime or on the social response to it. Only very rarely is an explicit connection made between the two. Indeed the academic commentators tend to define themselves as specialists in either criminology or penology. The former study the extent and causes of crime and offer theoretical explanations for it. The latter are more concerned with criminal justice and the ways in which the social reaction to criminality can best be organised in order to minimise its baleful effects and to maximise the ways in which offenders can be dissuaded from continuing their criminal activities. For example, the *Oxford Handbook of Criminology* (Maguire et al, 1994) deals separately with the themes of crime and its causation and crime control and criminal justice.

There are, however, some notable exceptions to this general tendency. The Home Office has published some 60 papers in the *Crime Prevention Unit Series* and, more recently, the *Crime Detection and Prevention Series*. These all adopt a decidedly practical approach to crime prevention strategies and a number focus explicitly on the retail sector. These include much that is relevant to the present study. The recent volume edited by Gill (1994) is also important, with retail-specific chapters on CCTV, electronic activated alarms (EAS or tags) and security shutters.

There is then an emerging literature on managing the criminal threat to safe shopping, which the present volume seeks to extend. The underlying premise is that criminology is best understood as an applied academic discipline. It should focus on real problems in the real world and the effort to 'understanding' can only be seen to be of value if it impacts on the 'policy' responses to a particular problem. To date there has been a rather general tendency to fight shy of elaborating what the social control implications of any particular study might be and how they could best be implemented, especially with regard to anything so prosaic as safe shopping!

Finally, the book seeks to make a contribution to the emerging field of studies in retail crime and to put particular emphasis on the ways in which empirical investigations can generate useful conclusions for crime risk management. This means that the intended audience is broader than conventional academic readers and includes those who take responsibility for managing and promoting a crime-free shopping environment: the retailers themselves, those who are employed to manage the retail environment (town-centre and shopping-centre managers), law enforcement agencies and those who are contracted-in to offer specific security services (eg uniformed guards) or to provide security hardware (eg CCTV).

A balance needs to be struck between 'understanding' and 'controlling' crime (where the former is a necessary condition for the latter, which reflects the overall purpose), and the whole concept of control needs to be re-defined to include both the provision of manned security services and the installation of security equipment – a major new dimension. The best estimates of the size of the private security industry from the British Security Industry Association (1994a and 1994b and see Chapter 5) suggest that the overall market is of the order of £2.8 billion a year, including the electronics sector (intruder alarms, CCTV and access control) and the guarding sector – which alone embraces some 1,280 companies with a turnover of £1 billion and around 80,000 employees. These latter figures compare with some 154,000 police officers in the police forces of the United Kingdom (Benyon et al, 1994 and 1995) at an annual cost of around £7 billion (Home Office, 1994a). Thus the private security industry, in terms of numbers, employs slightly over one-half as many persons as does public sector policing, and, in terms of expenditure, costs around 40 per cent as much. The image of law enforcement as a function exclusively of public policing no longer reflects the reality of crime control. The provision of private security, some of which impacts directly on the retail environment, is already of significant proportions (and growing by about 6 per cent a year) but remains a mostly unexplored area. Any investigation of crime in the retail context, especially one focusing on managing the risk to safe shopping, cannot but include an analysis of the contribution from this sector.

The aim in this volume is not to reject the traditional aims of criminological research but to extend them, and to do so in such a way that understanding crime can have real-life implications for its successful control – and to do so in a new area, that of the criminal and other threats to safe shopping. This is not an awkward compromise between two different endeavours, but a natural extension from one to the other. The new-style focus on the criminal threat to safe shopping and its control, however, requires some preliminary observations about the context of the study, the ways in which crime is conceptualised for present purposes and then made subject to empirical investigation.

The changing face of retailing

The routine and everyday connotation of the word 'shopping' obscures both its complexity and its importance. The retail sector is one of the largest and most dynamic parts of the United Kingdom's economy, although even recent commentaries fail to provide comprehensive and coherent data (Cahill, 1994; Guy, 1994). The best figures suggest that in 1992 retailing contributed 14 per cent of the nation's gross domestic product (GDP) and that over two million persons or 9 per cent of the British workforce was employed in retailing and distribution (O'Brien and Harris, 1991; House of Commons, 1994). It is also one of the fastest-changing parts of the economy which makes it all the more difficult to understand the complex problems of crime and nuisance within it, including the retailer-as-victim and the shopper-at-risk. The emerging profile of retail crime has to be seen against the back-drop of new forms of retailing.

Between 1945 and the mid-1990s the total number of retail outlets in Britain declined from over 500,000 to around 300,000 – a reduction of 40 per cent. There has also been an increasing concentration of total retail turnover in businesses with multiple rather than single outlets. In 1992–93 of a total UK retail turnover of £123.5 billion, retail businesses with 10 or more outlets, whilst only accounting for some 0.5 per cent of the number of concerns, generated over 60 per cent of total sales (Burrows, 1993; Burrows and Speed, 1994). In 1982 more than 2.3 million people worked in the British retail industry, the majority in small shops. By 1994 there were 300,000 fewer retail employees and the small shop had all but disappeared, 103,000 out of 188,000 having closed in twenty years. From another perspective, two-thirds of all the retail space occupied in the past 30 years has been developed in just 200 locations (Vidal, 1994).

Three interrelated factors are behind the changing face of retailing: the introduction of the supermarket or large single store; the creation of shopping centres in towns and cities – a collection of shops within a single, covered, purpose-built area; and the emergence of out-of-town retail parks or shopping centres on an even larger scale on green-field sites (Crossley and Murray, 1993). One commentator has called this the 'Americanisation' of British shopping (Poole, 1991). The opposite side of this coin is the threatened decline of the traditional high street.

The rise of superstores, shopping centres and retail parks

The first grocery superstore of more than 25,000 sq ft opened in 1964; there are now around 750 and there may be over 1,000 by 1996. The grocery trade is now dominated by just five multiple retailers – Argyll (Safeway and others), Asda, J. Sainsbury, Somerfield (Gateway) and Tesco. These stores have seen a rapid rise in their total market share of food and convenience-goods sales – from under 9 per cent in 1980 to over 50 per cent by 1990; and a marked shift to out-of-centre locations (Hamilton and Bernoth, 1994; House of Commons, 1994; Vidal, 1994). The two leaders, J. Sainsbury and Tesco, have a combined market capitalisation of £12 billion and annual sales of around £20 billion, about one-third of the market (Bernoth, 1995a). Sainsbury's attracts over three million shoppers a week and is planning to spend £650 million in the current year on opening 12 new supermarkets and remodelling 80 existing stores (Bagnall, 1995a). Tesco is planning to open 24 new stores in 1995, creating 4,000 full-time jobs (Cowe, 1995a). In 1983 there were 1,270 superstores of all types in Britain which took up 8.6 per cent of the retail space. By 1992 there were 3,500 such stores and they accounted for 19 per cent of retail space (Spillius, 1994). Supermarket stores alone had grown from around 300 in the early 1980s to over 900 in the mid-1990s – a growth of 200 per cent. And out-of-town sites accounted for well over three-quarters of all sales – Sainsbury's (72%), Safeway (84%) and Tesco (87%) (Erlichman, 1995).

By the mid-1990s competition between the big five market leaders was steadily intensifying. By early 1995 Tesco had launched a discount card scheme, Sainsbury and Safeway had tested so-called 'loyalty cards', and Safeway and Asda were poised to do so (Bernoth, 1995b; Gilchrist, 1995a; Mitchell, 1995a). It is as yet unclear whether the primary motivation of these schemes was to promote and retain customer loyalty (competition for customers by another name) or whether it was a form of payment to customers for handing over crucial marketing information about shopping habits, or both. There are fears that a food price war is being waged between supermarket chains so as to 'de-stabilise' the food market, with the prospect in the foreseeable future of increased competition and pressure on margins (Victor and Skipworth, 1993; Bernoth, 1994a; Clark, 1994; Dolan and Sivell, 1995). Early evidence suggested that the Tesco scheme attracted five million signed-up customers and that sales increased by over 4 per cent (Cowe, 1995a). The current battle for market share also extends to the provision of improved services for customers, such as crèches, baby-changing facilities and customer service desks – together with initiatives promising shorter queues at the checkouts, such as the 'One in Front' campaign by Tesco (Gilchrist, 1995b). A similar 'courtesy crusade' by J. Sainsbury is thought to be costing around £20 million a year, together with increases in the annual £16 million advertising spend (Bagnall, 1995b).

There is also increasing evidence that major supermarkets are promoting customer loyalty and their own credibility by offering so-called sub-brands – high quality, own-label merchandise in competition with traditional mega-brands or established market leaders. Sainsbury's, for example, has had considerable success with its Classic Cola and this has been followed with similar initiatives in ice cream, wine, beer, nappies and baby food (Mitchell, 1995b). And the steady rise of supermarket shopping is associated with a new form of purchasing – through debit cards – with 59 per cent of this 'electronic spending' taking place in supermarkets or garages (Thomas, 1995). In total there are 807 million transactions a year to a value of £22 billion and growth of 25 per cent a year.

Finally, the grocery superstore is now generating a new architectural vocabulary. For example, the new store for J. Sainsbury in Plymouth, designed by Jeremy Dixon and Edward Jones, architects of the Royal Opera House's extension, has a monumental entrance canopy of 11 twisted steel-lattice geometrical sails which has been described as belonging ideologically to the 'soft humane ... school of modernism' (Pearman, 1995). If the traditional corner shop has given way to the supermarket 'shed', the latter is now being transformed into a lavish 'civic amenity'.

The first shopping centres opened in Birmingham, Crawley, West Sussex and at the Elephant and Castle in London in 1964. Some 30 years later there are nearly 1,000 such complexes – five times as many as in 1972 and almost all of them away from town centres (Poole, 1991; Department of the Environment – URBED, 1994; Vidal, 1994). In 1982 over three-quarters of shopping centres were located in the middle of towns but by 1994 the proportion had fallen to 59 per cent. Shopping centres now account for 15 per cent of the UK's total retail space. In western Europe, 431 million sq ft of purpose-built shopping-centre floorspace has been built in the last three decades, most of it in Britain, France and Germany. The number of shopping centres rose from 1,372 in 1984 to 2,326 in 1993 – an increase of 70 per cent; and the number may double over the next ten years (*The Economist*, 4th March, 1995).

The first out-of-town retail park opened in 1982 and within 10 years there were 260 such parks, with another 173 similar, mall-type complexes to be found on edge-of-town sites. Brent Cross is regarded as the prototype and set the standard in 1976, to be followed by four other 'giants' – MetroCentre in Gateshead, Meadowhall in Sheffield, Lakeside in Thurrock, Essex and Merry Hill in the West Midlands (Crossley and Murray, 1993). There are plans for others, some of which are being vigorously opposed, near Bristol, Cambridge, Dartford, Leeds, Liverpool, Ludlow and Manchester (Warman, 1995). A 1994 survey by consultants DTZ Debenham Thorpe found that the three 'green-field malls' of Meadowhall, MetroCentre and Merry Hill had displaced London's Oxford Street as the country's busiest trading locations, because customers were choosing the convenience of the malls over the hassles of the high street (Rogers, 1994; *The Times*, 16th June, 1995). The Lakeside complex is valued at £454 million and 100,000 customers pass through the doors on a Saturday, each with an average £100 to spend – creating a one-day turnover of £10 million.

The MetroCentre, Europe's largest covered shopping centre, offers a case study in the rise of this form of retailing (Gledhill and Wilkinson, 1995; Hawkes, 1995a). The 120 acre site, formerly a dump for power station ash, was bought for £100,000 in 1979 and then jointly developed at a cost of £200 million by Cameron Hall and the Church Commissioners. It now offers 2.2 million sq ft of retailing space with some 350 shops and tenancies, together with Europe's largest indoor theme park, a multi-screen cinema, restaurants and a bowling alley. During the 1994 Christmas trading period 160,000 people a day visited the centre and around 100,000 shoppers visit each Sunday. In 1994 it had an annual income of £20 million and was valued at £200 million. Some 8,000 coaches roll up every year and the centre attracted 27.8 million shoppers in 1994. Annual rental income is expected to reach £30 million by the late 1990s. In February 1995 the centre was offered for sale and analysts predicted it could be worth up to £500 million, although Capital Shopping Centres (CSC) subsequently secured exclusive negotiating rights and bought the centre for £325 million in July. The sale was regarded as the largest single property transaction ever agreed in the UK (Mortished, 1995).

The Merry Hill complex, which opened in 1989, is another well known example. It has 1.4 million sq ft of sales space and employs 3,400 people, two-thirds employed on a part-time or casual basis. It is seen as the prime tourist attraction in the West Midlands and caters for nearly 3,000 coaches a year. It attracts between 50,000 and 70,000 visitors a day – around 22 million shoppers a year. Visitors spend an average of £42 per head and total sales have reached £350 million a year (Crossley and Murray, 1993; Joseph, 1993). By late 1994 Chelsfield, the property group which owns Merry Hill, had filed planning bids for a 650,000 sq ft extension which would transform it into one of the biggest centres in the country. The company plans to invest up to £100 million and create 2,000 permanent new jobs. The complex was then valued at £200 million – a 40 per cent increase on the purchase price of £121 million in 1993 (Mortished, 1994).

Figures from Verdict, a retail consultancy, show that more than one-quarter of retail sales are now made in out-of-town centres, compared with less than 5 per cent in the early 1980s, even though well over three-quarters of the total shopping space is still concentrated in town centres (Hobson, 1995). The 1994 report from the House of Commons Environment Committee confirmed this trend. In 1980, only 5 per cent of retail sales were in out-of-town retail developments; by 1991 the figure was 17 per cent; and by 1994 it had risen to 25 per cent (House of Commons, 1994). Another estimate suggests that one-third of shopping money, £47 billion, was spent in these centres in 1992 (Crossley and Murray, 1993). Verdict estimates that despite government attempts to revive shopping in the traditional high street, shoppers will still spend one-third of their cash in out-of-town stores by the late 1990s (Young, R., 1995). There is also evidence that legal work in retail property transactions, mostly relating to out-of-town or edge-of-town developments, is buoyant (Fennell, 1995). In 1995 the supermarket leader, J. Sainsbury, made a decision to invest £100 million in seven stores in Northern Ireland – all of which were to be built on edge-of-town or green-field locations (Byrne and Bernoth, 1995; Rodwell, 1995).

The 1980s also witnessed the rapid growth of retail warehouse parks – three or more large stores specialising in the sale of (bulky) household items such as carpets, furniture and electrical goods, catering mainly for car-borne customers and often in out-of-centre locations. There are now some 200 warehouse parks with a combined floorspace of 25 million square feet. And the 1990s is likely to see the introduction of up to 50 off-centre or out-of-town warehouse club stores, such as PriceCostCo, taking around 2 per cent of the retail turnover through bulk sales at reduced prices in unsophisticated buildings (House of Commons, 1994). There are, however, some contra-indications. The 'large shed' investment in Cargo Club by Nurdin & Peacock proved short-lived; it sold its three stores to Sainsbury soon after opening. And PriceCostCo has revised its strategy to target small businesses rather than individual shoppers (Hinde, 1995; Hosking, 1995).

There are many who take the view that international retailing is about to come of age – and a resonating new vocabulary has entered the lexicon of the trade. The word supermarket has an almost old-fashioned ring as newer terms such as hypermarket, superstore and retail park come into everyday use. There are even newer phrases such as warehouse club, air-craft-hanger-shopping, depot-shopping and shed-shopping. The latest manifestation of giant-size retailing is likely to adopt elements of a none-too-complex formula: very large stores of at least 45,000 sq ft with enormous product range. They will buy stock internationally on a big scale and will sell in bulk or in volume (or both) and at a price which is 10 to 15 per cent lower than can be found in high-street stores. They will target '*Which*-reading ABs looking for bargains' – customers with jobs, cars and precious little time (Spillius, 1994). The new style retail giants are evident in food, clothes, office equipment, shoes, sports goods and do-it-yourself products. These stores have the objective of cutting through the market they enter and are referred to in the trade as 'category killers'.

There is also likely to be an invasion of foreign competition. Alongside the established names of CostCo and Toys 'R' Us there will be other American giants such as Wal-Mart, K Mart, TJ Maxx and Staples. Wal-Mart is the largest American retailer reporting a 21 per cent increase in sales in 1993 to a total value of $67 billion, followed by K Mart with an annual revenue of $34 billion. The former is planning to open 60 of its huge mass-merchandise stores outside America by the end of 1995 with some likely to be located in Britain (Bernoth, 1994b and 1994c; Spillius, 1994). In addition, there is increasing competition from European giants. Aldi from Germany and Netto from Denmark were the first of the 'deep discounters' in food retailing to move into Britain, and these have been joined by Lidl the German discounter – with 11 stores opened in less than a week in late 1994, with a further 200 planned for the next few years. The group has

1,400 outlets in Europe, is the discount market leader in France and has an annual turnover of £4 billion. By mid-1995, however, analysts were commenting that the continental discounters were fighting for market share among themselves rather than winning market share from the big supermarkets (Hinde, 1995).

New definitions of shopping: the pleasure-dome

The seemingly inexorable drift towards large-scale, out-of-town shopping has a powerful rationale. Retailers with large units can achieve economies of scale which their smaller rivals cannot match – and the benefits can be passed on to customers in the form of lower prices. The new-style complexes also allow customers easy access to a number of different outlets at the same time and within the confines of a single, defined location. The concentration of sales is awesome. The Oxford Retail Group estimates that 100 companies now own or control over 60 per cent of all retail sales – by value not by outlet (House of Commons, 1994).

The motorist-as-shopper enjoys improved access and parking facilities. For example, there is parking for 10,000 cars at Merry Hill and some 3,000 coaches visit each year so that customers can shop in the 260 on-site stores (Joseph, 1993). The Automobile Association (AA) estimates that 87 per cent of car-owning households use the car at least once a week for shopping, whilst the Consumers' Association suggests that 50 per cent of people use their cars all the time for shopping (House of Commons, 1994). There is also the very practical consideration that modern retailing cannot easily adapt itself to the sometimes medieval street patterns of town centres. The late twentieth century shopper demands easy vehicular access and space to shop in comfort – and expects both to be provided at a high standard (Vidal, 1994). The rise of car ownership is an important variable. In the 1960s about 70 per cent of the British population did not have access to a motor vehicle, but by the mid-1990s some 70 per cent do have regular use of motor vehicles ('Shopping: The Supermarket', BBC2, 10th July 1995).

In addition, the so-called 'pleasure-domes' offer customers a new, triple-barrelled, turn-of-the-century definition of shopping. First, the customer has the option to shop in superstores for food and essentials in a way where the shopping can be accomplished quickly, with wide product choice and competitive prices. Secondly, the customer is offered the opportunity of 'browsing' or window shopping for clothes and luxuries in a range of more specialist outlets located in the same place. Thirdly, the retail parks and covered malls re-define shopping as a leisure activity and not just as something which has to be done. The new-style shopping is not simply a means to an end but it has become an end in itself – a major manifestation of the consumerism of the 1990s. And shopping centres have been described as the 'secular cathedrals' of the late twentieth century, dedicated to the twin gods of consumption and profit (Gardner and Sheppard, 1989).

Shopping as an activity has been broken down into two categories – shopping for 'needs' or the things which customers have to buy (for example, food and other essentials) and shopping for 'wants' or leisure shopping (Hawkes, 1995a). The retailers hope that consumers in shopping centres will be drawn from needs to wants shopping – thereby increasing total expenditure. Four types of shopper have been identified: the 'minimalist' who shops solely for needs and does so as quickly and inexpensively as possible; the 'traditionalist' who shops heavily but with a single-minded purpose; the 'grazer' who spends much of the time browsing and buying convenience foods; and the 'enthusiast' who engages at all levels. And for those who just soak up the atmosphere, lingering with no purpose other than enjoying the atmosphere, the activity is known as 'experiential consumption'. Mall-type shopping has developed its own vocabulary.

One commentator (Shields, 1992a) has argued that the mall offers a new architectural typology for the late twentieth century – huge covered spaces carefully punctuated with galleries and arcades, which offer the functional attractions of ease of access and controlled climate, together with reduced prices based on high market volume. Moreover, a new 'social logic' has entered design for shopping where the mall has symbolic value as a major site of social interaction as well as a venue for shopping. It becomes a new democratic centre for social intercourse. It caters for the shopper, the window shopper and the stroller, as well as for the perhaps less welcome 'hanger out' and adolescent 'mall-rat'. Its benefits, which derive from its internal environment, are seen as a public good and as something which is 'free' to the individual user – a key site for symbolic consumption and classless social interaction. Another commentator (Slater, 1993) has argued that the key feature of the shopping mall is its 'planned organicism' – the interiorisation of shoppers in a disciplined and controlled environment. It is the 'dreamscape' equivalent of Jeremy Bentham's panopticon, where firms can attract and control bodies within a rationalised framework in order to make profit. Others have likened the shopping mall to 'hyper-reality' or 'sanitised fantasy' – where everything is reduced to a set of agreed themes, so people feel more comfortable in the falsehood of the shopping centre than they do in the reality of the urban landscape outside (Gardner and Sheppard, 1988).

However it might be interpreted, the new-style emphasis on shopping is so great that some psychiatrists are now beginning to think that it can be a compulsive condition: it is estimated that up to 6 per cent of the American population, around three million people, mostly women, are on the brink of bankruptcy, divorce or both because of uncontrollable buying. The so-called 'shopaholic' is drawn to the shopping mall and will 'spend, spend, spend' – without having secured the benefit of a large football pools or lottery win. The condition is being taken so seriously that doctors are prescribing antidepressants as treatment for 'compulsive shopping' (Greig, 1994; Hawkes, 1994).

Finally, the technology-driven future of shopping is becoming evident with the experimental opening of retail facilities on the Internet, the worldwide computer communications network. The Barclays Bank initiative is modest, allowing customers to order wines from Sainsbury's, books from Blackwell's and gadgets from Innovations, as well as goods and services from Argos, Toys 'R' Us, Eurostar, The Car Shop and others – but the potential market is enormous. One million British users are already online, with a predicted growth rate of 10 per cent a month and estimates of global Internet transactions expanding to £380 billion by 1999. It is instructive to note that the Barclays initiative (BarclaySquare) is referred to as the 'mall on the Internet' or the 'electronic shopping precinct' – perhaps a case of tomorrow's retail idiom borrowing the dominant vocabulary from shopping in the mid-1990s (Hawkes, 1995b; Joseph, 1995; Lloyd, 1995; Preston, M., 1995).

Threatened town centres

One potential consequence of the emergence of shopping-mall and retail-park consumerism is what planners call the 'doughnut syndrome' – attractive and prosperous shopping developments around the outside of a town leaving a blighted hole in the middle. Customers ebb away from the town centres as the green-field site retail parks take away trade from the high-street stores (which then close) and the town centres become dreary, empty and desolate. One commentator has estimated that you can walk at least half a mile up and down the aisles of some superstores – about the length of an average high street (Pearman, 1995). Another suggests that the defining symbol of 1980s Thatcherism will turn out to be the out-of-town shopping centre – a monument to short-term consumerism when politicians believed that motorists should be granted their every wish, leaving a lethal legacy for town centres where shops are forced out of business and where the city centre is left to 'cheapjack shops and cafes, the elderly and the poor' (Jenkins, 1994a). The substitution of market forces for the use of planning regulations to deliver a balanced town-centre community has had the net effect of making the city centre:

> ... an Ozymandian ruin, devoid of a reason for existing, left with the ghosts of fame long past. Among its deserted caverns, a shadowy army of the poor, the transient and the dangerous pitch camp.
>
> (Jenkins, 1994a: *The Times*, 19th November)

The high street is left with an ugly legacy of 'boarded-up windows, deserted streets, discounted lines and perpetual sale signs' (Seaton, 1995). Ten years ago 59 per cent of all retail sales were made in the high street, but by 1994 this figure had shrunken to 48 per cent – a loss of nearly one-fifth of trade. One distinguished urban historian has pointed to a bifurcation between the 'affluent outer city' and the 'indigent inner city' (Fishman, 1993). These changes call into question the vitality and viability of town centres and the very future of the high street (Distributive Trades Economic Development Committee, 1988; Department of the Environment – URBED, 1994).

The doughnut syndrome

Dudley is often seen as a prime victim of the doughnut syndrome. Since 1987, when the Merry Hill Centre was built two miles away, luring away big-name shops, the town centre has almost died. Major stores such as C&A, Littlewoods, Marks & Spencer, Next, J. Sainsbury and Tesco have all moved out (Joseph, 1993). Many town-centre shops are vacant and among the remainder it is junk-shops, low-income shops and squat shops that predominate. This reversal of fortune is referred to as the 'consolidation of decline' as the big names move out to be replaced by low-quality outlets. Since 1987 the number of shops has dropped from 370 to 290 and about one-quarter of the space in the centre is vacant, even though rents have been reduced by about one-third (Crossley and Murray, 1993). Stanley Kalms, the chairman of the Dixons Stores Group, has pointed to the possibility that criminal 'entrepreneurs' will tend to move into vacated premises and that neglected high streets will soon offer no more than a network of squatter shops with a monopoly on supplying car boot sales (see Travis, 1993). These shops are being occupied by people who pay no rent, observe no safety standards and sometimes sell stolen goods. Kalms suggested that lawlessness will reign supreme: the local authorities will oppose the retailers' attempts to create high-street safety zones; the lawmakers are left in a time warp of indifference; and occasional shows of force by the police are reassuring for a time, but ultimately unconvincing. As crime takes over the remaining legitimate businesses will find it increasingly difficult to obtain insurance cover. Shops and households in high crime rate areas will be 'red-lined' by insurance companies and will either not get cover at all or will have to pay exorbitant premiums (Murray, 1994a). This acts as a further disincentive to staying in business and adds to the vicious downward spiral.

Estimates suggest that Dudley has lost 70 per cent of its market share to Merry Hill, and that towns such as Stourbridge and West Bromwich have also been hit hard, losing between 20 and 40 per cent of their trade (Vidal, 1994), with Birmingham losing up to 10 per cent of its trade (Hobson, 1995). Other shopping complexes are no less a threat to the nearest urban centre. The same fate is feared for Ludlow as it anticipates the possibility of a new Tesco superstore (McCrystal, 1995). A report for the Department of the Environment's Urban and Economic Development Group (1994) pointed to only 3 per cent of Britain's market towns as thriving, with three-quarters being stagnant or in decline. The House of Commons Environment Select Committee recognised the problems of 'receding shopping areas' in town centres as low-key and low-value encroachment fills the gap left by the departing big-name stores, but could offer little comfort other than the need to 'plan for decline' (House of Commons, 1994). The Association of Town Centre Management has also offered a bleak assessment:

> Out-of-town retail centres are now commonplace and they have become extremely popular. But that very popularity is, quite literally, draining the lifeblood from our traditional ... urban centres.
>
> (quoted in Hobson, 1995: *The Times*, 27th June)

Fighting back

The threatened town centres are trying to fight back. For example, there is a rival covered mall in Ilford town centre, together with a pedestrianised high-street and a new bypass, to compete with the nearby Lakeside Centre. This has had the effect of lessening the haemorrhage of trade to Lakeside from a predicted 10 per cent to less than one per cent, but it has required significant capital expenditure – £25 million of public money and £125 million of private investment (Crossley and Murray, 1993). In

London, the Crown Estate has invested heavily in revitalising Regent Street, spending £3 million on new street furniture – replacing Tarmac with York stone and putting up new bus shelters and lamp posts. New shop fronts have had to comply with guidelines laid down by English Heritage and Westminster City Council. In early 1993 nearly 19 per cent of the 1.2 million sq ft of shopping space was vacant, but by late 1994 vacancy rates were down to 5 per cent (Grigsby, 1994). And, at a national level, Marks & Spencer, one of the country's largest retailers with 283 stores and annual sales of £7 billion, added 500,000 sq ft of retail space in 1994, giving a total of 11.1 million sq ft overall, with two-thirds of the new space located in new stores or extensions to stores in town centres and city centres. The company is also planning to open the second largest store in the world in Newcastle in 1996, occupying 120,000 sq ft and incorporating a 30,000 sq ft food hall (Cowe, 1995b; Gilchrist, 1994 and 1995c). And Harvey Nichols, the prestige retailer, is to open its first store outside Knightsbridge in the centre of Leeds at the Empire Arcade – a £5 million investment to be completed by the end of 1996 (Wavell, 1995).

The refurbishment of existing town centres has received some support from the environment secretary, John Gummer, who suggested in December 1994 that town-centre car parks should be revamped and refurbished to meet the needs of modern shoppers, possibly by handing them over to private firms who would provide contract security and CCTV (Brown, 1994; Ezard, 1994). Ipswich town centre has already experimented with the provision of mini-parks for 30 to 40 cars so as to minimise the distance shoppers have to walk to shops. Investment has also been made in improved lighting and closed circuit television. The town's counter-measures have increased shopping by 5 per cent. Mr Gummer also suggested that town-centre shopping centres could be opened 24 hours a day. In addition, so-called 'modern convenience retailing' is re-asserting itself in the high street with the major retailers looking to establish or refurbish stores much closer to the town centres – such as Tesco's 'Metro' stores and Sainsbury's 'Central' stores (Ahuja, 1994).

More importantly, the rate of opening new, out-of-town superstores is slowing because of substantial changes in government policy (Verdict, 1994). The out-of-town retail boom received a significant setback in March 1994 when new guidelines were announced by the environment secretary which, without being law, will become planning gospel. The environmentalists cheered, the planners were bemused and the developers were dealt a severe blow to the body. The guidelines are aimed at restricting out-of-town developments, malls in the middle of nowhere and anonymous warehouses at motorway exits (Prynn, 1994; Vidal, 1994). As a consequence of the 1992 Rio de Janeiro conference on environmental pollution, the government is seemingly determined to curtail the use of motor vehicles (including for shopping) thereby reducing harmful emissions. Planning guidelines which restrict the use of motor vehicles for shopping could cut British fuel consumption and polluting emissions by 15 per cent over the next 20 years, whilst if no action was taken there would be a 100 per cent increase in the number of cars over the same period. Since 1982 the number of cars on the road has risen by 30 per cent and the average journey length has gone from five miles to seven miles. With a comment of unusual wit the environment secretary argued:

> ... car dependency makes us neither healthy (air pollution), wealthy (we are having to spend £23 billion on building new roads), nor wise (we destroy the countryside and leave a pretty sorry mess for future generations to sort out).
>
> (quoted in Vidal, 1994: *The Guardian*, 17th March)

Later in 1994 the report of the House of Commons Environment Select Committee confirmed the new-style thinking by demanding a campaign to revitalise high streets by making them more attractive to shoppers and suggesting the imposition of stricter planning controls on applications to build out-of-town stores (House of Commons, 1994). The committee was keen to promote better and more secure town-centre parking (for shoppers rather than commuters) and would like to see planning guidelines changed to ensure that superstores are built in or on the edge of town centres rather than on distant, green-field sites. More specifically, the committee recommended a double-barrelled test of acceptability for granting planning permission for out-of-town developments (House of Commons, 1994), including clarification of the use of the government's *Planning Policy Guidance Note 6 (1993)*. Planning permission should be withheld if there is a suitable site within or close to the town centre, or if retail impact studies show that the development is likely to cause 'demonstrable harm' to the vitality and viability of a nearby town centre. Both tests of acceptability should be applied in the future. This can only act as a brake on out-of-town developments.

By the spring of 1995, the environment secretary responded to the committee's concerns by ordering departmental officials to re-write planning guidelines and by commissioning research to assess the impact of out-of-town stores on town centres. He said he was committed to:

> ... using my planning powers to support local efforts to safeguard the vital-
> ity of towns and the economic viability of their retail centres in particular.
> (quoted in Brown, 1995: *The Guardian*, 23rd February)

This hardening attitude had already been reflected in increasing disen-
chantment with out-of-town retailing. Only four of the 50 giant shopping
centres proposed by developers in the 1980s have been built, and a number of high-profile schemes ran into difficulties. Plans for a huge mall with
space for 4,500 cars south of Cambridge were thrown out after local opposition and the Court of Appeal blocked the one million square foot
Trafford Centre in Dumplington, Greater Manchester – although both
developers immediately went to appeal (Kennedy, 1994a). Planning
consent for a superstore outside Ludlow had also been refused (Prynn,
1994). And, in November 1994, the environment secretary re-jected an
appeal by Safeway against the refusal of planning permission for an out-
of-town superstore near Andover, Hampshire. The stated reasons
included the potential inconvenience to people without cars, and the failure to meet the department's guidelines that stores improve the 'vitality
and viability' of town centres (Ahuja, 1994).

The supermarket giants in particular were disturbed by the extent to which
they were losing planning appeals. At the end of 1994, Safeway had won
just three out of 13 planning appeals for out-of-town sites, Tesco had won
four out of 14 and Sainsbury one of ten. The big retailers responded by ac-
cusing the environment secretary of trying to turn the clock back to a
(false) Utopian image of shopping in the 1950s; and argued that the new
guidelines and policy would in any case have the opposite effect to that intended – more not less pollution (Leake, 1994; Young, 1994a).

Other companies have taken the view that government concern has come
much too late and after out-of-town retailing has become firmly established. A spokesman for Somerfield, which owns the Gateway chain based
mainly in town centres, commented that the MPs were 'shutting the
garage doors after the Volvo has bolted' because so many planning applications for out-of-town complexes had already been approved (Leathley
and Prynn, 1994). The surveyors Hillier Parker estimated that by the time
the environment secretary sought to restrict development, some 30 million
sq ft of out-of-town shopping space had received planning approval, and
that if all these plans came to fruition the current 300 giant malls and retail parks would be joined by 400 more within the next few years
(Pepinster, 1994). And senior civil servants in the Department of the
Environment have conceded that with so many planning applications al-

ready granted, it is 'far too late in the day' to reverse the strangle-hold of the new superstores (Lean, 1995). And a political commentator argued that the reversal of policy had to be seen as a gross example of the stable door being hopelessly closed long after the damage was done (Jenkins, 1994a).

If the high-street retailers were becoming confident that the environment secretary had curtailed successfully out-of-town developments, they were certainly shaken out of their complacency in May 1995 by the unexpected House of Lords decision in *Bolton Metropolitan District Council and Others v Secretary of State for the Environment and Others* (*The Times*, 25th May) to permit the development of the £200 million Trafford Centre on a one million sq ft green-field site at Dumplington, west of Manchester (Hobson, 1995). Although the Trafford Centre may well prove to be the last of its size as a so-called sub-regional shopping complex, there are similar major developments being planned – for example, Bluewater Park, a 1.6 million sq ft shopping centre in Kent, designed to take advantage of the new rail route from the Channel Tunnel, and a 500,000 sq ft centre to be built at Braehead, 30 miles to the east of Glasgow.

Town centres, shopping centres and competition for customers

Alongside the new competition between out-of-town and city-centre retailers there is another conflict, one which has remained largely unnoticed. Within the town centre there is strong competition for customers between traditional city-centre stores or high-street shops and their neighbour-rivals in purpose-built, covered shopping centres and malls. This is some-times called the battle between the traditional high street and the edge-of-high-street developments, with particular reference to new shopping malls. Recent examples of the latter include the Glades in Bromley, Kent and Waterside in Lincoln, as well as 600,000 sq ft plus shopping centres to be developed in Glasgow and Southampton (Hobson, 1995). Evidence suggests that only the top 200 high streets are 'doing well'; and that in many areas there is a steady drift of customers towards larger city centres and shopping malls (Bagnall, 1995c). The 1995 closure of 285 Rumbelows stores, the decision of nine of the 12 regional electrical companies to leave their showrooms and the disappearance of Pentos (owner of Dillons, Rymans and Athena) all suggest that high-street retail competition is not without its casualties. According to KPMG, the town centre is vulnerable to 'fragile demand' and the first quarter of the year saw 58 retail concerns go into receivership compared with 51 in the corresponding quarter in 1994.

To some extent this is the micro-level equivalent of the larger retail strug-gle, but the competition is no less intense. There are unanswered ques-tions about how customers view these two types of town-centre retailing and the factors which influence the decision to shop in one rather than the other. Not least, to what extent is there a difference between the public's perceptions of crime, disorder and nuisance in new-style shopping centres and in more traditional town centres, and why? And, if there is a differ-ence, does this affect shopping behaviour? One important factor in the competition for customers between town centres and shopping centres may be the extent to which they can provide safe and secure shopping en-vironments. To date, this is a wholly unexplored area.

The current retail climate is such that these types of questions are assum-ing increasing importance. Consumer demand is currently estimated to be low and unlikely to improve in the foreseeable future so the outlook is 'great news for shoppers, but sobering news for retailers' (Verdict, 1994). In the late 1980s, with annual growth in sales of 5 or 6 per cent, retailers were the 'prospering giants' of the booming national economy. Today they are suffering from sluggish consumer demand and an increasingly compet-itive environment (Bassett, 1994 and 1995; Randall, 1994; Smith and Hamilton, 1994). A very modest sales momentum is only being achieved through price cutting and special promotions. When retailers are having to price into weak markets the high street becomes a zero-inflation zone.

There are a number of contributory factors. Recent increases in direct and indirect taxation and a reduction in relief have had the effect of reducing people's disposable incomes – with an immediate impact on all non-essen-tial retail sales. Pervasive and continuing job insecurity also operates as a disincentive to spending. This is compounded by the failure of the housing market to show any sign of regeneration, not least because the general deflation hits all consumer spending associated with the purchase of prop-erty. Finally, the mid-1990s consumer is increasingly debt-averse conscious as the 1980s increase in consumer borrowing has given way to fiscal re-trenchment.

The combined effect of these factors is to make retail customers more price-aware and price-sensitive – and decidedly more cautious about part-ing with whatever money they might have to spend. Increased competition has forced many retailers to lower their prices. But the mid-1990s con-sumer is an increasingly sophisticated animal with ever-rising expectations for both product choice and service. One enduring legacy of the 1980s is a customer-is-king mentality where purchasing power finds expression in consumer choice. The problem is that the wealth has diminished but the aspirations of customers remain on an upward curve. This puts the retailer under a double bind – to meet rising expectations at lower prices.

This directs attention not just to price but to the quality of service on offer to the would-be shopper. This means that retailers will not only have to become more efficient if they are to hold down or reduce prices, but that they will also need to pay increasing attention to their shopping environ-ments if they are to retain or attract customers – something referred to as 'excellence in execution' (*The Economist*, 4th March, 1995). One part of this will be the extent to which retailers meet customer expectations for a crime-free and nuisance-free shopping environment.

An emerging methodology

The purpose of the BRC's Retail Crime Initiative-sponsored survey of safe shopping in town centres and shopping centres is to clarify the com-plex relationship between crime and nuisance and retailing, and to do so in a way which takes into account not only the views of the customer-shopper, but also the views of those involved in the management of the re-tail environment; and to distinguish between the customers' views and the managers' views by type of shopping area – shopping centre or town cen-tre. The underlying assumption was that for anyone to be in a position to 'do something' about the problem of crime and nuisance in retail areas the first step was to listen to what the people most closely involved in shop-ping had to say themselves – in this case the shopping public and the town-centre and shopping-centre managers.

The findings are intended to enable those who have responsibilities for safety and security in shopping areas to address their problems in a con-crete and practical manner – and thereby make a contribution towards the development of 'best practice' in safe shopping. This directed attention to finding out not only what the crime and nuisance problems were but also what was being done to tackle them. The findings are of direct relevance to both town-centre and shopping-centre managers, as well as to the wider retail community.

Research design

Previous research had focused on shoppers' perspectives, especially in re-lation to their fear of crime and avoidance behaviour, but these were seen to merit further exploration. The existing research is reviewed in the following chapter. The current study offers an additional dimension by breaking customers' views down by type of retail environment and by making clearer distinctions between crime, nuisance and pollution.

No previous research had examined the managers' perspective, despite their formal responsibilities for security, so this is an innovation. There were three reasons for focusing on managers – one negative and two positive. To begin with, certain sources of data, which may have seemed to be obvious starting points (such as incidents recorded by retailers themselves or by the police) were thought to be incomplete indicators of the real levels of crime and nuisance. All the evidence from studies of the reporting and recording of official crime figures points to there being significant shortfalls. This is the underlying rationale for the successive sweeps of the British Crime Survey (Mayhew et al, 1993). In broad terms, only the most serious offences tend to be both reported and then recorded – which means, in the retail context, that lesser offences which were reported would not necessarily be recorded and that most nuisance-type behaviour would not be either reported or recorded.

For example, there is evidence that even for very serious offences, such as violent victimisation of staff in retail outlets, the official figures record as little as one per cent of the total (Willis, 1993; Beck et al, 1994). In addition, there would have been major problems in using police crime data, partly because of under-reporting and under-recording, but also because the areas taken as town centres and shopping centres for present purposes would not have been co-terminous with the areas for which police figures were available. Town-centre and shopping-centre managers were deemed to be persons who could offer the most informed perspective on crime and nuisance problems in their shopping environment. They would, for example, be in a better position to provide relevant information than retail staff on the shop floor. The managers' impressions of both the frequency and seriousness of incidents were taken as broad but reliable indicators of the underlying patterns of threats to safe shopping.

In addition, to the extent that one aim of the study was to explore the use of various security measures (uniformed guards, CCTV and security shutters) together with assessments of their contribution to security, the managers were the obvious points of first contact. They were seen to be the 'security experts' within their particular environments. Finally, by taking the views of similarly-placed managers across two retail locations, there was an opportunity for valuable comparative analysis.

This is not to argue that hard data on criminal and other incidents should not be studied, but the proper way to assemble these would be to undertake a substantial survey of shoppers and their victimisation. This would require a very large sample because of the relative infrequency of actual victimisation. These findings could then be compared with victim data compiled by town-centre and shopping-centre managers, as well as incident records compiled by uniformed security guards. These could then be set against the police figures. This would go some way to establish both the 'real' amount of victimisation and its attrition through the various stages of reporting and recording. But it would not obviate the need to explore the customers' fears of crime and nuisance (and their behavioural responses) or the managers' perceptions of its frequency and seriousness.

The research design is summarised below as Figure 1.1. The framework allows comparisons to be made of crime and nuisance and responses to the problems across town centres and shopping centres, broken down by shoppers and managers.

Figure 1.1 Key crime and nuisance variables in town centres and shopping centres: a comparative framework

Key variables	Town centres		Shopping centres	
	Shoppers	**Managers**	**Shoppers**	**Managers**
The problems of crime, nuisance and pollution				
Fear and risk Frequency Seriousness				
Responding to the problems				
Existing security measures Priorities in security				
Evaluating security options				
Effectiveness Acceptability				

The first objective of the survey was to explore the public's perceptions of crime and nuisance in town centres and shopping centres in order to enable a comparison to be drawn between two different shopping environments on a number of variables: the 'problem ratings' or the extent of concern about crime and nuisance; the incidence of actual criminal victimisation; the awareness of security measures; and the perceived acceptability of a range of security options. The second objective was to explore the perceptions of town-centre and shopping-centre managers of crime and nuisance in these two locations. This would permit a comparison to be drawn between the two shopping environments on a number of variables: the problem ratings for various types of crime and nuisance; the current levels of security provision – by range and type, as well as the priority given to them; and the views of managers on how to improve the safety and security of shoppers.

Sample

Data were collected from three different sources: shoppers in town centres and shopping centres, town-centre managers and shopping-centre managers (Table 1.1). A systematic random sample was drawn of shoppers throughout the trading period in the two types of shopping environment in six towns and cities in England during June 1994. The towns and cities were chosen because each had both a town-centre manager and at least one shopping-centre manager. In total some 622 shoppers were surveyed – 334 in town-centre locations and 288 in nearby shopping-centres. Face-to-face interviews were conducted in the shopping environment.

Table 1.1 Number of respondents by shopping environment

Respondents	Environment	
	Town centres	**Shopping centres**
Shoppers [1]	334	288
Town-centre managers [2]	40	–
Shopping-centre managers [2]	–	161

[1] Drawn as a systematic random sample of shoppers in six towns and cities in England.
[2] Drawn from a national survey of town-centre and shopping-centre managers throughout England, Scotland and Wales.

The Association of Town Centre Management provided a list of all current town-centre managers in England, Scotland and Wales, each one of whom was sent a postal questionnaire to complete. The response rate was at the 50 per cent level and this generated a sample of 40 such managers. From membership lists provided by the regional secretaries of the British Council of Shopping Centres, some 400 shopping-centre managers in the three countries were sent a postal questionnaire to complete. There were 161 responses – a response rate of 40 per cent.

The three groups of respondents (shoppers, town-centre managers and shopping-centre managers) were presented with identical or near-identical questions, with some variation to allow for special features in one or more of the sub-samples. In all the interviews carried out with members of the public, it was made clear that the questions related specifically to the shopping environment (town centre or shopping centre) in which the interview took place. Similarly, questions of town-centre and shopping-centre managers were location specific. Useful advice on the research design was offered by Martin Speed of the British Retail Consortium (BRC) and its Retail Crime Initiative, as well as by members of the Association of Town Centre Management and the British Council of Shopping Centres. The project was commissioned by the BRC's Retail Crime Initiative in March 1994. The research instruments were designed in April and were piloted in May, and data collection followed in June 1994.

Vocabularies of crime and nuisance

An assessment of crime and nuisance in the shopping environment requires careful consideration of which conventional categories of criminal victimisation may be relevant. To take some obvious examples, domestic burglary and the theft of household items are physically far removed from the shopping environment, whilst thefts of or from motor vehicles might well figure as shopping-related victimisation, as might thefts from the person or various forms of physical assault. It is also clear that there may be other unwanted or unwelcome near-crime activities which compromise the ability of shoppers to enjoy their shopping as a risk-free activity. The starting point for defining the particular threats to safe shopping involved a number of unstructured interviews with shoppers in and around a city centre. Respondents were invited to comment informally on 'anything at all' which they thought 'could make shopping less safe around here'.

The responses fell into three main types. First, a number of comments made reference to what might be called clear-crime categories:

> Well I don't feel safe around here [a pedestrian underpass]. This is the sort of place where folk can get attacked.

> I won't leave my car at the [named] car park any more. I park and ride, always – 'though I've never had it nicked.

> I'm glad you asked ... It's the drinkers and the dealers, the drugs you know, what makes it sort of ... oppression, like.

> They're putting up cameras soon, which I guess says it all ... And you never see a copper.

Secondly, there were a significant number of comments which alluded to unacceptable rather than criminal behaviour and, more pointedly, to unwelcome or undesirable co-visitors:

> This town is no different to any other, I guess. The scum seem to surface on Saturdays. I don't like my kids coming in on their own, but I don't mind if they're with friends.

> I never come in at night, not unless I'm with someone, 'cos you never know who's around.

> There's a problem getting from the shops [in the town centre] to the bus station. The quickest way is through the [named alley] but it's always crowded with drunks and layabouts.

> I don't really mind these people [pointing to street entertainers] but it's the drunks – always begging – that's a disgrace. The Council should do something.

> Well, last year I got my Christmas shopping done right early 'cos the [named shopping centre] gets so packed with gangs of kids – well you can't get through. They're a menace. All they do is hang around.

Thirdly, there was an undercurrent of complaints about litter, vandalism and graffiti:

> It's all so filthy. Litter, you know, and crisp packets everywhere ... and chips ... and them plastic boxes from [named burger outlet]. They should all be fined like when that kid got £1,000 – that'd teach 'em.

> I never come if I can help it, unless it's to go straight to the [named shopping centre] where at least it's clean. Even then, it's in and out and home.

The big problem, 'specially when it's wet, is the mess and the dirt. You spend more time looking at your feet than the shops. Tell 'em they need people with them bins and brushes like in the [named shopping centre].

These indicative comments were used to identify three broad areas or constellations of various impediments to safe shopping – to be termed 'crime', 'nuisance' and 'pollution'.

The *crime* category encompasses behaviour which would generally be taken to be clearly illegal. Such offending behaviour includes serious assaults and predatory street crime; drug-related offences, especially in relation to street-corner drug dealing; motor vehicle crime, particularly in city-centre and shopping-centre car parks; and criminal damage (vandalism) and graffiti.

The term *nuisance* is widely used as a convenient shorthand for members of the public being upset in any way whilst shopping. This may include shoppers being subject to behaviour which causes them distress, or it may involve the unwelcome and unwanted presence of certain persons in the shopping environment. It may be manifest through unpleasant or offensive gangs of threatening youths; children hanging around in town centres and shopping centres; people selling things on the street; and distress caused by prostitutes, vagrants, beggars, drunks or buskers. In some of these categories there is a fine dividing line between whether the presence of these people or their behaviour is criminal or not.

Finally, *pollution* is a term which may be used to describe the 'unacceptable face' of the retail environment. It includes dogs fouling public places, litter and untidiness, and the general image of an area as run-down and neglected – possibly as a consequence of criminal-type behaviour (for example, vandalism or graffiti) or simply because some of the people referred to above (for example, vagrants and drunks) are seen in themselves, irrespective of their actions, as 'contaminating' the environment.

The three broad categories were then sub-divided to incorporate the range of crime and nuisance problems identified by shoppers in the pre-investigation enquiries, as well as those which were already identified as relevant from previous research in this area (see Chapter 2). The categories listed below in Figure 1.2 must not be seen as definitive; they represent an attempt to impose a degree of analytic order on a range of very different types of behaviour and person, without which the task of data collection would be wholly unstructured.

Figure 1.2 A typology of crime, nuisance and pollution

Crime
Physical assault
Drug-related offences
Car crime
Vandalism/Graffiti

Nuisance
Threatening youths
Vagrants/Beggars
Drunks
Kids hanging around
Illegal street vendors
Buskers
Prostitutes

Pollution
Litter
Dogs fouling streets

In common with any such typology, the benefits of an ordered framework for collecting and analysing data need to be set against the possible costs of distorting the reality under investigation by imposing a specious structure on disparate categories. For example, although there is no doubt about physical assault, drug-related offences and car crime as falling under the heading of *crime*, there is some uncertainty about whether vandalism and graffiti would normally be seen by ordinary members of the public as meeting the formal criteria for illegal activities (see Johnston et al, 1994). Under the heading of *nuisance* the categories all relate to what may be defined as the unwelcome presence and unwanted behaviour of 'street people', although there is no clear-cut relationship between them and criminal activities. It is also possible that some of the persons (and, by implication, their behaviour) under the nuisance heading may be more of a threat to ordinary shoppers than activities which are more clearly criminal. Finally, and perhaps most clearly, the nuisance of litter and dogs fouling the streets can be regarded as falling under the heading of *pollution* or something which is seen as physically spoiling the shopping environment.

Presentation of findings

Throughout the following chapters the relevant tables are presented so as to permit comparisons to be made between the views of the shoppers in the two environments, of the managers in the two locations and of shoppers and managers in the same shopping environment. For the sake of simplicity, the majority of tables take the form of the distribution of responses expressed as a percentage, excluding the raw numbers. The figures in the tables are given to a single decimal place, but are rounded to the nearest whole figure in the text. Whenever it was appropriate to test for levels of significance, the relevant figures are given at the end of each chapter. Significant differences are referred to in the text.

Chapter 2 explores the existing and rather limited knowledge base on criminal and other threats to safe shopping. This includes an overview of the ways in which retailers are subject to criminal losses and their costs. Particular attention is paid to studies which have explored the fear of crime and, more importantly, the extent to which this can lead to 'avoidance behaviour' – that is, to people not shopping in an area which is perceived to be at risk or unsafe. Avoidance behaviour can occur whether or not the fear is well founded. Finally, a brief summary of the findings of previous research into safe shopping is presented, together with a critical assessment.

Chapter 3 concentrates on customers' perceptions of threats to safe shopping. It addresses a number of themes. Are members of the shopping public fearful of crime whilst shopping, and do they worry about criminal victimisation? If they are fearful, how do they rank the seriousness of the various threats to their safety and security? Do these concerns affect their shopping behaviour? Does crime, or the perceived threat of crime, affect whether people shop or where they choose to shop? Are there places and locations they avoid? Finally, what is the probability of actual criminal victimisation and who is at risk?

Chapter 4 then re-examines the perceived threats to safe shopping, including their seriousness and frequency, but this time from the perspective of town-centre and shopping-centre managers – that is, those people who have a professional stake in making the shopping environment a safe and attractive place for the customer. Do the two parties see the threat in similar ways? The focus here is on the frequency and seriousness of a range of threats to safe shopping.

Chapter 5 offers an audit of existing security measures, including the levels of protection afforded by police officers on patrol and private security guards, together with the use made of closed circuit television. Further data are offered on the perceived effectiveness and acceptability of these security measures from both the customers' and the managers' perspectives. This leads to an extended discussion of the role of conventional policing in town-centre security and the very substantial use made of private security guards in shopping-centre security. Chapter 6 develops this theme further by reviewing current controversies with regard to the regulation of the private security industry, with a particular emphasis on the role of security guards in the shopping environment.

Chapter 7 examines the priority afforded to the security of shoppers by both town-centre and shopping-centre managers. Significant differences emerge with town-centre managers promoting the commercial well-being of the town centre and shopping-centre managers highlighting the paramount importance of safety and security. The discussion seeks to find practical ways in which the profile of town-centre security can be raised and by whom, and how town-centre initiatives can be financed.

Chapter 8 concentrates on the burgeoning use of CCTV in both retail environments, including the extent to which systems were in operation and whether or not the equipment was noticed. Data are also offered on managers' perceptions of its effectiveness and customers' views on the acceptability of surveillance. The discussion focuses on the shortcomings in the assessment of the effectiveness of CCTV to date. Chapter 9 then explores the complexities of assessing costs and benefits and the dangers presented by the seductive appeal of CCTV as a 'high-tech fix' to the problems of crime.

Chapter 10 offers a case study of the use of security shutters in town centres, including managers' perceptions of them as an effective crime control option and the views of both shoppers and managers on their impact on the 'look' and character of the town centre. The discussion suggests that although shutters may be very effective in designing-out crime, there are unwelcome side effects in terms of a detrimental impact on the retail environment. The discussion is extended to review the crime and safety implications of urban regeneration and renewal.

The final chapter draws together the various threads of the enquiry. It offers a summary of the major findings together with an analysis of the implications for 'safe shopping' and recommendations which follow from the findings. It also points to areas seen as being in need of further research.

2 Criminal Threats to Safe Shopping

Crime, its consequences and how to handle the problem of lawlessness are rarely far from the top of the political agenda – not least because the statistics are daunting. In 1993, for example, there were 5.5 million notifiable offences recorded in England and Wales – a rise of 70 per cent over a 10-year period (Home Office, 1994a and 1994b). Alongside these official statistics of recorded crime there are an increasing number of victimisation surveys where members of households are asked about their experience of crime, whether or not reported to the police. The findings suggest that the 'real' amount of crime is up to four times greater than is recorded in the police figures – mostly because a significant proportion remains unreported. The various sweeps of the British Crime Survey (BCS) by the Home Office, which look only at household and personal victimisation, point to a recorded figure of around three million crimes per year and a total figure of 11.5 million offences (Mayhew et al, 1993 and 1994).

Both sets of data offer an incomplete perspective on crime. The annual *Criminal Statistics* tend not to provide information about crime by location, making it difficult or impossible to work out whether the offence took place at the victim's home, place of work or in a public place – such as a town centre or shopping centre. Nor is it clear with regard to offences against property whether the victim is a householder or is involved in business or commerce – such as a retail company, its employees or its customers. The retailer-as-victim and the shopper-as-victim are pretty well invisible in the national crime figures. The official statistics have the effect of concentrating concern about crime on individuals and their households and directing attention away from crime in the retail context. The British Crime Survey data are even less helpful because the samples are drawn from people living in private households, so that the focus is on personal victimisation. There is little or no information about the extent of crime committed against the business or corporate victim; and even personal victimisation is mostly not detailed by location – for example, home, work, street or shop. Crimes against retailers (burglary, robbery, fraud, theft by customers, staff dishonesty and violence against staff) remain largely unexplored.

Although the criminal statistics and BCS figures are extremely important in establishing the broad contours of criminal victimisation, they do little to provide a sound base for understanding either offending or victimisation in the retail context. There is a need for a radical reconceptualisation of the problems of law and order – so that the predominant thinking, in terms of household and personal victimisation, is matched with a parallel framework covering commercial and corporate victimisation, including the retail environment. It is arguable that the costs of crime in the latter areas are larger and impact more dramatically on the lives of ordinary citizens than does conventional crime. The Home Office has recognised this deficit and completed its first commercial crime survey in 1994, although the number of respondents (1,500) is far fewer than in the household surveys (16,000).

Recent research combining data from a number of different sources suggests that the total costs of crime nationally are of the order of £20.4 billion a year (see Travis, 1995a). But losses due to conventional crime are modest when compared with the costs of business crime and commercial crime and the costs of policing it. For example, the net loss from car crime is estimated at £775 million and for residential burglary at some £495 million – a total of £1.3 billion. Against this the costs of crime against businesses were of the order of £7.5 billion, or roughly six times as much as the losses due to more conventional offending. In addition, about £2 billion a year is being spent on private security. A previously neglected dimension of criminal victimisation is becoming apparent – one which includes the criminal threat to retailers and to their customers.

Crime: the threat to the retailer

Growing concern about the criminal threat to retailing and to the safety and security of shoppers has led to the establishment of the Retail Crime Initiative by the British Retail Consortium (BRC). One result is an annual report on crime in the retail sector – and its costs. The first report was published in 1994, covering the financial year 1992–93, and was based on a survey of 54,000 retail outlets in Great Britain, with a combined turnover of nearly one-half of all retail sales (Burrows and Speed, 1994). The retail crime survey revealed over two million criminal incidents in the course of a year – the equivalent of every one of around 300,000 retail outlets experiencing 6 such incidents in a 12 month period or one incident every two months, although neither the risks nor the losses were distributed evenly.

The total annual costs of retail crime, against annual sales of some £140 billion, were estimated to be £2 billion – £1.6 billion sustained as a result of known or suspected criminal incidents and a further £370 million of expenditure on security hardware and security services. This is equivalent to an annual average loss of £35 per head of population or about £100 a year from every family's budget. It was also estimated that retail profits would have been 23 per cent higher were it not for the costs of crime. The average rate of 'shrinkage', or loss due to crime and waste or error, was estimated at 1.2 per cent of annual turnover.

More specifically, retailers witnessed, or could quite clearly establish, over 1.5 million instances of customer theft and over one million shop thieves were apprehended. The gross loss due to customer theft was estimated to be £517 million, with only £45 million worth of stock recovered. Additional figures from the Home Office suggest that more than 80 people out of every thousand visiting a big store are likely to be engaged in stealing (Young, 1994b). There were also over 31,000 instances of staff theft, a gross underestimate of the real total because only detected cases could be counted. The total loss attributed to staff theft (detected and suspected) ran to £554 million, of which only £5 million was recovered. Of the 1.2 million customers and 28,000 staff who were detained by store managers or store guards for suspected theft during the one-year survey period, one-third were dealt with by the retailers themselves rather than the police. The BRC's chairman, Keith Ackroyd, has commented that if all known shop thieves were handed over to the police the criminal justice system would 'grind to a halt' (Travis, 1994a).

In addition, there were 57 burglaries for every hundred retail premises (57:100) compared with a residential burglary rate of seven per hundred households (7:100). The gross loss incurred as a result of burglary ran to £331 million. Home Office figures for recorded burglaries other than in dwelling houses (ie including shops) rose from 323,000 in 1980 to 647,000 in 1992 – an increase of 100 per cent, with a current detection rate of only 20 per cent (Shopfront Security Group, 1994). The BRC survey also found that there were 54 incidents of criminal damage per one hundred stores (54:100) accounting for £47 million worth of damage to property or stock.

Over 120,000 retail staff were subjected to physical violence or threats of violence – a figure which is bound to be an underestimate because it is derived solely from victims of violence who chose to report the incident. Finally, the combined losses due to payment card fraud, cheque card fraud and other fraud were £22 million, which includes only direct losses to the retailers and excludes the £165 million losses borne by the Association for Payment and Clearing Services (APACS).

The data are unequivocal – the criminal threat to the retailer is substantial whether this is measured by the number of incidents or the costs incurred. The chairman of the BRC, Keith Ackroyd, has summed up the findings and their implications:

> Crime is one of the most serious and costly problems faced by the retail industry in terms of direct losses of product, cost of preventive measures and, most worryingly, in the increase of violence and injury to staff. Ultimately it is the consumer and society at large that bears these costs.
>
> (quoted in Tendler, 1994a: *The Times*, 19th January)

Another important national survey of 297 retailers responsible for one-quarter of retail sales (£35 billion through nearly 20,000 shops) conducted in 1992–93 estimated that national retail crime losses were of the order of £2.3 billion. This figure included losses of £1.9 billion due to staff theft or customer theft and losses of £377 million caused by burglary, criminal damage, ram-raids and smash and grab raids (Bamfield, 1994). The average rate of shrinkage was estimated at 1.6 per cent of annual turnover. Dishonest customers were thought to be responsible for 43 per cent of shrinkage and staff theft accounted for a further 30 per cent, with the remainder being attributed to supplier theft (10%) or administrative error (17%). Some 657,000 customers were apprehended for theft by the retailers, of which 280,000 or 40 per cent were handed over to the police; and 31,000 dishonest staff were arrested. When administrative error and waste were deducted from the overall shrinkage figure, the total estimated loss due to crime was £1.9 billion or 1.4 per cent of annual turnover. Bamfield estimated that shrinkage reduced average retail profits by some 24 per cent.

The BRC Retail Crime Initiative research and the Bamfield study are important in three ways. First, they represent the first national efforts to quantify retail crime losses accurately and in detail. They are the leaders in opening up retail crime to empirical investigation. Secondly, in spite of using rather different methodologies, there is a striking congruence between the findings. In both studies national retail losses were estimated to be of the order of £2 billion. In the BRC survey this amounted to a 23 per cent reduction in profits, a loss equivalent to 1.2 per cent of annual turnover (Burrows and Speed, 1994). The Bamfield study indicated a 24 per cent reduction in profits, equivalent to 1.4 per cent of annual turnover (Bamfield, 1994). When rather different approaches generate near-identical data there are good grounds for believing that the figures are a reliable guide to the underlying reality of retail crime. Finally, even allowing for some distortion due to the very complex nature of the investigations, and the difficulties of making extrapolations from sample data to arrive at national estimates, there are no grounds for doubting that the losses incurred in retail crime are substantial. These costs are having to be borne either by the retailers in the form of lowered profits or by the customers in the form of increased prices, or both.

Under the umbrella of the British Retail Consortium and its Retail Crime Initiative, Speed, Burrows and Bamfield (1995) jointly contributed to the 1993–94 retail crime survey – the largest and most up-to-date one of its kind. This second sweep covered companies trading through 53,000 outlets with a combined turnover of £67 billion (or nearly one-half of the total UK sales). The findings corroborated those from the earlier studies. The total costs of crime amounted to £2.2 billion – an increase of 8 per cent on the 1992–93 figures. As in the previous studies, external crime (eg customer theft, burglary, robbery etc) accounted for two-thirds of the losses and one-third were attributed to internal crime (eg staff theft). The survey established that the retail sector suffered some 5.4 million criminal incidents during the course of a year or roughly 18 incidents per outlet on average. Customer theft rose by 40 per cent to a total value of nearly £750 million, with some 550,000 persons being apprehended – with the rise being partly attributed to more accurate recording of incidents.

The importance of the second Retail Crime Initiative survey is twofold. It confirms the earlier findings, namely that crime is an ingrained feature of the contemporary retail culture with very significant costs. The survey also found that the expenditure by retailers on crime prevention measures had reached some £580 million – a rise of 40 per cent on the previous year. This may reflect the size of the problem, but it also reflects the seriousness with which the problem is being taken.

A smaller 1994 survey, conducted by the Forum of Private Business (FPB) and involving a sample of its 23,000 members, who were representative of the interests of the 1.5 million small businesses in the country, pointed to broadly similar conclusions. The study estimated that crime cost small businesses around £500 million during the course of the year (Forum of Private Business, 1995). Retail outlets had a slightly above average burglary rate of 43 per cent and one in five of the burglaries resulted in losses of £1,000 or more. And only eight in ten businesses had insurance cover. Many businesses were found to be 'skimping' on insurance and crime prevention measures because they could not afford the cost. The forum is to press for discounted insurance cover for groups of businesses and to lobby government for tax concessions for members who take security precautions (Collett, 1995).

There is also increasing circumstantial evidence from security professionals about the dimensions of retail risk. For example, the head of security at Sears, which owns Selfridges as well as a string of other high-street names, has estimated that the annual increase in shop theft is of the order of 14 per cent, and that retail crime now accounts for over 5 per cent of all crime in Great Britain. Similarly, the head of public relations at Marks & Spencer has said that the annual costs of security for the company are £51 million – £21 million spent on security measures, together with annual losses of £30 million through shop theft. The 1992 security spend included £10 million on CCTV, £6 million on uniformed guards, £3 million on store detectives and £2 million on other electronic equipment (Rudnick, 1993; Frean, 1994). He went on to state that the annual loss to the retail trade nationally was equivalent to a Brink's-Mat bullion robbery every four days. Stanley Kalms, chairman of the Dixons Stores Group, with a turnover of £1.5 billion a year, has calculated that his company loses more than £20 million a year in over 10,000 recorded incidents of theft, violence and fraud (Bell, 1992; Horsnell, 1993). And the MetroCentre in Gateshead, Europe's largest indoor shopping centre, has reported losses of around £12 million a year due to thefts from its 350 stores (Tendler, 1995a).

These sorts of findings, together with earlier large-scale studies (Home Office, 1986; Touche Ross, 1989 and 1992) and smaller-scale studies (Ekblom, 1986; Ekblom and Simon, 1988; Hibberd and Shapland, 1993) are beginning to bring the problem of retail crime into perspective (see also Beck and Willis, 1994a, 1994b and Beck et al 1994). Crime is rapidly becoming one of the most influential factors in retailing. It is a cause of dramatically increasing insurance costs. It creates losses in revenue through lost stock and equipment. And there are consequential losses through expenditure on putting things right and instituting additional security measures, as well as costs incurred through the disruption to trade. Not only does crime increase overheads, it impacts directly on the 'bottom line' of profitability. Retailers are increasingly advised to see their security departments and their strategies less in terms of 'preventing crime' and more in terms of 'protecting profit'; and good risk management does this already. There is, however, another piece of the retail crime jigsaw which is still too little researched – the impact on the honest shopper of the fear of crime or crime itself.

Crime: the threat to the shopper

The retail environment has two components – the retailer and the shopper. If conventional crime figures tend to ignore the former, the criminal victimisation of the latter is even less well understood. A major concern is the extent to which the ordinary shopper is at risk of crime whilst shopping. There are occasional high-profile cases which attract enormous media interest, including: the murder of an assistant store manager at Woolworths, John Penfold, in November 1994 in Teddington (Berrington and Ford, 1994); the brutal assault on a pregnant woman whilst late-night shopping in London's Oxford Street (Pierce, 1994); the stabbing of 15 shoppers in a random attack in the Rackhams store in Birmingham in December 1994 (Ellam, 1994; Kennedy, 1994b); and the repeated slashing with a knife of two supermarket assistants at Budgens in Reading by robbers who were demanding the keys to the store's safe in early 1995 (Duce, 1995). Such cases are mercifully few and far between. Very little is known, however, about the ways in which the shopping public might be more routinely at risk from criminal victimisation. This is an almost wholly unexplored area.

An equally important concern is the impact of the fear of crime on shopping behaviour, even where the fear is out of proportion to the risk of victimisation. Preliminary attempts to answer these questions have only been made in the last ten years (Phillips and Cochrane, 1988; Poole, 1991 and 1994a). Such studies are important because the fear of crime can only place safe shopping in jeopardy and thus reduce sales – to the detriment of the retailer and the shopper alike. The crucial question is the way in which the fear and risk of crime can impact adversely on the individual and his or her willingness to go shopping.

The fear of crime and its consequences

Crime, nuisance and pollution – alone or in combination – may cause members of the shopping public to feel that being in a particular area is not pleasurable or safe, even to the point of acting as a disincentive to them going there at all. In recent years it has increasingly been acknowledged that the fear of crime:

> ... will grow unchecked. As an issue of social concern, it has to be taken as seriously as ... crime prevention and reduction.
>
> (Home Office, 1989: ii)

Where the fear of crime is reasonable it can be harnessed to fight the threat of crime; but where the fear gets out of proportion it becomes disabling and counterproductive – to the point where it becomes a social problem in its own right (Rosenbaum, 1988; Williams and Dickinson, 1993). The fear of crime has been seen as the product of an interaction between two variables – an evaluation or assessment of risk and a perception of personalised threat, including the perceived seriousness of the consequences of victimisation (Skogan, 1984). Increasing attention is also being paid to the ways in which the fear of crime can have behavioural consequences. Much of the evidence is to be found in successive reports from the British Crime Surveys.

The first BCS report (Hough and Mayhew, 1983) posed the question of the relationship between fear and behaviour directly; and the answer was unambiguous. Between 30 and 60 per cent of women, depending on their age, said that they felt very unsafe when walking alone after dark – and around one-third of all women added that they sometimes avoided going out on foot after dark in their neighbourhood for fear of crime. In inner-city areas, this figure rose to 51 per cent for young women, 54 per cent for middle-aged women and 58 per cent for older women. One in twelve respondents said that they never went out alone on foot at night because of the fear of crime.

Continuing work in the same area and using the 1984 BCS, Maxfield (1987; and see 1984) offers data on 'subtle adjustments' in behaviour to counteract the likelihood of criminal victimisation. The general point was that 'fear for personal safety is a major factor in limiting personal mobility'. The proportion of respondents who said that they would not engage in certain activities at all because of the fear of crime was small. Football matches were the most prominent of these events, cited by 7 per cent of all respondents, followed by 3 per cent who singled out cinemas or clubs and 2 per cent who avoided pubs. There were a number of precautionary measures which were less extreme, but which were much more routinely followed. For example, 44 per cent of respondents said that they always or usually stayed away from certain streets and areas; 47 per cent said that they avoided walking near certain types of people; and 13 per cent said that they avoided using buses and trains.

A report on the 1992 BCS, including data drawn from earlier sweeps of the survey, offers strong evidence of the fear of crime and its relationship to behaviour (Mayhew et al, 1993). The degree of fear, which could range from mild concern to pervasive anxiety, was measured by respondents' answers to the question 'How safe do you feel walking alone in this area after dark?' This is recognised as a reliable and valid indicator of fear for personal safety (Skogan and Maxfield, 1981; Maxfield, 1984). The level of concern about being on the streets alone at night was high. One in three of all respondents (32%) said that they felt, or would feel, very or fairly un-safe alone on the streets at night. This was the case for nearly one-half of female respondents (49%) but only 14 per cent of men felt the same way. The elderly were most fearful – 58 per cent of women and 23 per cent of men aged over 60 years felt very or fairly unsafe.

These findings broadly reflected the levels of concern identified in the 1984 survey (Hough and Mayhew, 1985; see also Gottfredson, 1984 and Maxfield, 1984 and 1987). The earlier research also found that one-third of those who felt unsafe did so because they were fearful of being mugged, with a similar proportion saying that they were worried that 'something might happen'. One in five were concerned about being troubled by strange people or gangs. One-quarter of the elderly said that they never went out after dark for leisure purposes and it was estimated that some 6 per cent of the elderly, and about 2 per cent of all respondents, stayed at home wholly, or in part, owing to the fear of crime.

One of the most recent studies reports a major Home Office inquiry into drugs and crime in Bradford, Glasgow, Lewisham (south London) and Nottingham (Leitner et al, 1994). Between one-quarter and one-third of young people aged 16-25 years and of low socio-economic status said that they never went out alone at night – Bradford (32%), Glasgow (28%), Lewisham (26%) and Nottingham (25%). This finding is particularly noteworthy because the so-called streetwise youngsters could be supposed to be those who would feel least intimidated by the thought of being alone on the streets at night. The authors comment that the 'figure is very high and suggests that people may ... be restricting their activities as a conse-quence of fear'. Of the whole sample of 4,000 respondents across all ages and social classes nearly one-half said that they never walked alone after dark – Bradford (49%), Glasgow (48%), Lewisham (46%) and Notting-ham (47%).

A January 1994 survey by MORI of 2,081 people aged 15 years or more in 148 constituencies throughout Britain found that there had been a dramatic increase in the fear of crime since 1987 and that there was a correlation between anxiety and avoidance behaviour (Ford, 1994a; MORI, 1994). Over four in ten respondents (42%) were fearful of going out at night on their own, a five point increase since 1987. Over one-quarter of the sample (26%) were afraid of using public transport at night, a rise of seven points. One in six of the interviewees (17%) were afraid of driving alone after dark. More than one-half (52%) were frightened about the possibility of being mugged on the streets. The levels of fear were much higher for female respondents than males – going out alone at night (67%), using public transport at night (38%) and driving alone after dark (28%). Overall, one-half of the sample were fearful of going out at night (51%), two-thirds were afraid of being attacked (68%) and four in five were frightened of having something stolen from them (80%).

The findings indicate that the fear of crime alone can have real consequences irrespective of the actual risk of victimisation. There are reasonable grounds to suppose that these sorts of fears for personal safety may be reflected in shoppers' anxieties about being at risk of crime in and around the retail environment, particularly whilst shopping in the evening. A recent survey by the Automobile Association (AA) of 1,400 members found that the quality of car parks determined where 70 per cent of the sample would shop. One in five motorists said that they avoided multistorey car parks altogether and three-quarters of the women surveyed said that they did not feel safe in them (*The Times*, 17th December, 1993). And in a similar survey the Royal Automobile Club (RAC) found that one-third of female drivers were anxious about driving alone at night (Jones, 1995).

Maxfield (1987) and others (Box et al, 1988) have also pointed to the ways in which environmental cues can make a contribution to the overall fear of crime. Such cues include incivilities, run-down neighbourhoods and housing and perceptions of a lack of social cohesion in an area. All of the categories under the headings of nuisance and pollution could be seen as incivilities – people or things which are seen to spoil the environment and its character. They have the effect of making an area seem crime-prone, which creates unease in residents or visitors. This then may have an independent effect on the fear of crime. Noise, drunks and graffiti can all contribute to a sense of decay and insecurity, as can groups of marauding youths, and yet none of these necessarily constitutes criminal behaviour. There is no clear and consistent definition of disorder. According to one definition it is a condition where there are constant and visible cues that there are uncontrollable dangers in the immediate vicinity (Kelling, 1986). The signs of physical disorder also tend to suggest that 'normal' regulating mechanisms are ineffective. The net effect is that run-down streets become seen as 'corridors of insecurity'. Kinsey, Lea and Young (1986) take the argument a stage further by suggesting that these not only contribute to the fear of crime and avoidance behaviour but give rise to crime itself. Uncongenial and disorderly behaviour if not controlled can lead to a spiral of decline in a neighbourhood – where informal social controls weaken and crime begins to rise.

The major implication of these studies is that there may be a causal relationship between perceptions of possible criminal victimisation and subsequent behaviour. It is also possible that anxieties about nuisance-type behaviour may have a similar effect. The data certainly point in the direction of the need for more detailed explorations of the ways in which the fears of crime and nuisance may be related to shopping behaviour. There is now a need to move away from the conventional questions about fears for personal safety, particularly those which relate to walking alone on the streets at night. Although they have near-universal currency and a tradition of standard usage, they only offer a general measure of fear and its consequences (Baumer and Rosenbaum, 1982; Maxfield, 1984). The broad indicator now needs to give way to more specific measures. These would include the fear of crime and its effects in specific contexts, such as shopping – broken down by type of crime and nuisance, and then by type of shopping environment.

Previous research on safe shopping

Some relevant data are available, but the studies tend to concentrate either on shopping centres or on town centres without offering any comparative analysis. Six relevant studies have been identified:

- a study of crime and nuisance in two shopping centres in the Midlands (Phillips and Cochrane, 1988);

- a Coventry study of crime and disorder and the effects of local byelaws to ban the consumption of alcohol in public places (Ramsay, 1989 and 1990);

- a study of the threat to safe shopping in and around the centre of Birmingham (Poole, 1991), and related research in North America (Poole, 1994a and 1994b);

- a survey in Nottingham conducted by KPMG Peat Marwick, with particular reference to the costs of crime to the retail community (KPMG Peat Marwick, 1991);

- a Leicester survey of shoppers' fears of terrorist attack whilst shopping and their avoidance behaviour (Beck and Willis, 1993a, 1993b and 1994a); and

- a nationwide investigation of the contribution of town centre management (TCM) to shopping undertaken by Donaldsons and Healey & Baker for the Association of Town Centre Management (Donaldsons and Healey & Baker, 1994).

Midlands study

A Home Office-sponsored study of crime and nuisance in a large shopping complex in the Midlands, where there were two shopping centres owned and managed by different companies, reported on 712 security-related incidents recorded by security staff over a four-week period (Phillips and Cochrane, 1988).

Nine in ten of the incidents (90%) were classified as 'nuisance' – a category used for cases of gathering, loitering or misbehaviour; disorder and fighting or the intimidation of security staff or members of the public; glue sniffing; truancy; vagrancy; fly-posting (the unauthorised selling of goods); and for when members of the public were found in private areas. Nearly one-half of the tenants (45%) of the 190 businesses said that 'young people hanging around' and loitering in the centre was their greatest problem – something which was perceived to be more of a problem than shoplifting (39%) or the harassment of staff (12%). Nearly twice as many tenants saw the primary role for shopping-centre security in terms of dealing with nuisance (78%) than saw it as dealing with crime (41%). One in ten of the incidents (10%) were classified as 'crime' – with a rough three-way split between shoplifting (retailer as victim) and theft from cars or theft from the person (shopper as victim). There were just three isolated cases of robbery or assault.

Although useful as the first investigation in this area, the study has its limitations. To begin with the definition of 'nuisance' is over-inclusive and certainly led to the recording of incidents which, although they may have been a nuisance, were also likely to involve breaches of the law – for example, public disorder, fighting and intimidation. In addition, the number of criminal episodes (N=68) was too small to allow any meaningful breakdown. Finally, the study paid no attention to the public's perceptions of crime and nuisance. There was, however, undoubted value in the research – especially the fact that 'nuisance' was deemed to be a more serious problem than 'crime' because it occurred more frequently.

Coventry study

In the course of a Home Office-sponsored project 1,200 users of Coventry city centre were interviewed to assess the extent of public concern about key aspects of crime and disorder (Ramsay, 1989). One aim was to establish whether people were afraid of becoming victims of crime whilst visiting the city centre. A second interest was the extent to which fear was triggered by 'indicators of crime' such as groups of youths hanging around or people drinking in the street. A third focus was the extent to which frightened shoppers modified their behaviour – for instance, by avoiding certain places. The project was part of a larger study looking at the potential effects of introducing local byelaws banning the drinking of alcohol in public places (Ramsay, 1990; and see Chapter 4).

In the previous 12 month period, the actual levels of criminal victimisation suffered by the respondents had been low – assaults (2%), muggings (3%) and one in eight visitors being insulted or bothered by strangers (12%). Young people were more at risk than the elderly. Of those assaulted, over one-half believed that the attacker had been drinking, whilst one-third of those mugged and almost three-quarters of those insulted by strangers thought their assailant had consumed alcohol before the incident. The fear of crime was considerably higher than the actual risk of victimisation. Over one-third of respondents said that they were worried about being insulted by strangers (37%); one-half were worried about being assaulted (50%); and nearly six in ten were worried about being mugged (59%). Certain themes emerged as particular problems in the city centre – rubbish and litter (89%), unruly young persons (66%) and public drinkers (52%).

Respondents were also asked if they had modified their behaviour in order to reduce the likelihood of becoming a victim. Nearly two-thirds (63%) stated that they sometimes kept out of the city centre; 59 per cent avoided certain people; 56 per cent avoided certain streets; and 39 per cent took a companion along for reassurance. The people most commonly avoided were drunks, winos and tramps (61%), groups (45%) and young men (20%). The report concluded that there was a high level of public support (86%) for bringing in a local byelaw which would ban drinking in public places. The value of the research is that it showed that public

47

drunkenness impacted significantly on both the fear of crime and actual victimisation, and was associated strongly with avoidance behaviour.

Birmingham study

One of the few large-scale British studies was a survey of 255 female shoppers aged 20 years or more, selected in city-centre locations in Birmingham, including four shopping centres (Poole, 1991: Appendix F). The principal findings, which are buried in a discursive text, can be presented in summary form as follows:

Fear of crime

- One-half of the shoppers (50%) said that they avoided the city centre at certain times of the day – for example, on winter evenings.

- One in eleven shoppers (9%) said that they carried something in their handbag to protect themselves – for example, a rape alarm.

Crime

- One in ten shoppers (10%) had had personal property stolen on some occasion whilst they were in the city centre.

- One in eleven shoppers (9%) had had their motor vehicle stolen or broken into whilst it was parked in the city centre.

Shopping behaviour

- The majority of shoppers were attracted to the city centre because of the presence of department stores (42%) or covered shopping malls (36%).

- Three-quarters of the shoppers (75%) visited covered malls regularly or on almost every occasion they visited the city centre.

Disincentives to shopping

- Two-thirds of the shoppers (65%) identified a single shopping centre (the Bull Ring) as the least popular of those in the city.

- The principal reasons offered were that it was intimidating and scruffy (42%), too crowded (29%) or that it made the shoppers afraid of crime (10%).

- The types of behaviour which shoppers found most distasteful whilst in the city centre included people loitering on restricted routes (40%), teenage males displaying rowdy behaviour (32%), people drinking openly in public (12%) and people begging or busking (10%).

Security measures

- Eight in ten of the shoppers (80%) said that private security guards were a welcome and useful presence in shopping centres.

- Over nine in ten of the shoppers (95%) said that private security guards did not inhibit their shopping.

- Nearly all shoppers (98%) said that CCTV helped to reduce crime and was to be welcomed.

The study adds an important empirical dimension to an understanding of the relationship between crime and nuisance and shopping behaviour; and it confirms that it is helpful to use the categories of crime and nuisance to study victimisation in the retail environment. The study also indicated that the levels of both crime and nuisance were far from negligible. Finally, the fact that the Bull Ring Centre was seen to be much less popular than the other three centres, together with the general view that young people hanging around was objectionable, is a strong indicator that there may be a constellation of environmental and behavioural variables which affect the decision to shop in one area or another. One-half of the sample said that they avoided particular places in the city centre mostly because some areas were seen to be intimidating, scruffy and crime-prone.

The study is weak, however, in two crucial respects. The sample of adult females were approached simply because they were deemed to be 'likely' respondents and do not constitute anything like a representative cross-section of the shopping public. The research also fails to make a proper comparison between crime and nuisance in the city centre and crime and nuisance in one or more of the shopping centres within the city centre. Most of the data refer to the city centre in general, with only isolated pieces of information relating to type of shopping area. This was something of a missed opportunity for comparative analysis.

Further work by Poole (1994a) took in the North American dimension. The research was based on short visits to 20 shopping malls in major cities in the United States and Canada during September and October 1992, including face-to-face interviews with mall managers and security personnel. As with the above British study, the findings do not conform to conventional canons of academic expression, but the general thrust can be summarised. A majority of 85 per cent of respondents highlighted shoplifting as the major problem, with the remaining concerns relating to firearms, drugs and juvenile gangs (Poole, 1994a: Appendix C). The author also refers to the *National Shopping Center Security Report*, conducted in 1992 by Hollinger and Dabney of the University of Florida, which was based on 352 responses to questionnaires sent to some 2,227 mall managers or security managers – a response rate of 16 per cent (Poole, 1994a: Chapter 4; see also Hollinger, 1992 and 1993). For all types of mall, the findings suggested that there were only three types of problem: firearms (40%), street gangs (45%) and loitering youths (84%). No further details were offered.

Although it is difficult to disentangle the hard data from what is essentially a travelogue-type account of mall security in North America, these findings do add some substance. Leaving aside gun-related problems (which have little or no relevance to the British shopping environment), the problems for American and Canadian shopping centres would appear to centre mainly on loitering youths and troublesome gangs. A further account of the North American scene (Poole, 1994b) adds nothing by way of quantitative data.

Nottingham study

The Nottingham Crime Audit was undertaken on behalf of the Nottingham Safer Cities Project by KPMG Peat Marwick (1991) between December 1989 and July 1990. The intention was to examine the nature and the costs of crime within the city and to provide the basis for new approaches to improving community safety and reducing crime. It was based on the premise that understanding crime is the first step towards responding to it and developing measures aimed at improving the quality of life in city areas, including the contribution of retailing.

The police crime figures showed that some 50 per cent of the total crime reported for the county was concentrated within the city boundaries. And almost one-quarter of all reported crime occurred within the central area of the city, 25 per cent of which related to shop theft and a further 25 per cent to motor vehicle crime. The concentration of crime was evident both by type and by area. Interviews with local people, local businesses and the local authorities added to the crime profile. Burglary, car theft, assault and vandalism caused particular anxiety. Other worries related to disorder on public transport, drunkenness and threatening behaviour. And non-crime factors, such as graffiti, litter and the poor environmental appeal of parts of the city, were also seen to be disadvantageous to its commercial and social well-being. The public showed a generalised concern about crime, which took the form of feeling 'vulnerable' rather than of being afraid of specific threats.

The survey also attempted to put figures on the direct costs of crime. It was estimated that burglary losses totalled some £2.6 million, that property losses associated with theft from or of motor vehicles were of the order of £4.4 million and that the costs of assaults, including lost wages and production, amounted to some £1.4 million. On the basis of known levels of city-centre spending and survey indicators of the numbers of people not visiting the central area as a result of concerns about crime (figures not given), the value of lost sales and lost profit to the city by reason of shoppers' avoidance behaviour was estimated. For present purposes this was one of the key findings. The study pointed to a figure of £12 million in lost turnover in the period of the study, which it was estimated represented some £840,000 in lost profit.

The overall conclusion from these data is that crime was an unavoidable fact of life in the city; that it created concern and intruded into the lives of local people; and that it absorbed significant public and private resources. More specifically, crime had an adverse impact on the attraction of new employment and inward investment into the area; and that it threatened continued recognition of the city as:

> a major retailing ... centre in the face of competition from newer, out of town centres.
>
> (KPMG Peat Marwick, 1991: 5)

Crime and the threat of crime, together with other anti-social forms of be- haviour and general unattractiveness, operated to prevent retailers in the city from competing on equal terms with those elsewhere. The report also suggested that the perceived threat of crime would act as a deterrent to people using the city for leisure purposes, including shopping. Moreover, the local authorities were identified as having 'no clear or consistent response', let alone inter-departmental strategies, to counter these threats to the commercial and retail sectors.

Although the research methodology is unclear and much has to be taken on trust under the KPMG Peat Marwick 'label' (for example, where there are figures they are offered only as conclusions), the study has much to commend it. It offers useful data because Nottingham is consistently near the top of the league table for reported crime among 57 major urban areas – and its problems can be taken as a rough guide to what might be happening, or might happen, elsewhere. The general profile of the fear of crime was not significantly different from that found in similar areas by various sweeps of the British Crime Survey. Most importantly, the study is one of the few to attempt to calculate the costs of crime and to do so specifically in relation to city-centre retailers. The clear but unstated inference from the data is that city-centre shoppers ought not to be taken for granted. If there is little or no inward investment to maintain and develop city-centre facilities, as well as to reassure anxious shoppers that it offers safe shopping, then crime, fear and unattractiveness will contribute to a migration of shoppers to out-of-town stores – locations perceived not to have the disadvantages of the city-centre environment.

Leicester study

The complex relationship between the fear of crime and changes in the pattern of shopping behaviour was the focus of a 1993 study of the terrorist threat to safe shopping (Beck and Willis, 1993a, 1993b and 1994a). The data derived from interviews with 849 shoppers in and around the city of Leicester in five different shopping locations – three in the city centre and two out-of-town retail parks. It was not surprising to find that nearly two-thirds of the shoppers (61%) had thought about the possibility of a terrorist outrage whilst they were shopping. It was more surprising to find that nearly four in ten of the shoppers (38%) claimed that they were very worried or worried about the possibility of a bomb exploding whilst they were shopping. It was very surprising to find that as many as one in eight of the sample (12%) stated that they had altered their pattern of shopping behaviour as a direct consequence of the perceived risk of a terrorist attack.

In all the cases where members of the public had changed their pattern of shopping, they had responded to the perceived risk by avoiding certain areas. One in three said that they had stopped shopping altogether in London. Two-thirds said that they now always shopped outside of city-centre areas, preferring to shop in out-of-town retail parks. The principal reasons offered were that city-centres were 'too crowded' and 'too noisy' and that they offered the terrorist too much scope to remain undetected within a large, shifting and anonymous population.

All of the shoppers were asked to identify the most vulnerable shopping area by location and to nominate the single store they perceived to be most at risk in or around the city. City centre locations were identified as highly vulnerable to attack by as many as 80 per cent of the shoppers, whilst out-of-town locations were seen to be vulnerable at only the 60 per cent level. The anxiety associated with the city-centre locations was corroborated when as many as 57 per cent of respondents volunteered the names of some 10 city-centre stores as being vulnerable, whilst only 3 per cent cited an out-of-town store as being at risk.

The major implication of this 'safe shopping' study is that there may be a causal relationship between shoppers' perceptions of possible criminal victimisation and subsequent shopping behaviour; and that city centres are seen to be more crime-prone than out-of-town shopping locations. Although the study focused on an extreme threat to safe shopping, it confirmed the view that a perceived criminal threat can act as a disincentive to shopping in a particular area. It is also possible that other (less extreme) forms of crime and nuisance may have a similar type of effect.

Association of Town Centre Management study

The Association of Town Centre Management (ATCM) is a body which was established in 1991 to forge a partnership between the private and public sectors to promote the standard of facilities, environment and financial well-being of town centres. In 1993 the Association commissioned a wide-ranging survey to assess the effectiveness of its town-centre initiatives, usually referred to as town centre management (TCM). Part of the study focused on a sample of 2,000 shoppers in eight town centres throughout the country who were asked questions relating among other things to safety in town centres – defined as problems of 'violence or crime' (Donaldsons and Healey & Baker, 1994).

Out of 13 listed features of the retail environment (including types of outlet, image, cleanliness, street furniture and public facilities) the problem of town-centre safety figured prominently. More than one-half of the visitors were not satisfied with safety measures (55%) which put it in fourth place in the rank order of shopping-related facilities seen to be deficient. The survey also addressed the contribution of non-shopping facilities to the town-centre environment – including security measures, leisure and sports provision, libraries, markets, crèches and street entertainment. Of nine listed items, security and safety was mentioned most frequently – by as many as four in five respondents (79%) – as being a 'very important' consideration in making the town centre more attractive for visitors. Finally, visitors were asked about changes in the quality of the facilities provided in the town centre over the previous few years. Over one in three respondents (34%) pointed to a deterioration in standards relating to the control of crime and violence.

This study again shows how crime-related concerns are articulated by shoppers and may be related to shopping behaviour. The strength of this research lies in the additional evidence it offers, although it is a pity that the findings and their implications were not discussed explicitly in the report. The study concluded that visitors recognise that town centres are being improved and that TCM is therefore effective in terms of measurable 'output'. This conclusion was not warranted as far as the problems of crime and violence as perceived by the shopping public are concerned. The data point in precisely the opposite direction – to a very high level of concern and a deteriorating perception of the quality of security provision, together with a strong sense that security ought to be seen as a major priority. More generally, the study found no significant differences between the four town centres with and those without TCM initiatives.

Previous research and its implications

When the findings from these various studies are taken together, they suggest the ways in which crime and nuisance – or the fear of them – may impact on town-centre and shopping-centre visitors; and the ways in which these problems could be explored in more detail. There would appear to be six broad conclusions.

First, the actual rates of criminal victimisation appear to be far from negligible. The Midlands study found that one in ten reported incidents were deemed to be criminal rather than merely nuisances (Phillips and Cochrane, 1988). The Coventry survey found a victimisation rate for assaults and muggings of 5 per cent for city-centre users in a 12 month period (Ramsay, 1989). And the Birmingham study discovered that one in ten visitors had had property stolen from them on some occasion whilst shopping, and that one in nine visitors had had their motor vehicle stolen or broken into whilst it was parked in the city centre (Poole, 1991). The scale of car crime was confirmed by the Nottingham survey which estimated that it constituted about one-quarter of all city-centre offending (KPMG Peat Marwick, 1991). These figures scarcely lead to the conclusion that shopping is a crime-free activity. Moreover, the surveys indicated that victimisation was likely to occur in both town centres and shopping centres, although none of the studies offered comparisons between the two retail environments.

Secondly, the studies pointed to the existence of a generalised anxiety or fear of crime among shoppers. For example, the Coventry survey found that one-half of the visitors feared being assaulted and even more were afraid of being mugged (Ramsay, 1989). And the study commissioned by the Association of Town Centre Management revealed that security considerations figured more prominently than any others in determining whether town centres were attractive for shoppers and that over one-half were dissatisfied with current levels of security provision (Donaldsons and Healey & Baker, 1994). The findings confirm the more general conclusions from the various sweeps of the British Crime Survey (referred to in detail above) that the public's concerns about crime exist in their own right, irrespective of the actual risk of victimisation. They are not something which can be simply discounted as an irrational concern, not least because even unfounded fears may have real consequences (see below).

Thirdly, there were even higher and more widespread concerns about nuisance-type behaviour whilst shopping. The Midlands survey found that nine in ten of all recorded incidents related to nuisance rather than crime, and that tenants were particularly concerned about 'young people hanging around' (Phillips and Cochrane, 1988). The Coventry study revealed that more than one-third of shoppers expressed concern about being 'insulted' on the street, particularly by unruly young persons and public drinkers (Ramsay, 1989). And the Birmingham research identified significant levels of public anxiety about people loitering on the streets and teenage males displaying rowdy behaviour (Poole, 1991).

Fourthly, the anxieties about nuisance-type behaviour whilst shopping confirm that it is appropriate to make a distinction between 'crime' (which is relatively serious but which occurs fairly infrequently) and 'nuisance' (which is less serious, but nonetheless disturbing and which occurs more frequently). It is necessary, however, to accept the need for caution and clarity in operationalising the concepts of crime and nuisance so as to avoid confusion or overlap. Although there is no clear dividing line between crime and nuisance, the terms appear to have more than a superficial plausibility; and it is certainly the case that shopper-respondents make useful distinctions between the two categories.

Fifthly, it is equally clear that worries about crime and concerns about nuisance can have an impact on shoppers' behaviour – in the direction of disinclining them from visiting retail environments deemed to be at risk from crime or frequented by persons considered to be unsavoury or uncongenial. This type of reaction to a perceived threat has been termed 'reduced patronage' (Atkins, 1991), but the more straightforward term 'avoidance behaviour' is used in the current study. The Coventry research offers some of the strongest evidence (Ramsay, 1989). Two-thirds of shoppers claimed that they sometimes avoided the city centre and more than one-half avoided certain streets – most often to minimise the chance of unwanted contacts with drunks, unruly groups and young persons. The Birmingham research pointed to the same conclusion (Poole, 1991). One-half of the shoppers stayed away from the city centre at certain times and two-thirds said that they avoided a single city-centre shopping complex. Finally, the Leicester survey of safe shopping found that one in eight shoppers had altered their shopping behaviour in response to the perceived threat of terrorist outrages – either by avoiding London altogether, or by preferring to visit out-of-town retail parks rather than the 'too crowded' and 'too noisy' high street (Beck and Willis, 1993a, 1993b and 1994a).

Finally, the studies are also highly suggestive of the possibility that customers' perceptions of, and attitudes towards, crime and nuisance may be different in shopping centres and in town centres. This directs attention to the need for rigorous comparative analysis. It is equally clear that customers and shoppers in both environments are ready to provide detailed information about their concerns relating to the various threats to safe shopping – and of doing so in a way which distinguishes between crime and nuisance. There is an established methodology which can be used to explore these matters further.

Managing the risk

The studies also point to a clear need for managing the risk to shoppers in the various retail environments. The diversification of British retailing, together with increased competition between its component parts, has led to the establishment of representative bodies to promote the interests of its various stakeholders. With regard to town-centre retailing there are two principal organisations which have an important role in improving the retail environment by eliminating or minimising the threats posed to safe shopping by crime and nuisance.

The British Council of Shopping Centres (BCSC) was established in 1983 to represent those engaged in shopping and shopping-centre development and management (British Council of Shopping Centres, 1993a). Membership is open to both individuals and corporations and there are currently about 840 members. The Council has a number of objectives: to advance the development and improvement of shopping facilities in the

UK; to promote the prestige and standing of members as reputable specialists in the field of shopping and shopping-centre development and
management; to represent the interests of shopping centres in respect of
any legislation affecting retailing and property; to encourage the exchange
of information; and to further education, training and research. The
Council publishes a journal *Shopping Centre Horizons*, has a regular programme of technical visits and seminars, organises an annual conference
in conjunction with the Centre for Advanced Land Use Studies and issues
a Diploma in Shopping Centre Management and various awards.

The Association of Town Centre Management (ATCM) was established
in 1991, with members from both the private and public sectors, as a
means of revitalising traditional town centres and promoting their 'social,
cultural and commercial well-being' (Association of Town Centre
Management, 1994). It has a membership of 89 town-centre managers and
nearly 200 others; with the total expected to grow dramatically as many
more town-centre managers are appointed. The Association has a number
of objectives: to encourage co-operation among those with a common vision for town centres; to act as a national forum for the identification and
exchange of best practice; to consider national and local government
policies and to seek priority for the funding of town centres; and to liaise
with other organisations having similar aims. A central theme is the concept of town centre management (TCM) which strives to create a partnership of effort at the interface between the public and private sectors and
town-centre users to address the commercial, social, environmental and
management aspects of making town centres successful. The Association
prepares guidance and it has commissioned research into TCM in order to
establish what is 'good practice', as well as to foster private sector and local authority participation in its initiatives (Donaldsons and Healey &
Baker, 1994). The House of Commons Environment Committee commended TCM as an 'impressive example' of partnership initiatives (House
of Commons, 1994).

There is a common denominator in the work of the BCSC and the ATCM,
namely to promote the commercial interests of the membership by achiev-
ing a competitive edge – not least by making the retail environment more
attractive to the consumer. There is, however, an important distinction to
be made between initiatives which improve the ambience and atmosphere
of shopping areas and strategies which focus on the management or elimination of factors, including crime and nuisance, which might compromise
the shopping experience. The former may involve improvements in the
environment or the 'street scene', including: comprehensive and aes-

thetically pleasing signs; the provision of easy access, with good parking and public transport facilities; adequate car parking adjacent to the shops; pedestrianisation where appropriate; all forms of urban renewal and regeneration, including the upgrading and refurbishment of existing facilities; and vigorous marketing of the 'image' of the town centre or the shopping centre. These types of initiative are intended primarily to enhance the attractions of shopping in the area, although they may also impact indirectly on the problems of crime and nuisance. The latter calls for a more crime-focused approach aimed at the elimination or reduction of anything which threatens the safety and sense of security of either the retailer or the shopper.

Whatever the undoubted benefits deriving from the work of the BCSC and the ATCM, their published literature pays far more attention to the promotion of a pleasant shopping environment than it does to the elimination of negative features, such as crime and nuisance. Given the ways in which crime and nuisance can impact on customers and their confidence in a particular area or location, this concentration of effort has obvious drawbacks. A more balanced approach would, while promoting the overall objective of creating a convivial shopping environment, recognise that the elimination of the threats posed by crime and nuisance was an essential part of that process – something which would operate in the interest of retailers and shoppers alike. The new approach would view 'promoting' the town centre or the shopping centre and 'eliminating' any threats posed by crime and nuisance as opposite sides of the same coin, and as objectives which should be afforded equal priority. In an increasingly competitive climate retailers cannot afford to ignore disincentives to shopping caused by crime and nuisance. This points to the need for an empirical investigation of the extent of such problems in town centres and shopping centres, and the ways in which shopping-centre managers and town-centre managers can take responsibility for resolving them. The need for high quality information cannot be overstated. The House of Commons Environment Committee found that although a lot of retail data may be available it is not necessarily collated and accessible, and that there are also difficulties with confidentiality. There appears to be a great deal of anecdotal but little empirical evidence on the effects of shopping-centre developments on town centres. The committee recommended independent research into the impact of developments in one sector on other forms of retailing, as well as surveys of consumers' attitudes towards different forms of retail development (House of Commons, 1994). The present study, the research for which pre-dated the Environment Committee's report, meets both of these criteria.

3   Crime and Nuisance: The Customers' Perspective

The public's concerns about crime and nuisance whilst shopping were measured in four ways. First, shoppers were asked whether or not they were worried at all by crime whilst shopping – and, if so, to what extent they were worried. Secondly, shoppers were asked to rate the seriousness of 12 specific types of crime and nuisance which could give them cause for concern. Thirdly, the interviews explored whether or not shoppers avoided certain places in order to minimise the risks from crime and nuisance. Finally, all shoppers were asked direct questions about whether they had witnessed any form of criminal victimisation whilst shopping or whether they themselves had been the victim of a crime whilst shopping in the previous 12 months.

Concerns about crime

Shoppers were asked if they were worried about crime in any way at all whilst shopping during the day (Table 3.1). The term worry was adopted as a general indicator of anxiety and unease, albeit unfocused and unrelated to specific criminal acts.

A significant minority of shoppers were worried about crime. The level of concern was higher in town centres (28%) than in shopping centres (22%). This difference was not statistically significant. Of those who were worried, however, far more were 'very worried' in town centres (26%) than in shopping centres (11%). This difference was statistically significant. Predictably, and in common with most other 'fear of crime' surveys, the highest levels of concern were expressed by female respondents and older shoppers. Around three-quarters of respondents were not worried about crime – 72 per cent in town centres and 78 per cent in shopping centres.

Table 3.1 The extent to which the public worried about crime in town centres and shopping centres during the day

Dimensions of concern	Town centres	Shopping centres
	Per cent	
Worried or not		
Yes	28.5	21.9
No	71.5	78.1
Total	100.0	100.0
Extent of worry		
Very worried	26.3	11.1
Quite worried	52.6	52.4
Only rarely worried	21.1	36.5
Total	100.0	100.0

Seriousness of crime and nuisance

Shoppers were then asked to rate the seriousness of a range of crime and nuisance problems in the area in which they were then shopping (Table 3.2). Whereas the term worry was used as a general indicator of concern about crime, the exploration of perceived seriousness covered criminal acts, nuisance-type behaviour and pollution. This approach offered the principal means of investigating concerns which could be broken down both by type (crime, nuisance and pollution) and by weight (a range from 'very serious' to 'not serious at all').

The striking finding was that, for all types of crime, nuisance and pollution combined, the problems were seen as very serious or serious by far more shoppers in town centres (37%) than in shopping centres (11%). More than three times as many town-centre shoppers viewed crime and nuisance as a serious problem than did shopping-centre respondents. This was a statistically significant difference. There were also striking differences by type of crime and nuisance problem.

Table 3.2 The public's perception of crime and nuisance in town centres and shopping centres by type of problem and seriousness[*]

Problems	Very serious/ Serious		Not very serious/ Not serious at all	
	Town centres	Shopping centres	Town centres	Shopping centres
	Per cent			
Crime				
Physical assault	27.9	8.4	40.2	53.9
Drug-related offences	22.2	7.7	35.7	55.5
Car crime	51.2	15.3	25.5	56.6
Vandalism/Graffiti	43.7	13.5	53.6	84.0
Nuisance				
Threatening youths	29.4	14.3	65.5	79.8
Vagrants/Beggars	49.1	11.8	47.0	85.1
Drunks	41.6	8.0	53.8	88.1
Kids hanging around	34.7	24.0	61.9	70.8
Illegal street vendors	15.3	5.6	81.7	89.2
Buskers	15.0	1.4	83.0	96.5
Pollution				
Litter	56.3	19.8	43.1	79.1
Dogs fouling streets	54.4	5.2	38.4	88.6
All problems	36.7	11.2	52.4	77.3

[*] All 'Don't know' responses have been excluded from this table for the sake of clarity, so in most cases the percentages do not total 100.

In town centres, a substantial minority of one in four or more of the shoppers identified the crime categories of physical assault (28%) and drug-related offences (22%) as serious problems. And over one-half of the shoppers rated car crime as a serious problem (51%). Between 40 and 50 per cent of the shoppers thought that vagrants and street beggars (49%), vandals (44%) and drunks on the streets (42%) were serious problems.

Around one-third of town-centre shoppers were concerned about children hanging around (35%) and threatening youths (29%). Only a minority of shoppers thought that illegal street vending (15%) and busking (15%) were problems. Finally, more than one-half of the respondents expressed environmental concerns about litter (56%) and dogs fouling the pavement (54%).

In shopping centres, only three problems were rated as very serious or serious by one in six or more of the respondents – children hanging around (24%), litter (20%) and car crime (15%). Few shopping-centre respondents saw the crime categories of physical assault (8%) or drug-related crime (8%) as serious problems.

Table 3.3 The public's perception of very serious or serious crime and nuisance problems in town centres and shopping centres by type of problem showing the factor by which town-centre problems exceeded shopping-centre problems

Problems	Town centres	Shopping centres	Factor by which town centres exceeded shopping centres
	Per cent seen as very serious or serious		
Crime			
Physical assault	28	8	x 3
Drug-related offences	22	8	x 3
Car crime	51	15	x 3
Vandalism/Graffiti	44	14	x 3
Nuisance			
Threatening youths	29	14	x 2
Vagrants/Beggars	49	12	x 4
Drunks	42	8	x 5
Kids hanging around	35	24	x 1
Illegal street vendors	15	6	x 3
Buskers	15	1	x 11
Pollution			
Litter	56	20	x 3
Dogs fouling streets	54	5	x 10
All problems	37	11	x 3

Far more town-centre shoppers expressed the view that crime and nuisance was very serious or serious than did shopping-centre respondents. Table 3.3 offers a simplified presentation of these remarkable findings – focusing on the crime and nuisance problems which were identified as very serious or serious, and showing the factor by which the seriousness ratings of problems in town centres exceeded those of problems in shopping centres. In all cases bar one (kids hanging around) the differences were statistically significant.

Overall, the four crime categories of physical assault, drug-related offences, car crime and vandalism or graffiti were perceived as very serious or serious by three times as many town-centre shoppers as shopping-centre visitors. With regard to nuisance-type problems, far more town-centre shoppers perceived these as very serious or serious than did shopping-centre visitors – buskers (x 11), drunks (x 5), vagrants or beggars (x 4) and illegal street vendors (x 3).

Avoidance behaviour

A central concern was whether the fear of crime and nuisance impacted on shopping behaviour (Table 3.4).

Table 3.4 Avoidance behaviour in town centres and shopping centres

Avoidance behaviour	Town centres	Shopping centres
	Per cent	
Areas avoided or not		
Yes	13.0	4.9
No	87.0	95.1
Total	100.0	100.0
Areas avoided		
Pubs and clubs	39.5	42.9
Car parks	27.9	28.6
Shopping centres	18.6	–
Fast food outlets	14.0	21.4
Toilets	–	7.1
Total	100.0	100.0

Shoppers were asked to state in their own words whether or not there were areas within the shopping environment which they avoided; and, if so, which particular places they tended not to visit. A minority of shoppers said that they avoided certain places – but, as might have been predicted from the earlier findings, the proportion was much higher in town centres (13%) than in shopping centres (5%). This difference was statistically significant. Nearly three times as many town-centre shoppers said that they would not enter certain areas as did respondents in shopping centres. The two groups agreed that the places to be avoided above all were pubs and clubs – 40 per cent of town-centre shoppers and 43 per cent of shopping-centre visitors. They also agreed that car parks were to be avoided – 28 per cent of town-centre and 29 per cent of shopping-centre shoppers.

Risk of crime

Whatever the levels of anxiety about criminal victimisation, the only 'hard' measure of crime is whether shoppers had seen a crime being perpetrated whilst shopping (Table 3.5) or had been the victim of crime themselves whilst shopping (Table 3.6).

Table 3.5 Criminal victimisation witnessed in town centres and shopping centres in previous 12 months by type of crime

Witnessed crime	Town centres		Shopping centres	
	Number	Per cent	Number	Per cent
Witnessed a crime or not				
Yes	28	8.4	2	4.5
No	306	91.6	275	95.5
Total	334	100.0	288	100.0
Type of crime witnessed				
Shoplifting	12	42.9	10	76.9
Fighting	6	21.4	–	–
Shooting	1	3.6	–	–
Assault	2	7.1	1	7.7
Muggings/Snatches	5	17.9	1	7.7
Car crime	2	7.1	1	7.7
Total	28	100.0	13	100.0

These data relate to criminal victimisation in a 12 month period immediately prior to the interview, but only to crimes witnessed or to
victimisation suffered whilst shopping. In both cases the number of real-
crime incidents was small. This means that caution needs to be exercised
in drawing any inferences from the data. With regard to witnessed
criminal victimisation (Table 3.5) only 28 out of 334 town-centre shoppers
(8%) and only 13 out of 288 shopping-centre shoppers (5%) had seen any
form of criminal activity. Although the numbers were very small and the
differences were not significant, the data tend to confirm the earlier
findings that the problems of crime and nuisance are greater in town
centres than in shopping centres. In both locations the largest single
category of crimes witnessed was shoplifting – 43 per cent in town centres
and 77 per cent in shopping centres. It is also interesting to note that one-
half of all crimes witnessed in town centres (50%) were crimes of a violent
nature – fighting, assault, mugging and a single shooting. In contrast, 15
per cent of crimes witnessed in shopping centres fell into the category of
violent crime.

**Table 3.6 Criminal victimisation in town centres and shopping centres
in previous 12 months by type of crime**

Criminal victimisation	Town centres		Shopping centres	
	Number	**Per cent**	**Number**	**Per cent**
Victim or not				
Yes	19	6.0	2	0.7
No	315	94.0	286	99.3
Total	334	100.0	288	100.0
Type of criminal victimisation				
Car crime	8	42.0	1	50.0
Assault	8	42.0	–	–
Robbery	3	16.0	1	50.0
Total	19	100.0	2	100.0

With regard to actual criminal victimisation (Table 3.6) there were even
fewer incidents. Only 19 out of 334 town-centre shoppers (6%) and just
two out of 288 shopping-centre shoppers (1%) had themselves been vic-

timised whilst shopping in the 12 months prior to being interviewed. Although there were only a small number of victims the difference in the overall level between town centres and shopping centres was statistically significant; but the very small number of cases precluded any useful comparisons between the two shopping environments in terms of type of victimisation.

Indicators of crime and nuisance

The impact of crime and nuisance on shoppers in the two shopping environments was assessed in three interrelated ways: the extent to which visitors were 'worried' about crime whilst shopping during the day; 'seriousness' ratings for 12 types of crime, nuisance and pollution; and the amount of victimisation suffered or witnessed whilst shopping. The first two are indirect indicators of levels of crime and nuisance, whilst the third is a direct measure. All the findings point to the same conclusion – namely, that town centres are far more crime-prone and nuisance-prone than shopping centres. The weight of the evidence is considerable. Given the complexity of the data it may be helpful to restate some of the findings, and compare them with earlier research, before moving on to suggest a possible explanation of them.

Fear of crime

Over one-quarter of town-centre visitors (28%) were worried about criminal victimisation during daytime shopping, compared with one in five visitors to shopping centres (22%). There were significant differences in the seriousness ratings for four categories of crime. In town centres over one-half of respondents rated car crime as serious compared with 15 per cent of the respondents in shopping centres. Vandalism or graffiti was rated as a serious problem by over four in ten town-centre visitors. Over one-quarter of town-centre respondents rated physical assault as a serious problem compared with just one in twelve respondents in shopping centres. And drug-related crime was seen as a serious problem by one in five town-centre shoppers. In all categories, three times as many town-centre shoppers rated crime as a serious problem as did shopping-centre shoppers. There were also significant differences in the seriousness ratings for categories of nuisance – unwelcome or unwanted persons in the shopping environment. Town-centre respondents were significantly more concerned than shopping-centre respondents about vagrants or beggars (49%), drunks (42%) and threatening youths (29%).

The only category of crime and nuisance (excluding pollution) which was rated as very serious or serious by more than a tiny proportion of shopping-centre visitors was that of kids hanging around (24%). For them this was by far the most serious problem. The finding is roughly in line with earlier studies. For example, the Birmingham data (Poole, 1991) indicated that a minority of shopping-centre customers felt intimidated by people hanging around on restricted routes (40%) and by teenage males displaying rowdy behaviour (32%). Phillips and Cochrane (1988) found that 45 per cent of respondents identified young persons hanging around as a major problem; this was deemed to be more of a problem by tenants than shoplifting. Both studies suggested that shopping centres had a particular problem with regard to the intimidating presence of young persons, something which is confirmed by the present study.

Town-centre shoppers identified all types of crime as significant problems and were also concerned about nuisance-type behaviour. In contrast, shopping-centre visitors were relatively untroubled by either crime or nuisance, with the sole exception of kids hanging around. The findings have major implications for town-centre managers and shopping-centre managers. The former will need to face the uncomfortable truth that their shoppers and customers perceive town centres to be blighted by both crime and nuisance – and to a significant degree. The latter can take considerable comfort in the finding that the only identified problem in shopping centres was that of kids hanging around.

Criminal victimisation

Both town-centre and shopping-centre managers may be reassured by the relatively small number of incidents of criminal victimisation witnessed or suffered by shoppers whilst shopping in the two environments over a 12 month period. This finding is in line with the evidence from successive sweeps of the British Crime Survey which show consistently that levels of anxiety are out of all proportion to the risks of victimisation. The findings for actual rates of victimisation were much lower than those identified by Poole in the Birmingham city-centre survey where one in ten female shoppers had had property stolen and one in eleven had had their motor vehicle stolen or something stolen from it (Poole, 1991).

There are, however, few grounds for complacency because even though the number of incidents was small, any rate of criminal victimisation must be considered undesirable and unacceptable. Nor should the clear differences between town centres and shopping centres in this respect be overlooked. There was twice as much crime witnessed in town centres (8%) as in shopping centres (4%). And there was six times as much victimisation suffered by shoppers whilst shopping in town centres (6%) as in shopping centres (1%). This latter difference was statistically significant. The data on victimisation witnessed and personally experienced offer a hard measure which corroborates the findings on both worry and seriousness – namely that the problems of crime and nuisance are substantially greater in town centres than in shopping centres.

Behavioural consequences

It would also be unwise to discount or write off the weaker indicators of crime and nuisance (the worry and seriousness findings) because they are an imprecise or incomplete assessment of the range and scale of the problems. Admittedly, it is fashionable to argue that a preoccupation with the fear of crime, which is almost invariably unrelated to the actual risk of victimisation, is dangerous in itself because it encourages a sense of insecurity (Jenkins, 1994b; Toynbee, 1994). It is argued that the inexorable rise in the 'tide of terror' has the effect of creating a real problem out of a non-problem. A recent joint paper by the Police Foundation and Policy Studies Institute (1993) suggests that the more attention that is paid to crime and the greater the emphasis on security, the more likely it is that the fear of crime will rise. There is increasing academic support for this view (van Dijk and Mayhew, 1993; Bottoms and Wiles, 1994; Mayhew, 1994). Pearson makes the point that because there are so many mathematical unknowns in both police statistics and victimisation surveys, a certain crime-myth perpetuates itself, a:

> ... myth granted numerical certainty by the criminal statistics which, obeying their own grammar of continuity, spiral relentlessly upwards ... and obligingly confirm our worst fears of social ruin.
>
> (Pearson, 1983: 213)

Although this is an important point of caution it does not necessarily follow that the perceived fear of crime is wholly unrelated to actual victimisation, or that all fears should be discounted as unreasonable (Young, 1994). Where anxiety takes the form of considered judgements and where these show differentiation between respondents (by location and by type of fear) it becomes more difficult to sustain a case for ignoring them. The prudent course is to take what respondents say at face value, even though their assessments may be informal or untutored. The fear of crime may be an incomplete and imperfect measure but it can be taken as an indicator of well-founded concerns which merit attention.

Evidence from the earlier studies of shopping behaviour indicates clearly that the perception of being at risk – even where this is unfounded or exaggerated – can have real behavioural consequences. Worried or frightened shoppers may elect to avoid those locations where their anxiety is greatest. This is a crucial point for retailers; a precondition for profit is the presence of customers. Four studies offered hard data on avoidance behaviour:

- The Coventry survey identified one-half or more of respondents as stating that they had modified their behaviour to avoid possible criminal victimisation – nearly two-thirds sometimes kept out of the city centre, 59 per cent avoided certain people and 56 per cent avoided certain streets (Ramsay, 1989).

- The Birmingham city-centre research found that one-half of all shoppers (50%) said that they avoided certain areas, especially in the evenings; and that a minority regularly carried personal alarms whilst shopping (Poole, 1991).

- The Nottingham audit suggested that the costs of crime to the city, including the losses due to worried shoppers taking their custom elsewhere, were of the order of £12 million in lost turnover and £0.8 million in forfeited profits over an eight-month period (KPMG Peat Marwick, 1991).

- The Leicester 'safe shopping' survey found that as many as one in eight shoppers (12%) said that they had changed their shopping behaviour in response to the perceived threat of terrorist attack. Of these 'avoiders' the majority said that they now preferred to shop in out-of-town retail parks because the town centres were too noisy and too crowded (Beck and Willis, 1993a, 1993b and 1994a).

Whilst the current study confirms this phenomenon in general, it also points to the fact that town centres are significantly more at risk of losing customers than shopping centres. As many as one in seven of the town-centre shoppers (13%) said that they avoided certain areas of the town centre (mostly around pubs and clubs) compared with 5 per cent of the shopping-centre shoppers. Nearly three times more shoppers in town centres said that they avoided certain places than in shopping centres. The clear inference is that the perceived lack of security in town centres acts as a disincentive to shopping there.

Towards an explanation

The conclusion that crime and nuisance is substantially greater in town centres than in shopping centres in the same town or city requires explanation. There are a number of possibilities. There may be factors which predispose town centres to crime and nuisance and there may be other variables which effectively insulate shopping centres against such problems. Another possibility is that shopping centres can exercise control over access in a way which is not available to town centres. Finally, there may be real differences in the ways in which social control and policing is exercised in the two retail environments. These possibilities are discussed briefly here, and then again later with the benefit of further research findings.

It may well be the case that town centres are by their nature more at risk of crime and nuisance than shopping centres. It would be unwise to overlook the obvious, namely that the town centre is a public and open environment with few or no controls over access. Everyone, however uncongenial and undesirable they might be, is at liberty to use the public spaces of the town centre up to the point where they break the law. The town centre is usually a complex network of shops, businesses and offices, with numerous leisure facilities (including pubs, clubs and off-licences) and sports venues, such as football grounds. The town centre also has a range of local authority-funded public amenities, including facilities for visitors by road, rail and bus.

The town centre is liable to suffer all the problems associated with nuisance and disorder in public places. It typically throngs with visitors pursuing different objectives and with different reasons for being there. The sheer scale of the town centre, together with its multiplicity of roles for different users, simply makes the area exposed to crime and nuisance. It acts as a magnet for a wide range of people, not all of whom observe conventional canons of good behaviour. And the very structure of the town centre means that it is vulnerable to certain types of crime – for example, car-related offences, predatory crimes of assault and those related to drug use or drug dealing. Finally, certain parts of town centres can be seen as the natural repository for drunks, beggars and the like. And the shadow home secretary, Jack Straw, has pointed to what he calls the 'brutalisation of Britain's high streets' by the aggressive begging of 'winos, addicts and squeegee merchants' (Travis, 1995b), although he is rather less specific about how to deal with the problem – other than by re-stating the need to reclaim the high streets for law-abiding citizens (Ford, 1995a).

In contrast, the shopping centre is a smaller and more coherent place where most of the visitors have a focused purpose in a structured environment. It is dedicated to attracting purposeful shoppers and to meeting their needs. Ironically, the same factors which make the shopping centre an agreeable and attractive place for the modern shopper may act as a disincentive to would-be troublemakers. The spaciousness, good lighting, airiness and cleanliness of the shopping centre may prove less than captivating to the street-scene troublemaker who prefers the more volatile atmosphere of the town centre and its 'richer' mix of crime and nuisance possibilities. Relative to the town centre, the less fragmented structure of the shopping centre may make it unattractive to anyone other than those who visit for the express purposes of browsing, buying and indulging in associated activities. To this extent it is unsurprising that the only problem which was identified by shopping-centre visitors was that of young kids hanging around.

The shopping centre is also a more private and regulated environment than the town centre – with greater control over the type of person who is admitted or allowed to stay. And the shopping centre may elect to exercise control over access to private property on grounds other than those of lawlessness. Policing in the town centre will normally take the form of low-level preventative patrols with more vigorous action being taken only when an offence has been committed or is threatened. Private policing in the shopping centre may have a lower level of tolerance, with private security guards excluding people whose behaviour or demeanour constitutes a nuisance, even though this falls well short of criminal activity. In effect, undesirable 'street people' can be excluded from the private spaces of shopping centres and possibly displaced to the public places of the town centres.

There is an important distinction to be made between 'public places' in town centres and 'private spaces' in shopping centres. In general, shopping malls retain their status as private property and all activities – including entry – take place with the consent of the owner. A recent legal decision confirmed the 'private' status of shopping centres. In the case of *CIN*

Properties v *Rawlins and Others* (*The Times*, 9th February, 1995), the central question was the right of the public to use pedestrian malls within a town-centre shopping complex. The decision was that the public at large had no right to enter the mall and that the owners had a right to determine what licence the public might have to enter it. These issues are explored further in Chapter 5 where particular attention is paid to the role of private security guards and the exercise of discretion in restricting access and ejecting undesirable visitors, as well as the criteria which govern decision making in these areas.

This suggests that there are real differences in the ways in which the two shopping environments are policed. In particular there is an important distinction to be drawn between reliance on traditional, bobby-on-the-beat policing in town centres (public policing) and the use of in-house or contract security guards in shopping centres (private security). Whereas public policing in the town centre is a multi-faceted service of which the safety and security of shoppers is but one aspect, private security in the shopping centre is dedicated solely to protecting shoppers and the shopping environment. Private security in the shopping centre is a one-dimensional task when compared with the many and competing demands placed on conventional policing in the town centre. This allows private security to be a more focused activity than public policing. Chapter 5 reveals significant differences between public policing in town centres and private security in shopping centres. These findings give rise to an extended discussion in Chapter 6 of the use, growth and regulation of private security personnel in the retail environment.

Tests of significance

Table 3.1

Worried or not $\chi^2_c = 3.6$, 1 df, p = 0.0576
Extent of worry $\chi^2 = 7.2$, 2 df, p < 0.05

Table 3.2

Crime
     Physical assault $\chi^2_c = 37.1$, 1 df, p < 0.0001
     Drug-related offences $\chi^2_c = 38.9$, 1 df, p < 0.0001
     Car crime $\chi^2_c = 95.4$, 1 df, p < 0.0001
     Vandalism/Graffiti $\chi^2 = 85.9$, 1 df, p < 0.0001

Nuisance
     Threatening youths $\chi^2 = 20.2$, 1 df, p < 0.0001
     Vagrants/Beggars $\chi^2_c = 102.2$, 1 df, p < 0.0001
     Drunks $\chi^2_c = 92.7$, 1 df, p < 0.0001
     Kids hanging around $\chi^2 = 7.8$, 1 df, p = 0.0053
     Illegal street vendors $\chi^2 = 14.5$, 1 df, p < 0.001
     Buskers $\chi^2 = 35.9$, 1 df, p < 0.0001

Pollution
     Litter $\chi^2_c = 68.5$, 1 df, p < 0.0001
     Dogs fouling streets $\chi^2 = 179.0$, 1 df, p < 0.0001

All problems $\chi^2 = 62.7$, 1 df, p < 0.0001

Table 3.4 $\chi^2 = 11.9$, 1 df, p < 0.001

Table 3.5 $\chi^2 = 3.7$, 1 df, p = 0.052

Table 3.6 $\chi^2 = 12.7$, 1 df, p < 0.001

4 Crime and Nuisance: The Managers' Perspective

The next logical step in the exploration of crime and nuisance in town centres and shopping centres was to examine the views of town-centre and shopping-centre managers. It is arguable that the managers had a rather more informed perspective on crime and nuisance than had ordinary members of the public, partly because they had formal obligations in the fields of safety and security. The questionnaires made it clear that respondents were to answer the questions on the basis of their professional experience in the particular environment in which they were currently working.

It was possible, therefore, to ask town-centre and shopping-centre managers rather more direct questions about crime, nuisance and pollution than were asked of members of the public, but still using mainly the same categories of problems. One question was concerned with the frequency with which criminal and nuisance-type incidents occurred – daily, weekly, monthly or less frequently. Another question required respondents to identify the single most serious crime and nuisance problem from their point of view. The data permit comparisons to be made between the two retail environments on the nature and extent of crime and nuisance problems.

A second objective was to enable comparisons to be drawn between the views of the shopping public and the views of the managers. To the extent that the public and the managers have similar perceptions of crime and nuisance in the same location (town centre or shopping centre) this would constitute corroboration of the other's view – which could then be taken as strong indirect evidence of the types and scale of the real problems.

Frequency of crime and nuisance

Town-centre and shopping-centre managers were asked to estimate the frequency of a range of crime, nuisance and pollution problems in the area for which they had responsibility (Tables 4.1 and 4.2).

Table 4.1 Town-centre managers' perception of crime and nuisance in town centres by type of problem and frequency

Problems	Daily	Weekly	Monthly/Less than monthly	Never
			Per cent	
Crime				
Physical assault	3.6	17.9	78.5	–
Drug-related offences	11.5	23.1	65.4	–
Car crime	59.3	33.3	7.4	–
Vandalism/Graffiti	25.0	46.4	28.6	–
Nuisance				
Threatening youths	3.7	44.4	48.1	3.7
Vagrants/Beggars	53.3	16.7	26.7	3.3
Drunks	30.8	46.2	23.1	–
Kids hanging around	40.0	15.0	30.0	15.0
Illegal street vendors	17.2	37.9	24.1	20.7
Buskers	43.5	30.4	17.5	8.7
Prostitutes	15.4	–	23.1	61.5
Pollution				
Litter	56.0	20.0	24.0	–
Dogs fouling streets	28.0	12.0	52.0	8.0
All problems	29.8	26.3	34.5	9.3

Using 'daily' as the strongest measure of the frequency of crime and nuisance, and taking 'all problems' as a generic or composite measure of crime and nuisance, a major finding was that these problems were seen as occurring on a daily basis much more in town centres than in shopping centres. For all types of crime, nuisance and pollution combined, the problems were seen as a daily occurrence by far more town-centre managers (30%) than shopping-centre managers (10%). Three times as many town-centre managers considered crime and nuisance to be an endemic feature of their shopping environment than did shopping-centre managers. This difference was statistically significant. There were also striking differences for each type of crime and nuisance.

Table 4.2 Shopping-centre managers' perception of crime and nuisance in shopping centres by type of problem and frequency

Problems	Daily	Weekly	Monthly/Less than monthly	Never
			Per cent	
Crime				
Physical assault	0.8	3.8	51.0	44.4
Drug-related offences	3.0	6.8	54.9	35.3
Car crime	1.6	23.0	58.7	16.7
Vandalism/Graffiti	9.4	21.7	63.8	5.1
Nuisance				
Threatening youths	2.9	19.7	57.7	19.7
Vagrants/Beggars	12.6	9.6	40.8	37.0
Drunks	4.9	23.2	57.8	14.1
Kids hanging around	15.4	24.4	35.8	24.4
Illegal street vendors	3.0	5.3	24.0	67.7
Buskers	3.9	11.6	22.0	63.5
Prostitutes	0.8	–	5.5	93.7
Pollution				
Litter	58.1	11.6	11.7	18.6
Dogs fouling streets	–	–	–	–
All problems	9.7	13.4	40.3	36.7

For town-centre managers, using the average figure for 'all problems' estimated as occurring daily (30%) as a baseline, the categories of crime and nuisance which figured most prominently were, in ascending order: drunks (31%), kids hanging around (40%), buskers (44%), vagrants or beggars (53%) and car crime (59%); and there was substantial concern about litter (56%). For shopping-centre managers, using the average figure for 'all problems' estimated as occurring on a daily basis (10%), the categories of crime and nuisance which figured most prominently were just vagrants or beggars (13%) and kids hanging around (15%); and here too there was substantial concern about litter (58%). There were statistically significant differences between the two samples with regard to eight out of the twelve categories of crime, nuisance and pollution: car crime, vandalism/graffiti, vagrants/beggars, drunks, kids hanging around, illegal street vendors, buskers and prostitutes.

More specifically, as regards the four categories of crime (excluding all types of nuisance and pollution) there were differences in the managers' perceptions of frequency of occurrence. The percentage of town-centre managers who estimated that crimes occurred on a daily basis were: for physical assault (4%), drug-related offences (12%), vandalism and graffiti (25%) and car crime (59%). In contrast, the percentage of shopping-centre managers who estimated that crimes occurred on a daily basis were: for physical assault (less than 1%), car crime (2%), drug-related offences (3%) and vandalism and graffiti (9%). The differences with regard to car crime and vandalism/graffiti were statistically significant.

Although the first step was to consider the differences between town-centre and shopping-centre managers' perceptions of the frequency of crime, nuisance and pollution (combined), it was also possible to look for differences between managers' perceptions of the more serious categories of crime and nuisance (excluding pollution) and the most serious category of crime (taken on its own). The relevant data are presented in Table 4.3. Far more town-centre managers saw all problems combined as a daily 'fact of life' than did shopping-centre managers, but the differences were more marked at the 'crime' end of the spectrum (most serious) than in the 'nuisance' part of the spectrum (less serious).

Table 4.3 Managers' perceptions of crime, nuisance and pollution occurring on a daily basis in town centres and shopping centres by type of problem and the factor by which town-centre problems exceeded shopping-centre problems

Problems	Town centres	Shopping centres	Factor by which town centres exceeded shopping centres
	Per cent of problems seen as occurring daily		
Crime, nuisance and pollution	30	10	x 3
Crime and nuisance	28	5	x 5
Crime	25	4	x 6

When the data on pollution are excluded, the difference in terms of perceived frequency becomes much more dramatic. Over one-quarter of the town-centre managers (28%) saw crime and nuisance as daily events. In contrast, only one in twenty shopping-centre managers (5%) saw crime and nuisance as occurring daily. And if the data on both pollution and nuisance are excluded and the four criminal offences only are considered, the difference between the two groups of managers' perceptions of frequency increase still further. One-quarter of town-centre managers (25%) estimated that crime occurred on a daily basis compared with just one in twenty five of the shopping-centre managers (4%). With everything but the most serious categories of crime excluded, six times more town-centre managers thought criminal activities pervasive than did shopping-centre managers.

Single most serious problem

The managers' perceptions of the frequency with which crime and nuisance occurred cannot be divorced from their views on the seriousness of these problems. One way of addressing this was to ask the managers in the two shopping environments to identify what they regarded as the single most serious problem in their town centre or shopping centre (Table 4.4).

In terms of seriousness, problems of pollution (litter and dogs fouling the streets) and most types of nuisance faded into relative insignificance, although they had previously figured prominently as occurring on a daily basis. Crime rather than nuisance or pollution emerged as the most serious problem. Combining the four categories of crime into a single sub-total, nearly two-thirds of town-centre managers (64%) and nearly one-half of shopping-centre managers (47%) saw criminal activities as their most serious problem. The differences between town-centre and shopping-centre managers' concerns as reflected in the sub-totals relating to both crime and nuisance were statistically significant.

The distribution of perceived seriousness was rather different for the two samples when the three sub-totals (crime, nuisance and pollution) were compared. Nearly two-thirds of town-centre managers highlighted crime (64%) and one-third emphasised nuisance (32%). For shopping-centre managers there was an equal split between crime (47%) and nuisance (47%) as the most serious problem. Differences were also apparent between the individual categories which comprised these sub-totals. Perhaps predictably, car crime was identified as the most serious type of crime by both town-centre managers (39%) and shopping-centre managers (18%).

**Table 4.4 Town-centre and shopping-centre managers'
perception of the most serious problem**

Most serious problem	Town-centre managers	Shopping-centre managers
	Per cent	
Crime		
Physical assault	3.6	6.7
Drug-related offences	7.1	10.9
Car crime	39.4	18.5
Vandalism/Graffiti	14.3	10.9
Sub-total	64.4	47.0
Nuisance		
Threatening youths	3.6	26.0
Vagrants/Beggars	6.9	5.0
Drunks	14.3	11.8
Kids hanging around	–	3.4
Illegal street vendors	7.1	–
Buskers	–	0.8
Prostitutes	–	–
Sub-total	31.9	47.0
Pollution		
Litter	3.6	5.9
Dogs fouling streets	–	–
Total	100.0	100.0

Less predictably, and perhaps more worryingly, there was also a strong undercurrent of opinion in both groups of managers that drug-related offences were the single most pressing problem – an opinion offered by one in fourteen town-centre managers (7%) and one in nine shopping-centre managers (11%). There was also a minority view that violent crime or physical assault was the most serious problem – held by 4 per cent of town-centre managers and 7 per cent of shopping-centre managers. If these latter two categories are combined then drug-related and violent crime was seen to be the most serious problem by one in nine of town-centre managers (11%) and by one in six shopping-centre managers (18%). Although in the overall picture persons who caused a nuisance were seen to be generally less of a problem than those involved in criminal behaviour, a minority of both groups of managers saw drunks as the single most pressing problem – with one in seven town-centre managers (14%) and one in eight shopping-centre managers (12%) taking this view. In addition, over one-quarter of shopping-centre managers (26%) highlighted threatening youths as the single most serious problem compared with just 4 per cent of town-centre managers.

Indicators of crime and nuisance

On the assumption that town-centre and shopping-centre managers are well placed to comment with authority on the general and specific problems of crime and nuisance in the shopping areas for which they have responsibility, the findings on both 'frequency' and 'seriousness' are compelling and point unequivocally in the direction of town centres having a significantly worse problem than shopping centres. Three times as many town-centre managers (30%) as shopping-centre managers (10%) thought that crime, nuisance and pollution were everyday occurrences. If the four categories of crime are taken on their own, then six times as many town-centre managers (25%) as shopping-centre managers (4%) thought that crime was commonplace. And nearly two-thirds of the town-centre managers (64%) and one-half of the shopping-centre managers (47%) pointed to criminal behaviour as their most serious problem. Nuisance was much less evident and pollution faded into relative insignificance. The seriousness of motor vehicle crime was highlighted by both groups, but there was a significant undercurrent of feeling about the gravity of physical assaults, drunkenness and drug-related criminality.

Shoppers and managers: a comparison

In addition and more importantly, although a direct comparison between the public's perceptions of the seriousness of types of crime and nuisance and the managers' estimates of the frequency with which crime and nuisance occurred is problematic, on the assumption that both offer a reasonable indicator of threats to safe shopping, there was a striking congruence between the views of the shoppers and those of the managers (Table 4.5).

Using the figures for 'all problems' as a composite measure of the various crime, nuisance and pollution risks to safe shopping, over one in three members of the public in town centres (37%) rated them as serious compared with one in nine customers in shopping centres (11%). That is, more than three times as many town-centre shoppers as shopping-centre shoppers viewed crime and nuisance as a serious problem. Again, using the figures for 'all problems' as a composite measure, one in three managers in town centres (30%) saw crime, nuisance or pollution as occurring on a daily basis compared with one in ten managers in shopping centres (10%). That is, three times as many town-centre managers as shopping-centre managers viewed crime and nuisance as endemic. Shoppers and managers saw the problems of crime and nuisance in near-identical terms. The data point unequivocally to the conclusion that the problems of crime and nuisance are significantly greater in town centres than in shopping centres.

Table 4.5 Perceptions of crime, nuisance and pollution by seriousness (the public) and by frequency (the managers) and the factor by which town-centre problems exceeded shopping-centre problems

Perceptions of problems	Town centres	Shopping centres	Factor by which town centres exceeded shopping centres
	Per cent		
Public Seriousness (Very serious or serious)			
Crime	36	11	x 3
Nuisance	31	11	x 3
Pollution	55	12	x 5
All problems	37	11	x 3
Managers Frequency (Daily occurrence)			
Crime	25	4	x 6
Nuisance	29	6	x 5
Pollution	42	58	–
All problems	30	10	x 3

All of the indicators reviewed in this and the previous chapter point in this direction. The public's worry about crime and nuisance, their ratings in terms of seriousness and their tendency to avoid certain areas suggest that shopping in town-centres is much less safe than in shopping centres. The findings on victimisation witnessed and personally experienced corroborate this view. And the comments from town-centre and shopping-centre managers on both the frequency and the seriousness of crime and nuisance also suggest that the town centre is more at risk than the shopping centre. Finally, where there are points of comparison between them, shoppers and managers in the town centre clearly articulated the view that this shopping environment was more susceptible to crime and nuisance than shoppers and managers in the shopping centre. The congruence between the views of shoppers and managers within the same shopping environment was of the order of a mirror image.

Managing the risks

The starting point for action to minimise the threats to safe shopping is to acknowledge the extent of the problem and to accept that 'owning' the problem is a necessary condition for responding to it. No matter how uncomfortable it may be, particularly for town-centre managers and for retailers with a major stake in town centres, unless there is a general recognition of the difficulties and their dimensions there can be no progress towards solutions. Failure to accept this may result in an increase in the migration of worried town-centre shoppers (the avoiders) to the more congenial environments offered by shopping centres and retail parks. The town-centre retailer will not need reminding about a steady drift of customers away from the high street, but is now in a position to include crime and nuisance disincentives to shopping as one factor to be considered in taking remedial action.

It would be naive, however, to underestimate the strong pressures which militate against the acceptance of uncomfortable findings; and recent research by the Association of Town Centre Management offers a conspicuous example (Donaldsons and Healey & Baker, 1994). The study was intended to provide an independent evaluation of TCM initiatives and the overall conclusion was a blanket assertion that 'TCM is effective'. There was some evidence for this view, but major findings on the public's perceptions of the criminal risks to safe shopping remained largely unexplored in the text and were not subject to analysis or commentary. For example, over three-quarters of the 2,000 shoppers who were interviewed (79%) highlighted the importance of measures against crime and violence in making town centres attractive for visitors. These aspirations were not being met. More than one-half of the visitors identified security deficiencies

(55%) as cause for concern and over one in three said that they were aware of a deterioration in standards relating to crime and violence in recent years (34%). Perhaps inadvertently, these three negative findings were buried in a text which sought – in the authors' own words – 'to prove' the effectiveness of the TCM initiative. If they had been given due prominence, the favourable and generalised conclusion about the effectiveness of TCM would have been much more difficult to sustain.

If disquieting findings are faced up to, further analysis of the data may begin to suggest solutions; and crime and nuisance problems can be converted into safety and security opportunities. A closer examination of some of the current findings together with previous research which permits some inferences to be drawn about crime problems as they affect the retail environment, may offer useful pointers for security risk management.

Motor vehicle crime and car parking

Motor vehicle-related offences were highlighted by both town-centre managers (39%) and shopping-centre managers (18%) as the single most serious crime problem. But whereas well over one-half of town-centre managers (59%) saw car crime as a daily occurrence, only 2 per cent of shopping-centre managers thought of it as an everyday event. These figures are reflected in national and international data on car crime. For example, during 1993 in England and Wales, from a total of nearly 20 million vehicles, there was a total of 1.5 million recorded offences – 926,000 thefts from vehicles and 598,000 thefts of vehicles; and overall, car crime accounted for 28 per cent of the 5.5 million recorded offences (Ford, 1994b). Additional data from the BCS show that a significant proportion of car crime remains unreported – 69 per cent of thefts from motor vehicles and 8 per cent of thefts of motor vehicles (Home Office, 1994b), as well as over 90 per cent of criminal damage to motor vehicles (Laycock, 1988).

The British Crime Survey estimated that 22 per cent of thefts of cars and 20 per cent of thefts from cars take place in private or municipal car parks – though local data show that these figures can be much higher (Drury, 1992; Webb and Laycock, 1992; Webb et al, 1992). The 'car theft index' developed by the Home Office suggests that the most vulnerable vehicles are the ones parked in public places with little security (Houghton, 1992). The overall cost of car crime was estimated to be £700 million. And the International Crime Survey (ICS) of 20 countries found that England and

Wales topped the league table for thefts of motor vehicles with 3.3 per cent of cars or one in thirty being stolen in 1992 (van Dijk and Mayhew, 1993). Whatever the source of the data the motorist appears to be very much at risk.

The 1992 BCS offers data on motor vehicle crime by setting (Mayhew et al, 1993). The general finding was that there are around 3.8 million offences a year (thefts of motor vehicles, thefts from motor vehicles and attempts), roughly three times as many as are recorded by the police. In the course of a year, some 3 per cent of the car owning population can expect their vehicle to be stolen, a further 12 per cent will have something stolen from their car and 5 per cent will be subject to unsuccessful or attempted car crime. For all categories of motor vehicle crime and combining the data from the 1982, 1984, 1988 and 1992 surveys, rather more than one-half of car crimes took place at or near the household of the owner (57%), whilst over four in ten offences took place elsewhere (43%). Of this latter figure, 9 per cent took place at or around the place of work and 33 per cent in car parks or streets not near the home or place of work – that is, places which might be associated with shops and shopping. This permits the broad inference that there are up to roughly 1.2 million motor vehicle offences a year in or around the shopping environment.

The authors also suggested that the risk of victimisation is high for motor vehicles left in car parks to which members of the public have access. And the ratio of thefts to hours at risk is an important factor. Parallel research found that some 12 per cent of motorists who parked in public car parks conceded that they sometimes left the doors or the boot unlocked and 9 per cent admitted to sometimes leaving the windows open (Webb et al, 1992). Luxury cars appear to be increasingly at risk, because they give the impression of containing valuables or because they can be 'cannibalised' for expensive spare parts which are then sold on (Harlow, 1995). Research has also pointed to the fact that the design of car parks and security surveillance can affect levels of crime (Poyner and Webb, 1987; Laycock and Austin, 1992; Tilley, 1993a).

Even allowing for the fact that it is easier to restrict the opportunities for motor vehicle crime within the physical parameters of a shopping-centre complex than it is in the wider and more diffuse environment of an average town centre, there may be much to learn from the ways in which shopping centres have planned vehicular access and the ways in which they organise parking, including surveillance. This discussion, however, needs to take into account current government ambivalence about the use of motor vehicles in town centres.

For example, the House of Commons Environment Committee expressed concern about the government's *Planning Policy Guidance Note 13 (1994)* which seeks to promote shopping in existing locations offering a choice of access, particularly for those without the use of a car. Local planning authorities were instructed to reduce parking provision or to keep it to a minimum, and to concentrate development in those areas which have good access other than by motor vehicle. There was a clear inconsistency between that and *Planning Policy Guidance Note 6 (1993)* which seeks to promote town-centre development. The committee called for clarification and the minister suggested that *Planning Policy Guidance Note 13 (1994)* was intended to discourage the use of cars for commuting rather than for shopping. The committee was not reassured. The importance of car parking for town-centre shoppers was a recurring theme – mostly on the grounds that if there is inadequate parking in a town centre, consumers will simply go elsewhere for their purchases (House of Commons, 1994).

The importance of car parking for shopping centres has been usefully highlighted in a trade paper which argues that the multi-storey car park is the point of first contact or 'front door' of the shopping complex – and therefore something which determines the shopper's attitude to the whole centre (Dundec Contracts Limited, 1994). If the car parks are dark, intimidating and uninviting they will act as a disincentive to the shopping public. At the very least the public will enter the shopping facility with a feeling of unease. At worst they will seek an alternative place to shop. Darkness, in particular, can contribute to feelings of intimidation and danger. The fact that these fears are ungrounded is little consolation if the customer has already chosen to go elsewhere. The customer who feels unwelcome may prove not to be a customer at all.

The British Council of Shopping Centres (1993b) has also recognised in a *Guidance Note* that the car park is 'an important and integral customer service which will reflect the quality of the centre'. Thefts of and from motor vehicles while in car parks add to customers' concerns about their personal safety as well as that of their property, and these insecurities can lead to the loss of repeat business. Concern must also be shown towards staff use of car parks, especially during unsocial hours. The core assertion is that security in shopping centre car parks requires the same level of attention by owners and management as do the malls and other pedestrian areas.

Informal discussions with shopping-centre managers confirmed that they conceived of their centres not just in terms of store-based facilities for shoppers but also in terms of the associated infrastructure for getting the shoppers in, moving them through and allowing them to leave – all needing to be done with the maximum of ease and the minimum of disruption. Convenient vehicular access and good parking arrangements were seen not so much as a vital pre-condition for safe shopping, but as a core part of the overall service for customers. In contrast, some town-centre managers tended to the view that transport and parking was one concern and that what the town centre and its shops had to offer was another, quite separate matter. These comments revealed two very different styles of thinking. Town-centre managers defined parking and shopping as having a linear relationship (the one coming before the other). Shopping-centre managers saw car parking as an integrated part of customer services, on a par with what the shops had to offer and subject to the same security imperatives. This global vision of safe parking and safe shopping has much to commend it and there is increasing evidence of the importance attached by customers to the provision of convenient and secure parking facilities (Beck and Willis, 1992).

Finally, there are two practical suggestions which may be of benefit in reducing car-related crime in both town-centre and shopping-centre car parks. The House of Commons Environment Committee has commended the 'secured' car parking scheme of the Automobile Association (AA) and the Association of Chief Police Officers (ACPO) as an example of good practice in town centres. The aim of the scheme is to improve the standards of car park security by assessing them against a list of criteria such as lighting, signing and staffing levels. At present some 100 car parks have achieved 'secured' status (House of Commons, 1994). The British Parking Association (BPA), founded in 1967, takes a lead role in advancing the standards of design, planning, construction and manning of all motor vehicle parking facilities. It holds three or more seminars a year for representatives from local authorities and commercial organisations, and publishes a regular journal, *BPA Parking News*.

Another suggestion from the RAC and the Consumers' Association, which is commented on favourably by the Environment Committee (Drury, 1992; Webb et al, 1992) is that the Office of Fair Trading should reconsider its decision that car park owners are not supplying either goods or services but simply a licence to park. This allows operators to disclaim liability for damage or personal injury to customers except in cases of negligence. The RAC is pressing for changes to the Fair Trading Act to give car park owners an economic incentive to improve security and services – namely, the prospect of having to pay compensation to non-negligent victims. The comments of shopping-centre managers in the present study point to the conclusion that they already see themselves as taking responsibility for safe and secure car parking as an integrated part of the shopping experience. A very clear statement was offered by one shopping-centre manager:

> People in cars are not simply motorists, they are our customers. I want to see them drive in easily and park with confidence ... and leave later with the boot full of shopping.

Public drunkenness

There is substantial evidence of the role of alcohol in crime and nuisance-type behaviour. Recent research in Nottingham, conducted under the auspices of the King Edward Hospital Fund, estimated that alcohol was a factor in 88 per cent of incidents of criminal damage and 78 per cent of all assaults – both of which have a strong town-centre profile (KPMG Peat Marwick, 1991). The 1992 BCS also indicated that in some 44 per cent of the 2.6 million violent assaults a year the offender was drunk at the time, rising to 47 per cent for violent offences in shops, 50 per cent for offences on the street and 86 per cent for offences in and around pubs and clubs (Mayhew et al, 1993).

The Home Office study of 1,200 visitors to Coventry city centre found only a small proportion of people who had been assaulted (2%), mugged (3%) or insulted by strangers (12%) in the previous 12 month period. All three forms of crime and harassment tended to happen more to young people than to the elderly. The role of alcohol, however, in these offences was prominent. Over one-half of the assault victims believed that their assailant had been drinking prior to the attack, whilst one-third of those who had been mugged and almost three-quarters of those who had been insulted by strangers thought that the offender had consumed alcohol. As stated above, nearly two-thirds of respondents (61%) said that they took steps to avoid any contact with drunks, winos and tramps in and around the city centre (Ramsay, 1989).

In the present study, a substantial and near-equal minority of one in seven town-centre managers (14%) and one in eight shopping-centre managers (12%) identified public drunkenness as their single most pressing problem; but there was a marked difference in relation to its perceived frequency. While only a tiny proportion of the shopping-centre managers (5%) estimated that drunkenness was an everyday event, as many as one-third of the town-centre managers (31%) thought that it occurred routinely. This six-fold differential suggests that the problems of public drunkenness and associated misbehaviour are being better controlled in the shopping-centre environment than in the town centre.

The most likely reason is that access to a shopping centre can be controlled in a way which is simply not possible in a town centre – either by refusing entry or by ejecting unwanted persons (see Chapters 3 and 5). In the shopping centre the skid-row drunk or lager lout identified by demeanour or behaviour is likely to be moved on or denied access. This raises the possibility that the unwelcome drunk may be thrown out of the shopping centre and displaced to the high street. One manager's solution can then become another manager's problem, as was pointed out by one town-centre manager:

> The shopping centres move them out and the police move them on, but when there's nowhere else to go they always end up somewhere on the street.

The identification and exclusion of known or suspected drunken persons in shopping centres is a proactive and focused approach to risk avoidance, but this is not an option which is open to town-centre managers. They are not in a position to turn public places into private spaces, but it may be possible to persuade the local police to apply the letter of the law to undesirable drunks on the street. This is not straightforward because among the many and competing demands on police resources minor drink-related offences are unlikely to command a high priority. Police officers also have to judge the point at which insalubrious and unsavoury conduct associated with public drunkenness crosses the threshold of illegality.

It may be worthwhile for those with responsibilities for town-centre shopping to explore the available legal options for reducing the opportunities for the consumption of alcohol on the streets. Managers or owners may not be able to control access to town-centre streets, but it may be possible to regulate the behaviour which is allowed on them. It is certainly worthwhile for responsible agencies (local authorities, the police and the retailers) to explore the ways in which unacceptable behaviour can be prevented by placing a legal restriction on the consumption of alcohol. Interestingly, as many as 10 per cent of town-centre managers in the present study said that they were currently looking at 'alcohol byelaws' to restrict drinking in public places, and there is some evidence that these have been used to good effect.

Following serious public order problems with late night revellers in Coventry city centre during Christmas 1984, the Coventry City Alcohol Related Crime Project was established. By 1988, the year of the 'lager lout', the multi-agency partnership was pressing the Home Office for authority to introduce byelaws to ban the consumption of alcohol in public areas in the city centre, other than in or close to licensed premises. Approval was given for a two-year experiment beginning in October 1988; and by 1st May 1991 the Secretary of State had given the initiative a permanent statutory footing (Ramsay, 1989 and 1990; Vincent, undated). The ban was introduced with the consent of all the private owners in the designated area (inside the inner ring road), and with support from 86 per cent of the general public. Warning signs were erected advising that the area was an 'Alcohol Free Zone' and that the public consumption of alcohol was an offence. Enforcement became a police responsibility, but only after someone had been requested to refrain from drinking. This was done so as to avoid the possibility of persons being arrested who were not aware of the ban. Offenders are liable to a Level 2 fine on the standard scale (£200), although in the five years between 1988 and 1993 the police made only six arrests under the drinking byelaws. Any local authority can make an application to the Home Office for similar powers under section 235 of the Local Government Act 1972 in order to promote 'good rule and government' and for 'the prevention and suppression of nuisances'.

The results of the initiative appear to be startling. The head of Coventry City Centre Development (Vincent, undated) claims that drinking in unauthorised places has been totally eliminated, as has the problem of homeless people loitering and drinking during the day. Surveys indicate that the public feel safer in the city centre. Although no evidence was found to indicate a reduction in crime levels during the two-year experimental period, the longer-term view is that the byelaws have had a 'dramatic' effect on reducing crime, vandalism and levels of abuse and insults, thereby improving the image of the city centre. The city centre is now claimed to be the 'safest' part of Coventry. This is reflected in increased inward investment especially in evening entertainment facilities. Ironically, the net effect may be that total alcohol consumption had increased – but only in and around licensed premises and not in public places.

A rather more measured assessment suggests that these positive findings should be treated with some caution (Ramsay, 1990). To begin with, the centre of Coventry is a relatively small and clearly demarcated zone (within the central ring road) and it is questionable whether similar initiatives would be effective in larger and more diffuse urban areas. Studies to date have also not looked at the possibility of 'problem drinking' being displaced elsewhere. Finally, the byelaws were introduced coincidentally with the introduction of all-day drinking, which may have had the effect of taking the drinkers off the street anyway. These are important caveats because they suggest that the initiative may have simply moved the problem elsewhere or made no difference at all. A more thoroughgoing study would seem to be necessary.

Violent crime and drug-related offending

There was a minority view that violent crime or physical assault was the most serious problem facing managers – town-centre managers (4%) and shopping-centre managers (7%). And over one-quarter of the public in town centres (28%) and one in twelve shopping-centre respondents (8%) highlighted assault and violence as a matter of concern. These anxieties were reflected in the victimisation data where over 50 per cent of the offences in both locations took the form of physical assaults or robberies. The combined data suggest a strong undercurrent of anxiety about violent crime.

These concerns are confirmed by recent research commissioned by the Association of Town Centre Management (Donaldsons and Healey & Baker, 1994). The ATCM report offers compelling data on an unmet need for security against violence in town centres. The study found that as many as 79 per cent of respondents rated safety and security as a 'very important' factor in making town centres more attractive places for visitors, that more than one-half were not satisfied with safety measures (55%) and that one-third pointed to a deterioration in standards relating to 'crime and violence' in recent years (34%). The British Crime Survey of 1992 provides figures broken down by the context in which violent assaults took place. The survey estimated that in a year some 2.6 million crimes of violence were committed (Mayhew et al 1993), of which:

- 760,000 or 30 per cent were classed as domestic or home-based incidents involving partners, ex-partners, household members or relatives; or none of these but still taking place in or around the home;

- 510,000 or 19 per cent took place in the streets, on public transport or in other public places;

- 420,000 or 16 per cent were incidents in or around pubs and clubs, including discos;

- 350,000 or 13 per cent were violent assaults at work;

- 260,000 or 10 per cent comprised muggings – robberies or snatch thefts; and

- 300,000 or 11 per cent were violent incidents at sporting events or in shops and leisure centres.

The data do not yield a precise figure for violent criminal victimisation in the retail context, but they do offer a useful indication. If the categories of domestic or home-based violence and work-related violence are excluded, then the remaining 1.5 million offences (56%) cover those where members of the public, including the shopping public, could be said to be at risk – on the streets, around pubs and clubs or whilst shopping. Given the large number of cases in these categories, even if shopping-related acts of violence comprised only a tiny proportion, there would still be a significant number of incidents.

Additionally, in over four out of ten violent incidents (44%) in the 1988 survey the victim said the offender was drunk at the time of the attack (Mayhew et al, 1989 and 1993). A large proportion of assaults in pubs and clubs were likely to involve drunken assailants (86%), as were attacks on the street (56%). A final category of assaults, which included attacks in shops, found that nearly one-half of the victims claimed that the offender was drunk at the time of the attack (47%). In these cases the victims were punched, slapped, grabbed or pushed. The data suggest that the violence was largely unpremeditated with drunkenness as a critical variable. The crime prevention implication is that the precipitating problem of drunkenness should be dealt with (see above) rather than the violence in which it finds expression.

Finally, the survey offered data with regard to so-called muggings – the 260,000 robberies or snatches which fall into the category of predatory street crime. Only one in eight or 12 per cent of these offences were committed by drunken assailants but, where the victims were male, one-half involved the use of weapons – most commonly stabbing implements such as a knife or a screwdriver. These findings suggest that the predatory attacks were more purposeful, or even premeditated, than the drunken assaults – and therefore perhaps less susceptible to a crime reduction strategy by town-centre or shopping-centre managers. There is some evidence, however, that highly-focused, intensive policing can reduce the incidence of street robberies (Barker et al, 1993); and the Criminal Justice and Public Order Act 1994 (section 60) makes provision for additional police powers under which uniformed officers are able to stop and search pedestrians, or vehicles and their occupants, for offensive weapons in the anticipation of violence. This power can only be exercised for a 24 hour period at a time and only on the authority of a senior officer. Any weapons found during such a search may be seized. Police officers do not need grounds for suspicion before stopping and searching a person once the initial authority has been given. It is an offence to refuse to stop which can attract a maximum penalty of three months imprisonment and a fine. These provisions may help to control street-level violence.

A significant and near-equal minority of one in fourteen town-centre managers (7%) and one in nine shopping-centre managers (11%) identified drug-related offences as their single most serious problem; but again there was a marked difference in relation to its perceived frequency. Where only a tiny proportion of 3 per cent of shopping-centre managers estimated that drug-related offences were commonplace, as many as one in eight town-centre managers (12%) thought that they were an everyday occurrence. The four-fold differential suggests that the problem may be easier to control or contain in the shopping centre than on the high street. This is probably due to the ways in which access to shopping centres can be controlled, although it may also reflect the natural preference of the drug abuser for the 'street scene'. And in a social climate where there is a 'creeping decriminalisation' of the use of soft drugs and where policing policy is increasingly premised on user (but not supplier) toleration, it is difficult to see drug-related offending as anything other than a problem which is likely to worsen.

The present research did not explore the nature of these offences – for example, whether they involved drug use or drug dealing or criminal acts (theft or robbery) carried out to provide the money to purchase drugs. The interrelationship between drug-related offending and crimes of violence warrants more detailed investigation. If the two categories of drug offences and violent crime are combined then one in nine town-centre managers (11%) saw them as the single most serious problem, compared with one in six shopping-centre managers (18%). This is one of the few areas where the data suggest that the shopping centres may have more of a problem than the town centres. This could point to a real difference but it could also be a product of differences in the managers' attitudes towards and willingness to tolerate problems relating to violence and drugs in the shopping environment. The shopping-centre manager may find the whole idea intolerable and unacceptable; and he or she may be in a relatively strong position to take action to ban or eject drunken, doped or violent visitors. The data to be presented in Chapter 5 are highly suggestive of a widespread practice of rigorously excluding known and suspected trouble-makers. The town-centre manager does not have this option and may be compelled to fatalistically accept these offences as an inevitable part of the complex town-centre mosaic. As one manager commented with regard to violence and drunks:

> It's not a huge problem in itself ... but it's the unpredictability that creates trouble. Things can flare up at anytime – usually when there's no police around.

Threatening youths and kids hanging around

Perhaps surprisingly, two nuisance-type problems were identified as matters of particular concern by shopping-centre managers. Threatening youths stood out at the top of the list as the single most serious problem (26%) and kids hanging around were cited as the most frequent example of crime and nuisance occurring on a daily basis (15%). It would be an exaggeration to assert that problematic youths are the only problem for shopping-centre managers, but not by very much – which must make town-centre managers envious! These findings are reflected in earlier studies, two of which were specific to shopping centres:

- The British Crime Survey of 1984 identified ways in which troublesome youths could have a negative impact on those who witnessed their behaviour. Groups of boisterous young people contributed to a generalised sense of insecurity and their presence appeared to conjure-up feelings that those who witnessed them were somehow at risk themselves (Maxfield, 1987).

- The Midlands study of two shopping centres found that nearly one-half of respondents (45%) said that 'young people hanging around' and loitering in the centre was their greatest problem – something which was perceived to be more of a problem than shoplifting (Phillips and Cochrane, 1988).

- The Coventry investigation highlighted unruly young persons (66%) as being one of the strongest themes to emerge under the heading of city-centre problems (Ramsay, 1989).

- The Birmingham city-centre and shopping-centre research discovered that teenage males displaying rowdy behaviour (32%) was amongst the types of behaviour which shoppers found most distasteful (Poole, 1991).

- The Nottingham audit found that the public showed a generalised concern about 'threatening behaviour' which led to feelings of being vulnerable (KPMG Peat Marwick, 1991).

One possible explanation is that, because the overall crime and nuisance profile of shopping centres was much lower than that for town centres, what are really low-level, nuisance-type problems in shopping centres tend to assume a disproportionate significance. When there is so little else to worry about, the problems of loitering youths rise to the top of the agenda. To some extent this problem may reflect the absence of genuine risks to the safety and security of visitors to shopping centres. Moreover, the same features which make shopping centres attractive to shoppers (protection from the elements and a clean and attractive environment) may also make them something of a magnet for young persons. Many managers offered the view that shopping centres acted as a focal point for young people. They could be present legitimately – shopping with their parents, shopping on their own or with friends, or simply hanging around browsing and 'taking in the scene'. They could also be there rather less legitimately either as an over-large and unwelcome group of rowdy youngsters or as a more threatening gang-like presence. Concern has grown about young persons gravitating to shopping centres on unauthorised absence from school – even to the point of establishing special 'truancy watch' schemes in such areas and encouraging retailers to refuse to serve children during school hours (O'Keeffe, 1993; O'Leary, 1994).

There is something of an irony here, namely that the same factors which draw in (highly desirable) customers may also pull in (less desirable) young people who wish simply to 'hang around' or to cause trouble rather than to shop. The point was well made by managers:

> The shopping centre offers a free, dry and warm environment – a popular place to socialise and not just for shopping. It can attract an undesirable element who gather and then deter shoppers from remaining for their intended purpose.

As part of a refurbishment of this centre all the seating was removed temporarily. As a result of having no seating the threatening gangs of youths moved to other town-centre locations.

The general irritation appeared to be as much a function of the fact that the youths were non-shoppers as of the assessment that they posed a threat, although some managers made reference to gangs of youths being involved in orchestrated shoplifting attacks on stores. The problem in controlling these young persons seemed to arise from a difficulty in judging accurately whether their presence was entirely innocent and lawful (and spending oriented) or whether they constituted an unacceptable threat to good order or even a criminal menace. Shopping centre managers are far from alone in being unable to fathom the interests and intentions of the young.

Tests of significance

Table 4.1

Crime

Physical assault	$\chi^2 = 1.5$, 1 df, p = 0.2208
Drug-related offences	$\chi^2 = 3.8$, 1 df, p = 0.0525
Car crime	$\chi^2 = 71.2$, 1 df, p < 0.0001
Vandalism/Graffiti	$\chi^2 = 5.3$, 1 df, p < 0.05

Nuisance

Threatening youths	$\chi^2 = 0.1$, 1 df, p = 0.8286
Vagrants/Beggars	$\chi^2 = 25.5$, 1 df, p < 0.0001
Drunks	$\chi^2 = 18.0$, 1 df, p < 0.0001
Kids hanging around	$\chi^2 = 6.8$, 1 df, p = 0.01
Illegal street vendors	$\chi^2 = 9.2$, 1 df, p < 0.01
Buskers	$\chi^2 = 34.4$, 1 df, p < 0.0001
Prostitutes	$\chi^2 = 14.6$, 1 df, p < 0.001

Pollution

Litter	$\chi^2 = 0.2$, 1 df, p = 0.6429
Dogs fouling streets	$\chi^2 = 179.0$, 1 df, p < 0.0001

All problems $\chi^2 = 16.0$, 1 df, p < 0.001

Table 4.4

Difference between sub-totals $\chi^2 = 2.4$, 1 df, p < 0.01

5 Existing Security Measures: An Audit

If the sensible first step in responding to crime and nuisance in the shopping environment was to acknowledge the size and scale of the problems (from the point of view of shoppers and managers), the next step is to conduct a 'security audit' of existing measures and practices. This provides a basis for thinking creatively about improvements in security strategies. Making comparisons of security cover for shoppers and managers in two retail environments is complex. The types of security measures being used in town centres and in shopping centres are not always directly comparable; and the public may not be aware of the technical aspects of some options. To minimise these difficulties and to permit comparative analysis the security options were compressed into four broad categories:

- police on patrol
- security guards on patrol
- closed circuit television (CCTV)
- 'Watch' schemes such as Business Watch, Pub Watch, City Watch, Retailers Against Crime, etc.

Additionally, town-centre and shopping-centre managers were encouraged to comment on location-specific security measures. This allowed managers to add texture and useful detail even though it does not necessarily permit direct inter-location comparisons. Although broad comparisons are made between the four categories for present purposes, the most important data relate to differences between public policing and private security. These are discussed in full. A more detailed review of the contribution of CCTV to safe shopping is reserved for later examination in Chapters 8 and 9. The audit was undertaken in four ways. First, both sets of managers were asked factual questions about the range of security measures currently being used in their environment. The answers are used as a basis for a comparative analysis of the type and extent of existing security provision.

Secondly, members of the public were asked whether or not they were aware of a range of security measures. This was necessary because the effectiveness of some security options is predicated on their visibility. For example, customers can scarcely be comforted by the supposed reassuring presence of security guards if they fail to see them. Equally, it would not be possible to claim any deterrent value for CCTV if would-be offenders were unaware of its installation and use. This question was only put to those respondents who were shopping in areas where it had previously been established that the relevant security measures were being used.

Thirdly, town-centre and shopping-centre managers were asked to rate the effectiveness of the four categories of security measures. This question was put to all managers, whether or not an option was in use, so as to obtain a general view of its effectiveness from as large a sample as possible. Although this question did not provide comprehensive data on effectiveness, which would have required a very different methodology, it is reasonable to suppose that whether or not town-centre and shopping-centre managers have confidence in security equipment and security personnel is a reliable, albeit indirect, indicator of performance.

Finally, members of the public were asked to comment on the acceptability of the security options. This question was put to all shoppers, whether or not the options were in use, so as to establish a general view of their acceptability from as large a sample as possible. With regard to CCTV, for example, there is some evidence that a majority of the general public (72%) think that cameras could be 'abused and used by the wrong people', and that one in three people suppose that cameras invade people's privacy (Honess and Charman, 1992). Equally, there is increasing concern that 'officers in brown uniforms' exercise much the same sort of powers as officers in blue uniforms, but without the same responsibility and accountability (Campbell, 1994). These were matters of recent concern to the House of Commons Select Committee on Home Affairs (1995a and 1995b), and it was thought useful to make an empirical contribution to a growing debate.

The audit of existing security measures generated information on a number of aspects – extent of use, public awareness, effectiveness and acceptability. It is arguable that where a security measure is in widespread use and where managers and the public agree that it is both effective and acceptable, the measure is making a valid contribution to resolving the problems of crime and nuisance in that particular environment. Conversely, where there is a substantial lack of congruence between the level of use of a security option and its perceived effectiveness and acceptability, the measure may need further consideration. And it is by no means self-evident that the 'best' solutions for town centres will also be the options of first choice for shopping centres. The complex inter-relationship between these variables is discussed after a presentation of the findings.

Extent and awareness of security cover

Town-centre managers (Table 5.1) indicated that the most prevalent security measures involved a conspicuous police presence – either police on patrol (97%) or dedicated police squads serving the town centre (93%). Four in five managers (79%) also pointed to the use of private security guards, employed by shopping-centre management, retailers or other private companies rather than the town centre itself. Over three-quarters of the town centres (77%) had CCTV and, where it was used, two-thirds of the managers (65%) estimated that it was being used extensively. Four in ten managers (40%) indicated the presence of 'Watch' schemes. These covered a wide range, including large-scale, town-centre-wide schemes through to very small and specific schemes which focused solely on particular types of outlet – such as pubs or small businesses.

Table 5.1 Security measures used in town centres by extent of coverage

Security measure	In use	Extent of coverage		
		High	Medium	Low
	Per cent			
Police on patrol	96.6	21.4	64.3	14.3
Private security guards	79.3	13.0	52.2	34.8
CCTV	76.9	65.0	25.0	10.0
'Watch' schemes	40.0	–	–	–
Dedicated police squads	92.6	48.0	40.0	12.0

In contrast, shopping-centre managers (Table 5.2) indicated that the most prevalent measures were in-house security – private security guards (90%)

and staff using radios to maintain contact with each other (96%). No managers made reference to police officers on patrol. Nearly all managers (89%) pointed to the use of CCTV and, where it was used, over two-thirds of them (70%) estimated that it was being used extensively. One in five managers (20%) indicated the presence of 'Watch' schemes.

Table 5.2 Security measures used in shopping centres by extent of coverage

Security measure	In use	Extent of coverage		
		High	Medium	Low
	Per cent			
Police on patrol	–	–	–	–
Private security guards	89.5	49.7	40.7	9.7
CCTV	88.7	69.6	27.1	3.4
'Watch' schemes	20.5	–	–	–
Staff radio link-up	96.2	77.1	22.0	0.8
Retailer/Police radio link-up	54.5	35.2	37.1	27.8

The public's awareness of security measures broadly mirrored the information offered by town-centre and shopping-centre managers (Table 5.3).

Table 5.3 Public awareness of security measures in town centres and shopping centres by type of measure

Security measure	Aware		Not aware	
	Town centres	Shopping centres	Town centres	Shopping centres
	Per cent			
Police on patrol	82.0	30.3	18.0	69.7
Private security guards	20.2	84.4	79.8	15.6
CCTV	49.6	60.2	50.4	39.8
'Watch' schemes	16.6	9.4	83.4	90.6

In the town centres the public were most aware of police officers on patrol (82%) and the use of CCTV (50%). Only one in five shoppers pointed to the presence of private security guards (20%). In the shopping centres the public were most aware of private security guards (84%) and the use of CCTV (60%). One in three shoppers pointed to the presence of police officers on patrol (30%), although this was not mentioned at all by shopping-centre managers.

Effectiveness and acceptability of security measures

Town-centre managers (Table 5.4) were of the view that the most effective security measure (defined as being either 'excellent' or 'good') was CCTV (82%). The next most highly-rated option was dedicated police squads (70%). The least highly-rated measures were police on patrol (43%) and private security guards (52%).

Table 5.4 Perceived effectiveness of security options by town-centre managers

Security measure	Excellent/ Good	Average	Poor
		Per cent	
Police on patrol	43.3	46.7	10.0
Private security guards	52.1	32.4	15.4
CCTV	82.3	11.8	5.9
Dedicated police squads	70.3	25.9	3.7

Table 5.5 Perceived effectiveness of security options by shopping-centre managers

Security measure	Excellent/ Good	Average	Poor
		Per cent	
Police on patrol	–	–	–
Private security guards	85.3	11.3	3.3
CCTV	84.6	13.5	1.8
Staff radio link-up	88.5	11.6	0.0
Retailer/Police radio link-up	56.9	29.4	13.7

In contrast, shopping-centre managers (Table 5.5) indicated that there were three security measures which they saw as being equally effective – staff radio link-up (88%), private security guards (85%) and CCTV installations (85%).

The acceptability to members of the public of three types of security measure is detailed in Table 5.6. In town centres, the most acceptable security measure was police officers on patrol (97%), followed by CCTV (91%). In shopping centres, the most acceptable security measure was CCTV (96%), followed by private security guards (92%). In effect, police officers on patrol were most acceptable in town centres and private security guards were most acceptable in shopping centres, whilst CCTV received a striking vote of confidence in both shopping environments. Putting things the other way round, in town centres private security guards were deemed to be unacceptable by one in three shoppers (34%) and in shopping centres police officers on patrol were deemed to be unacceptable by one in five shoppers (23%).

Table 5.6 The perceived acceptability of security measures by the shopping public

Security measure	Very acceptable/ Acceptable		Unacceptable/ Very unacceptable	
	Town centres	Shopping centres	Town centres	Shopping centres
	Per cent			
Police on patrol	97.0	77.1	3.0	22.9
Private security guards	66.2	92.4	33.8	7.6
CCTV	90.6	96.0	9.4	4.0

Town-centre and shopping-centre security

The most important theme to emerge from the audit was the contrast between the use of publicly-funded police officers in town centres and the use of privately-funded security guards in shopping centres. Although the protection of the shopping public might be considered a task which would be carried out in a similar or near-identical way in the two shopping environments, the data indicate that this is not so; and the differences are substantial. Another prominent finding was the extensive use of CCTV in the two locations and the widespread confidence in its deployment. This is discussed in detail in Chapters 8 and 9.

In town centres, the security of the shopping public was seen to depend largely on the visible and reassuring presence of police officers on patrol. A publicly-funded agency was being used to protect the interests of the private shopper – albeit someone who was also a member of the public and shopping in a public place. For shopping centres, the security of the shopping public was based mainly on the deployment of private security guards funded by the shopping centre itself or by its retailers. The interests of the shopper were being protected by 'private policing'. These findings are summarised in Table 5.7.

Table 5.7 Use, awareness, effectiveness and acceptability of police on patrol in town centres and private security guards in shopping centres

Police on patrol or private security guards	Police on patrol in town centres	Private security guards in shopping centres
	Per cent	
Managers' views		
Measure in use	96.6	89.5
High level of perceived effectiveness	43.3	85.3
Public's views		
Awareness of measure	82.0	84.4
High level of perceived acceptability	97.0	92.4

Nearly all town-centre managers pointed to police officers on patrol (97%) as the dominant security measure. The majority of shoppers were aware of this feature of the retail environment (82%) and found it highly acceptable (97%). Nearly all shopping-centre managers highlighted private security guards as the primary security option (90%) and saw them to be effective (85%). The majority of shoppers were aware of this feature of the retail environment (84%) and found it highly acceptable (92%).

Initially, the findings appeared to be only what was to have been expected. It was assumed that there would be a stronger private security presence in shopping centres than in town centres, and that conventional policing would be more apparent in town centres than in shopping centres. It was surprising, however, to find that on all four variables (for the managers on use and effectiveness and for the public on awareness and acceptability) the distribution of responses was near-identical – the only difference being that the data referred to public policing in town centres and private security in shopping centres.

The findings from the survey indicate clearly that for the public in shopping centres significant 'privatisation' of policing has already taken place, and that it commands the support of both the shopping-centre managers and the shopping public. There is evidence here not so much of an ongoing debate as of one that has been resolved firmly in favour of private security. This is now a taken-for-granted, everyday feature of one part of the retail environment. The bobby on the beat may still patrol the town centre but he or she has been superseded by the private security guard in the shopping mall. This directs attention to a discussion of the contrast between public policing in town centres and private security in shopping centres, and to a more specific review of the implications for town-centre and shopping-centre managers.

From public policing ...

The debate about the balance between public policing and private security is intense and shows little sign of producing a consensus. One commentator argues that the state's displacement by the private sector in the area of policing is impossible because it would mean undercutting the legitimacy of the state itself (Cohen, 1983). Other commentators have suggested that displacement is well advanced – and point to a new feudalism where huge spheres of public space (and the activities in them) are controlled by private corporations (Shearing and Stenning, 1983). For others, something is clearly afoot, but the public–private dichotomy has generated a complex and often contradictory web of 'ambiguities and fuzzy edges' (Johnston, 1992).

There is growing evidence of large-scale retrenchment in public policing. Part of the explanation is an increasing awareness that police activity has a limited impact on the incidence of crime. Home Office research has shown that a police officer on foot patrol passes within 100 yards of a burglary in progress only once every eight years, and that classic detective work is instrumental in clearing-up only one in six known crimes (Clarke and Hough, 1984). Studies have also shown that increasing the numbers of police officers would have relatively little impact on crime (Clarke and Hough, 1980 and 1984; Morris and Heal, 1981; Heal et al, 1985). Figures from the Audit Commission (1993) reveal that between 1982 and 1992 the number of recorded crimes per police officer rose from 26 to 42 – an increase of 62 per cent. In the same period, the number of crimes cleared up per officer dropped from 41 to 26 – a decrease of 36 per cent. By 1994 the best figures for crimes cleared up per officer were recorded in Nottinghamshire (14 primary detections per officer each year) and the worst in the Metropolitan Police area, with just seven detections per officer (Audit Commission, 1994). There is also evidence that public support for the police is far from strong. A recent national Gallup poll found that only 55 per cent of the public had confidence in the police; and three-quarters thought that the police were unlikely to catch a domestic burglar. Most victims do not expect to see their stolen possessions again (Willis, 1992; Shrimsley and Darbyshire, 1993). A survey by MORI found that only one-third of respondents (36%) were happy with policing in their area, whilst one-half (48%) were dissatisfied with the police (Ford, 1994a).

There are increasing concerns about the high levels of expenditure on policing and the low 'measurable return' on this investment. At the present time law enforcement costs £6 billion a year or about £110 per head of population (Home Office, 1994a), a rise of 50 per cent in real terms over the past 15 years (Jenkins, 1994b). These facts have led to a critical reassessment of what the general public can expect to be made available from the public purse and what they might legitimately be asked to provide or pay for themselves. Following the report on Sir Patrick Sheehy's inquiry into police responsibilities and rewards (Sheehy, 1993) and a recent Home Office white paper on police reform (Home Office, 1993a) the debate is ongoing, but it looks certain that the balance between 'public policing' and 'private security' will be adjusted in the direction of the public having to provide privately some of what formerly was offered as a wholly public service.

The white paper recognises that every policing task cannot be given the same degree of priority and points to the need to define more clearly what the police service should regard as its core responsibilities and what may be considered as ancillary tasks (Home Office, 1993a). The starting point was that well under one-half of police time and money is devoted to fighting crime – with only 18 per cent of all calls to the police being about crime and only 40 per cent of officers' time being spent directly dealing with crime. A subsequent Home Office review was established in February 1994 to make recommendations about the most cost-effective way of delivering core policing services and to assess the scope for relinquishing ancillary tasks (Home Office, 1994c and 1995a).

The review, headed by Ingrid Posen of the Home Office, identified a number of areas where current police responsibilities could be relinquished, including ones of direct concern to the retail sector. In an interim report, ancillary functions are seen to include parking and static traffic enforcement, and automatic alarm calls are identified as a possible 'waste of police time'. In the field of public order, broadly defined, much of present police work in relation to gaming and betting, lotteries, late-night refreshments, billiard halls, street collections and pedlars is seen as ancillary. The policing of large public events, such as pop concerts and football matches, is considered to be the responsibility of the organisers. And a whole range of crime prevention-related tasks are seen as indeterminate (neither core nor ancillary) such as work with multi-agency partnership groups, crime prevention publicity and the sponsoring of local initiatives. Finally, 'commercial risk analysis' is defined as an ancillary task – something which does not need management or delivery by the police (Ford, 1994c; Home Office, 1994c).

A further report, which was published in mid-1995, broadly endorsed the earlier thinking by identifying 26 police tasks which could be hived-off to local authorities or to the private sector (Ford, 1995b; Home Office, 1995a). The study supported the view of senior police officers that service functions are part law enforcement and part 'social service', and that there is little scope for the police to withdraw from any major areas of work, but it also sought to relocate responsibilities which were deemed to be peripheral away from conventional policing. Some of these proposals would impact directly on the retail sector. For example, charges could be introduced to meet the costs of maintaining the lists of keyholders at commercial premises with burglar alarms, and builders and developers could be compelled by law to include crime prevention measures in new developments. Both would have the effect of shifting crime control responsibilities to owners and users – a degree of privatisation in crime control. And, as expected, the use of 'private security stewards' at major public events received a strong endorsement. In itself this would not impact directly on the retail sector, but the implication is clear – namely that manned guarding services have received a 'vote of confidence'. This could have an indirect impact on retailing in that elements of what might be called 'public order self-policing' are seen to be the responsibility of those who are in the business of organising events-for-profit. Policing the high street and the shopping mall could well fall under any broad conceptualisation of what constitutes an activity where security is thought to be the primary responsibility of owners, managers and organisers. All the recommendations are in the direction of transferring a range of current police responsibilities to the private sector.

There are other indicators, too, of the drift towards private policing. For example, the Audit Commission has launched a national efficiency study of police car and foot patrols to see if they could do their job better (Tendler, 1995b). Foot and car patrols by some 25,000 police officers in England and Wales account for 20 per cent of all police work and cost around £1.1 billion a year. The aim is to establish whether police time could be spent more advantageously on specific tasks rather than routine patrols; and the ways in which civilian patrols, such as security guards funded by local authorities and residents, might be used to reduce demands made on the police.

In addition, the new arrangements set up under the Police and Magistrates' Courts Act 1994 confirm the suspicion that central government is keen to take greater control over policing and to do so, in part, in the interests of saving money. The Secretary of State has powers to determine and direct both policing objectives and performance targets in order to secure 'an efficient and effective police force'. It is instructive to note that considerations of efficiency come before those of effectiveness. There are also powers to amalgamate or alter police force areas, which might be used to seek economies of scale; and others to become directly involved in the appointment of members of police authorities, possibly to bring a more business-like approach to local decision making. Finally, there are provisions for police budget requirements to be limited; and for forces to seek or accept commercial sponsorship and to 'sell' their services. All these provisions point in the direction of public sector-wide restraints on expenditure (Slapper, 1995).

Similarly, a report by the Home Office police research group in 1995 suggests that it is impossible for the police to service properly the needs of some 130,000 Neighbourhood Watch schemes nationwide with five million members. They propose that the schemes should become in part self-financing (Tilley, 1995; and see Ford, 1995c). In high-crime areas the telephone companies should help scheme co-ordinators with their telephone bills. In medium-crime areas the report recommends that local fund-raising events should be held and that the membership should pay small subscriptions. And in low-crime areas, such as middle class housing developments, householders should pay modest regular sums for passive police support. It is instructive to note that Neighbourhood Watch was initially conceived as a 'partnership' between the police and the responsible public, but that it is now being converted into a service for which the more affluent can pay.

These developments make it difficult not to conclude that the sphere of public policing is contracting. This means that the responsibility for protection against crime is increasingly becoming something which individuals must assume and provide for themselves. This has been termed the 'rebirth of private policing' (Johnston, 1992); or the more cynical might see it as the privatisation of policing by stealth. Speaking at the annual Police Federation conference in 1995, David French, of the 97,000-strong constables' section, said that it would not be long before private patrols in shopping malls moved to the streets outside:

> Not long ago we were told that the patrolling policeman was the frontline officer, the back bone of the service. Now we are being told that someone else can do the job ... British policing is being downgraded by stealth. We already know that the growth of private security services means those who can afford it are looking to hired hands to protect them, using the police only as the necessary back-up when arrests need to be made.
>
> (quoted in Tendler, 1995c: *The Times*, 17th May)

All of these factors are pushing retailers into providing their own security. According to the chairman of the Dixons Stores Group, Stanley Kalms, the epidemic of retail crime is not being touched by conventional policing. The police have withdrawn from certain traditional roles and are no longer a force for the detection and prosecution of crimes against property. They have become no more than a 'data collecting agency' and routinised inaction against store-related crime has become 'an obscene travesty of the law' (see Horsnell, 1993). The consequence of this is that the larger retailers are turning their stores into 'fortresses' and are employing private security on an 'unprecedented' scale. It is interesting to note that senior police officers are now resigned to the prospect that 'para-policing' will become increasingly common, simply because people want more policing than the public purse can provide (Blair, 1994), even though the Home Secretary has stated vigorously that he is 'not in the business of creating a secondary police force' and condemns any drift towards vigilantism (Dutta and Ford, 1994; Wynn Davies, 1994). What he has failed to realise, or has chosen to ignore, is that so-called secondary policing has already become primary policing in the nation's shopping centres.This radical transformation requires elaboration and explanation.

... To private security

Statistical data on the size of the private security industry are notoriously unreliable. This is partly due to conceptual confusion over the boundaries within the industry (physical security, eg locks and grilles; electronic security, eg alarms and CCTV; and manned services, eg security guards). The industry is also complex and fragmented. And there is an absence of any industry-wide or central agency for collecting relevant data. Any figures therefore need to be treated with some caution (Johnston, 1992), but indicative data are available.

The UK security market is the second largest in Europe after that in Germany and is forecast to grow from £2.2 billion in 1992 to £2.6 billion by 1995 (Rudnick, 1993; Harris, 1994). The British Security Industry Association has estimated that the overall private security market is of the order of £2.8 billion a year, including the electronics sector (intruder alarms, CCTV and access control) and the guarding sector (British Security Industry Association, 1994a and 1994b). The Home Office and the Department of Trade and Industry accepts the figure of over £2 billion a year as 'fairly accurate' (Home Office, 1994d). Sir John Smith, as Deputy Commissioner of the Metropolitan Police, has suggested that the private security sector has between 100,000 and 250,000 employees (Campbell, 1994). Another estimate puts the total at 300,000 personnel (Hobson, 1994).

The provision of manned guarding services is a major component of the overall market. Of the industry-wide total spend of £2.8 billion a year, the British Security Industry Association estimates that over £1 billion or 36 per cent is spent on manned security services. The Association suggests that the guarding industry includes some 1,280 companies and around 80,000 employees (British Security Industry Association, 1994a and 1994b). The Home Office also accepts these figures as accurate (Home Office, 1994d). Other estimates indicate that the provision of manned security services is on a much larger scale. Figures from the Policy Studies Institute suggest that there are some 130,00 security guards, of whom 91,000 are employed as in-house security officers (Jones and Newburn, 1994). The trade union APEX (1991) points to a figure of over 100,000 people employed in manned security services – with roughly 40,000 directly employed by shops and businesses and a further 60,000 employed on a bought-in basis from contract security companies (Button and George, 1994).

The British Retail Consortium (1995) calculates that the retail sector alone accounts for 9 per cent of the total custom for the provision of manned security services. And out of some £400 million a year spent by retailers on crime prevention (security equipment and security personnel), around £150 million or 40 per cent is on manned security services – £63 million a year on contract security staff and £87 million a year on internal security staff (Burrows and Speed, 1994). The retail industry itself estimates that it employs around 50,000 security staff – or roughly one in five of all such staff in Britain (Shopfront Security Group, 1994).

The private security sector had a total market size of £807 million in 1987, rising to £2.1 billion in 1992 – an increase of 63 per cent (Campbell, 1994). Bruce George MP, well known for his interest in the private security industry, estimates that the security industry has a turnover of £4 billion a year, employs some 300,000 persons and is expanding at a rate of between 6 and 10 per cent per year (George and Button, 1994). One of the largest companies, Securicor, with an annual turnover of £700 million and 25,000 employees in the UK, has estimated that the number of persons employed in all forms of private security will increase from about 128,000 to 200,000 persons by the year 2002 (Securicor Security Services, 1994). On the assumption that the average rate of growth of 5.8 per cent a year between 1970 and 1994 is maintained, the manned guarding market is likely to expand from around 80,000 to about 125,000 persons in the same period – an increase of 56 per cent.

Although the figures vary, probably because they are drawn from rather different sources and use different definitions of what constitutes private security, there is general agreement about the size of the industry, including manned guarding services. The best estimates of the size of the private security sector are:

Total security market	£2.8 billion
Manned guarding services	
Number	80,000
Value	£1.0 billion
Annual growth	6 per cent

Finally, there is an interesting comparison to be made between the size of the private security market and the provision of public policing. There are 154,000 police officers in the police forces of the United Kingdom

(Benyon et al, 1994 and 1995) compared with about 80,000 private security guards. Public policing is provided at an annual cost of around £7 billion (Home Office, 1994a) compared with a private security market turnover of nearly £3 billion a year. Thus the private guarding industry employs slightly over one-half as many persons as public sector policing; and the annual spend on all forms of private security is of the order of 40 per cent of that on conventional policing.

It is also worth noting that the police themselves are beginning to take an interest in the provision of private security. For example, a recent discussion paper, prepared by the Police Foundation and the Policy Studies Institute (1994) on the roles and responsibilities of the police, tentatively suggests that the balance between public sector and private sector policing could change in another way. The paper puts forward the idea that there could be a 'core' of sworn police officers with conventional powers alongside whom 'unsworn police patrols' would operate. They would wear some sort of uniform (perhaps with a local insignia) and the 'work could be conducted under licence by ... private security companies'. The boundaries between public sector policing and private security are indeed becoming blurred.

On a projection of annual growth at around the 6 per cent level, the UK manned security sector will employ nearly as many guards as there are police officers by the turn of the century; and the security industry as a whole will employ some 30 per cent more persons than conventional policing. The 'rise and rise' of private security would appear to have an unstoppable momentum. It is also clear that while the Home Office is exploring the balance in police activity between core and ancillary tasks, and whilst the House of Commons (1995a and 1995b) Select Committee on Home Affairs has opened up a debate on the regulation of the private security industry, the 'privatisation' of policing in one part of the retail sector has already taken place. Not least because of government concern to minimise the burden on the public purse, this trend is unlikely to be reversed. There are immediate implications for both town-centre and shopping-centre managers (discussed below) and wider issues with regard to industry-wide regulation (discussed in Chapter 6).

Implications for town centres

The shift by owners, retailers and managers of shopping centres towards the use of private security has placed local authorities, shopkeepers and managers in town centres in something of a dilemma – whether to argue the case for a stronger police presence in the town centres or to follow the example of the shopping centres and provide it themselves.

If managers are to persuade already hard-pressed police forces to provide a more conspicuous presence in town centres, they will need to convince them that shoppers' safety in town centres should be afforded a higher priority. But any such claim would constitute a new demand on police resources and the recent move to divide police work into core, indeterminate and ancillary tasks suggests that the chances of its being accepted are not good (Home Office, 1993a and 1994c). In a climate of increasing fiscal restraint simple pleas for 'more police' are unlikely to carry any weight. There might be a better chance of success, however, if the pressure could be orchestrated around the more serious offences relating to drug abuse, predatory street crimes and motor vehicle crime. Emphasis on these crimes may enable retailers to mobilise stonger, even widespread, public support behind their demands for additional public policing. Data from the current survey could well be used to support such demands. The danger with this strategy is the possibility that by highlighting the insecurities of the town centres retailers might fuel the very anxieties which they are seeking to eliminate.

Retailers could also elect to spell out more clearly the costs incurred when the shopping environment becomes severely compromised by crime and nuisance. A study conducted in Nottingham sought to assess the local economic consequences of city-centre crime and the fear of crime. The report estimated that avoidance of the city centre by shoppers led to annual losses of £12 million in turnover and nearly £1 million in profit for the retail sector alone (KPMG Peat Marwick, 1991). And as the focus of the national economy moves from manufacturing to the service and retail sectors, retailing assumes additional importance. At present the retail sector provides employment for over two million people, or roughly 10 per cent of the total UK workforce (Burrows and Speed, 1994). Anything which damages the retail environment will have an adverse impact on the country's prosperity. Economic arguments could thus be used to exert pressure for additional policing in town centres. Against this, Home Office figures for 1995 show that 38 out of 43 police forces are under strength; and there are plans to cut another 2,000 officers during the course of the year (Tendler, 1995c).

Another option would be not to press the claim for additional officers in the town centres (which is unlikely to be heard sympathetically) but to seek adjustments within the present levels of policing and how officers are used in and around the retail environment. The current research shows that town-centre managers are of the view that dedicated police squads (70%) are much more effective than police officers on patrol (43%). This may reflect their informed and professional view that 'policing with a purpose' is a greater security asset to both retailers and members of the public than are police officers on patrol who offer little more than what one respondent described as 'a token visual presence'.

Alternatively, the local authorities, shopkeepers and managers in town centres may choose to follow the example set by the shopping centres and accept that securing the safety of shoppers (and paying for it) is an integral part of the retail enterprise. The motives here are strictly commercial. If town-centre retailers do not wish to witness what appears to be an increasing 'retail migration' to shopping malls, shopping centres and out-of-town retail parks, they will have to offer their customers the same sense of safety and well-being as is found in these environments. The sense of security of the shopping public is a necessary condition for successful retailing, where dealing with the problems of crime and nuisance is seen in terms of protecting profit. The town-centre retailers may have no option but to follow the lead of the shopping-centre retailers and invest in private security. Market forces may be driving town-centre retailers in this direction, but it is naive to suppose that there are no difficulties.

On the one hand, if town centres are to redress the balance against crime and nuisance then those with ultimate responsibility (often the local authority) will need to review the emphasis placed on security. Even then it may be far from easy to secure the co-operation of all the interested parties – the police, local authorities and large (multiple) and small (singleton) retailers. Town-centre security has to contend with multiple ownership and the confusion of public spaces and private places, making an orchestrated initiative that much more difficult. And an increased emphasis on the security of shoppers in town centres will require a commensurate level of funding. These points are discussed further in Chapter 7.

On the other hand, even assuming that town centres are willing to follow the lead of the shopping centres, there is the further difficulty that not all town-centre retailers are equally able to purchase their own security. As government promotes so-called ancillary policing, which is also sometimes called 'fantasy' policing, two questions arise – What form should it take? and Who should pay? The probable answer to the former is that new-style officers will resemble security guards rather than Guardian Angels; and, with regard to the latter, privatised rent-a-cop schemes will be funded by investors who know that private security is one of our few growth industries (Moore, 1994). No-one else is really in a position to offer para-policing services. The expansion of private security will be driven by market forces where only those who can afford to purchase ancillary policing will have the benefit of it. Provision will depend on the ability to negotiate a contract. David French, of the Police Federation, made the point forcefully at the 1995 annual conference:

> We already know that the growth of private security services means those who can afford it are looking to hired hands to protect them ... Private policing will be policing for profit; policing at the least cost for the maximum price, money palmed out of the insecure citizen by slick salesmen with a friendly smile and the persuasive powers of a side-handled baton.
>
> (quoted in Tendler, 1995c: *The Times*, 17th May)

The most likely consequence for retailers is that household-name, multiple stores in prestige, town-centre locations will be best placed to provide in-house security, whilst the more numerous single outlets are unlikely to be able to afford it. The security-spend options are stacked heavily in favour of the retail 'giants', whilst the smaller, independent retailers are unlikely to be able to pay for either security equipment or security personnel. And if the smaller town-centre retailer is seen to be failing to meet the rising standards of customer care, the owners will risk a migration of trade to the larger competitor stores – in effect, a redistribution of trade within the town centre. This could fuel a vicious spiral where perceived insecurities lead to fewer sales, making security improvements less likely with a further detrimental impact on sales. There would then be a real risk of an increasing divide between the security 'haves' and 'have nots' in the town centre.

More optimistically, there is an outside possibility that major retailers will be prepared to pay for services to be provided across the whole town centre. This principle has been reflected in funding to date for town centre management (TCM) initiatives; but there is also evidence that the 'goodwill' factor should not to be taken for granted (Donaldsons and Healey & Baker, 1994). One possible solution is to combine private finance with public policing (a 'mixed economy' of policing), with private companies or local authorities buying-in conventional police officers for specific security purposes. The president of the Association of Chief Police Officers (ACPO), John Hoddinott, is on record as pointing to a 'widening of commercial interests within the service', suggesting that there are market-place opportunities for both buying-in or purchasing services from non-police sources and for selling or providing police services on a commercial basis – that is, hiring out police officers for those who can pay the market rate (Weeks, 1994). This is possible under the Police and Magistrates' Courts Act 1994. Hoddinott gave the example of the South Wales Constabulary who were actively considering 'marketing' their services. In effect, traditional policing could offer a narrow security function on a commercial basis in addition to, or as an alternative to, its public policing functions; and this would allow town centres, hospitals and councils to pay for their own police (Gibbons, 1995), something which has already happened in relation to the policing of large public events such as football matches and pop concerts (Lightfoot and Leppard, 1995).

For example, by early 1995 the council in Corby, Northamptonshire, had contracted the services of four community constables specifically to patrol the streets, over and above ordinary levels of policing, at a cost of £110,000 a year (Murray, 1995). And if local authorities are beginning to buy-in their own policing, then retailers themselves could also think along these lines. But this would still leave unresolved the matter of Who pays? and Who can afford to pay? And if we can now look forward to policing sponsored by whichever company makes the best offer – 'a cigarette company, a bank or a second-hand car firm' (Slapper, 1995) – the next question is What happens when the police have to investigate an alleged crime by their sponsor? The notion of buying-in policing raises as many questions as it answers. It is also interesting to note that part of the police motivation for going down this route, which the chief constable of Leicestershire, Keith Povey, has acknowledged, is that the public would prefer to see hired police officers on patrol rather than private security guards, although he also conceded that any move in this direction will mean that 'people who have the ability to pay for more will get more' (Gibbons, 1995).

Whilst these sorts of option are being explored, there is some evidence that major town-centre retailers are beginning to think that if they cannot or will not be protected by the conventional police, then they will have to find their own protection. Stanley Kalms, the chairman of the Dixons Stores Group, is on record as advocating that private vigilante groups be given semi-official status for the purpose of protecting high-street stores. He has stated that there is a need 'to legitimise the meaning of vigilantism' because self-protection is honourable when there is no other protection available (Travis, 1993). And he admitted that his store chain, frustrated by the lack of official action against shop squatters (who paid no rent, observed no standards and sold stolen goods), had employed 'heavies' to evict them from premises close to his own.

There is also considerable public support for vigilante action. Gallup conducted 1,095 interviews nationally in 1993. It found that three-quarters of those questioned believed that people were sometimes justified in 'taking the law into their own hands', and that two-thirds believed that those not properly protected by the police had a right to organise patrols to deal with criminals themselves (Shrimsley and Darbyshire, 1993). The widespread support for do-it-yourself justice was attributed to despair caused by rising crime and the inability of the police to do anything about it. The representatives of the professional and managerial classes in the sample were only slightly less keen on vigilantes than lower middle-class people and manual workers. The support for vigilante action from retailers and members of the public raises the question of what the permissible boundaries to DIY protection against high-street crime should be – something which is discussed further below in relation to shopping-centre security and banning known or suspected troublemakers.

Implications for shopping centres

It may have been the case initially that shopping centres had to recreate a form of conventional policing for a new shopping environment – the reassuring presence of 'officers' on patrol, albeit privately funded and operating exclusively in a private place. There is now evidence that the visible presence of private security guards is increasingly a response to customer-led expectations for a safe shopping environment; and retailers cannot afford to be unresponsive to such feelings. They run the risk otherwise that their customers will haemorrhage away to competitors' stores. Where crime or the fear of crime is thought to have an adverse impact on profit, the entrepreneur becomes increasingly responsible for providing – and paying for – crime control.

It is important to note the high and rising levels of public support for private security guards. In one of the earliest studies, based on visits to 34 shopping centres in Europe, 20 of them in the UK, Poole found that almost 60 per cent of customers said that they welcomed the sight of security staff because this signified to them that they were in a safe place to shop; but others said that they felt 'intimidated' or that the guards were 'too bossy' (Warren, 1992). In a study, conducted in Birmingham, 80 per cent of the sample said that private security guards were a welcome and useful presence in shopping centres; and 95 per cent said that private security guards did not inhibit their shopping (Poole, 1991). And in the current study, 84 per cent of shoppers were aware of guards and 92 per cent thought that they were an acceptable feature of the retail environment.

These data suggest that private security guards in shopping centres are commanding increasing support – up to a near-universal level. In addition, the earlier research by Poole found that 'guard baiting' was a popular pastime in some shopping centres – where the figures in uniform were treated as something of an 'Aunt Sally' by mischievous and rebellious troublemakers intent on cocking a snook at authority. Shopping-centre managers in the current study offered no evidence of this phenomenon, although it remains possible that interviews with security guards could have identified this type of behaviour.

It is also arguable that private security may be better placed to undertake what was formerly a public obligation. The British Retail Consortium found that of 1.2 million apprehended and detained shoplifters in 1992–93 only 120,000 or 10 per cent were found guilty or cautioned. This does not inspire confidence in the ability of the criminal justice system to offer redress. Equally, of the £517 million worth of stock stolen by customers, only £46 million or 9 per cent was recovered (Burrows and Speed, 1994). The shopping-centre retailers may think that they can do better, and they may well be right; and they are better placed to do so than their colleagues in the town centres.

To begin with, as was pointed out in detail in Chapter 3, policing the shopping centre is less complex than policing the town centre. Whereas security in the shopping centre is concerned solely with protecting its shops and shoppers, public policing in the town centre is a multi-faceted service of which the security of shoppers is only one dimension. Private security in the shopping centre is a straightforward task compared with the competing demands placed on conventional policing in the town centre. The city centre is a public and open environment with few or no controls over access, whilst the shopping centre is a private and more regulated environment where there is more control over the type of person who is admitted or who is allowed to stay. This is one of the most important reasons for the difference between town-centre and shopping-centre policing. In certain cases, however, shopping centres may be subject to 'walkway agreements' made under section 35 of the Highways Act 1980 (Johnston, 1992). These allow designated throughways to be treated as highways and thus subject to public byelaws. In effect, the owners can assign private property to a measure of public control.

With this single exception shopping centres are private places and this has been confirmed by a recent legal decision. In the case of *CIN Properties* v *Rawlins and Others* (*The Times*, 9th February, 1995), the central question was the rights of the public to use pedestrian malls within a town-centre shopping centre – the Swansgate shopping centre in Wellingborough. The owners (CIN) alleged that 13 young men who lived in the area frequented the centre and caused a nuisance. The young men were sent letters revoking any licence they might have to enter the centre and, when they continued, CIN started an action seeking appropriate declarations and injunctions. The initial judgement at Wellingborough County Court held that the public had an irrevocable right to enter and use the mall whenever its doors were open, subject to reasonable conduct. On appeal, Lord Justice Balcombe held that there were no rights in favour of the public at large to enter the mall, except under section 20 of the Race Relations Act 1976, and in the absence of any dedication as a highway or of a walkway agreement. The owners had a right to determine any licence the defendants might have to enter the centre. This decision considerably strengthens the long-standing belief that the owners of shopping centres have the authority to determine access even where the centre appears to be a public place.

Shopping-centre managers in the current study were firmly of the view that their private security officers were empowered to exercise discretion in order to prevent unwanted and undesirable people from entering the shopping centre, or from staying there once they had entered. One of their most important security options was security guards being proactive in excluding or moving on people whose behaviour or demeanour constituted an unacceptable nuisance, even though this might fall well short of criminal activity. This revocation of the public's licence to enter at will meant that undesirable 'street people' and 'known troublemakers' were vigorously excluded from the private spaces of shopping centres – and possibly displaced to the public places of the town centres. Shopping-centre managers summarised this frequently-used strategy:

> Periodically we carry out a high profile blitz on undesirables. This effectively moves them on to somebody else's area of responsibility.

> Most groups are well known to us. They are speedily identified on entry to the centre and kept on the move. The numbers are not allowed to grow.

> We identify and interview ring-leaders – and we are not afraid to issue trespass notices.

Banning may be made easier because the government has shown an interest in a national identity card scheme in the interests of promoting police efficiency (Home Office, 1995b). Such a scheme could help in tackling 'plastic card' crime, social security fraud and terrorism, together with car-related crime if identity cards were linked to the Driver and Vehicle Licensing Agency (DVLA) in Swansea (Leppard, 1994b). If a compulsory scheme is introduced, and some police chiefs are confident that something will be in place within two or three years, identity cards could have a role in the banning of troublemakers from shopping centres. This would make it that much more straightforward to turn suspected troublemakers into known troublemakers. It is too early to predict whether any identity card scheme will be implemented. In contrast, one shopping-centre manager questioned the wisdom of banning known troublemakers:

> A banning policy has proved ineffective. It is a challenge to troublemakers and it becomes a 'badge of honour' to be banned.

Whatever the merits of banning troublemakers, a robust but legal approach to excluding unwanted persons, and however successful it might be, it is by no means self evident that it is acceptable (Willis and Beck, 1994a). Some members of the public are being penalised for who they are (or the sort of person they appear to be) rather than for how they behave. It is possible that security guards will draw inferences about a person's behaviour from his or her looks and demeanour. On rather different grounds some persons will be excluded on the basis of what they might do, rather than on the basis of what they are doing or have already done. While this sort of strategy may receive public support, it must be recognised that it is premised either on personalised assessments of character or on prospective judgements about likely behaviour. In these respects the exclusion of undesirables from shopping centres is in marked contrast with the use of the criminal law by conventional police officers – which is largely predicated on formal criteria and based on actual behaviour. Banning suspected troublemakers is an exercise in largely unfettered discretion, although security guards will no doubt claim a breadth of experience which validates their judgements. This is an area which requires further research.

There would appear to be something of a twin-track policy on access to shopping centres. On the one hand, for the majority of consumers, the mall offers a 'surrogate town square', the new natural meeting place for the community. In addition, as credit is increasingly offered through bank and store cards, those with money to spend are made to feel welcome. The consumer-spender is a welcome guest in the pleasure-dome. On the other hand, those who do not conform to the acceptable stereotype – the 'new marginals' – are increasingly being told, with the benefit of legal authority, that they are not welcome, being:

> ... denied access, based on the flimsiest of judgements and reasoning, by security guards (private armies who ensure retailers conform and shoppers 'behave').
>
> (Shields, 1992a: 5)

The language is strong, and the same author has talked of 'draconian' regimes of private security (Shields, 1992b), but it points clearly to the shopping centre being defined as a 'public' place for those whom the owners wish to entertain, but defined as a decidedly 'private' place for those who are not welcome. Underwritten by shopping-centre management policy, the private security guard becomes the arbiter of acceptability. The use of banning orders and trespass notices in shopping centres offers a possible model of crime control which is underpinned by the civil law rather than the criminal law – and it may be that this option is under-utilised by both town-centre and shopping-centre managers. In mid-1995 security staff at the MetroCentre, Europe's largest indoor shopping centre, became the first to ban known shoplifters for life, in an effort to cut losses from theft approaching £12 million a year. The centre owners served exclusion orders on seven well-known thieves, with more than 50 others expected to be banned in the following 12 months (Tendler, 1995a).

The major advantage of using the civil law is that it requires a lower standard of proof than the criminal law. An injunction may be obtained on affidavit evidence alone without cross-examination of witnesses – and imprisonment can follow a breach if this is proved beyond reasonable doubt and it is shown that the breach was wilful and deliberate. There are suggestions that some criminal offences where the police are reluctant to prosecute and where the courts are disinclined to impose custodial sentences should be made civil nuisances, thus opening the way to injunctions and possible committals to custody for contempt. Retail-sector crime control could benefit from this sort of approach being used, although it could only be deployed against relatively well-known offenders and trouble-makers.

There is a weakness in the current trend to re-define more and more forms of misbehaviour as criminal – the conversion of that which is anti-social and offensive into that which is illegal (Jenkins, 1994b). We become less tolerant of 'vandals, rowdies, sneak thieves and foulmouths' – and criminalisation heightens the sense of moral disapproval and denunciation. Many of the sections in the Criminal Justice and Public Order Act 1994 fall into this category. And the Police Foundation and Policy Studies Institute (1994) point to the increasing tendency of governments to introduce new criminal legislation to combat 'every passing law and order exigency'. It is by no means self evident, however, that social control is necessarily improved by making behaviour illegal. The lager lout, the beggar, the inveterate drunk and the threatening youth in the retail environment will not disappear simply because some legislation has been passed and the statute will not cause an abrupt change in behaviour. The age-old problem with the blunt instrument of making things illegal, however well intended, is that where the costs of enforcement outweigh the burden on the public of the activity, the law will remain incompletely enforced or not enforced at all. This lends some support to the police view that retail crime is a retail problem. In the main it does not threaten the structure of society or its institutions. Paradoxically, criminalisation may make matters worse rather than better because the net effect is that little or nothing is done. And, given that so many of the crime and nuisance problems in town centres and shopping centres (particularly the latter) tend to the 'objectionable' rather than the 'dangerous' end of the spectrum, civil remedies along the lines of trespass notices and banning orders – backed by the threat of more severe penalties in the event of non-compliance – have a great deal to commend them.

As part of the 'banning process' there could be scope for more use of police photographs to enable shopkeepers to identify and then exclude known or suspected troublemakers. This has recently received the approval of the courts. A late 1994 judgement in the case of *Hellewell* v *Chief Constable of Derbyshire* (*The Times*, 13th January, 1995; Whitaker, 1995) allowed an application by the chief constable to strike out a claim by the plaintiff, Paul Hellewell, for declaratory relief and an injunction restraining the disclosure to the public of any photograph taken of him whilst in custody at the police station. Traders in a Shop Watch scheme, following a complaint about the level of shoplifting and harassment experienced by shopkeepers, had requested the police to provide photographs of individuals known to be causing problems, primarily because in some shops new staff might not recognise such troublemakers and as a result fail to bar or ban them from the premises. The plaintiff had been photographed in accordance with the Codes of Practice established under the Police and Criminal Evidence Act 1984 and copies of the photograph, which by its nature indicated that it had been taken in police or prison custody, were distributed to Shop Watch members. Guidelines were issued to the effect that the photographs were not to be publicly displayed and that only shopkeepers or their staff should see them. The plaintiff had learned that his photograph was in circulation and had brought proceedings.

The court held that this did not involve a breach of confidence. The police might make reasonable use of such a photograph for the purpose of the prevention and detection of crime, the investigation of alleged offences and the apprehension of suspects or persons unlawfully at large. They might do so if the person was wanted for arrest or was a suspected accomplice or anyone else – provided they had only these purposes in mind and they made no more than reasonable use of the photograph. Although there was no absolute benchmark for testing reasonableness, the honest judgements of professional police officers in the fight against crime were the key. Providing these principles were not transgressed, there would be 'an obvious and vital public interest' in the use of such photographs, which the courts would uphold. The police would have a public interest defence against any action brought against them for breach of confidence. The plaintiff was a criminal with 32 convictions, including 19 for dishonesty, which permitted the inference that he had caused trouble in local shops. The circulation of the photograph was limited to shops in the Shop Watch scheme. And the police had acted in good faith for the prevention or detection of crime and to a limited and specific extent by distributing the photograph only to persons who had a reasonable need to make use of it.

The validity of a public interest defence over the use of a suspect's photograph is a significant decision. It underwrites the principle of police-shopkeeper collaboration and it does so specifically in the retail context. More importantly, the definition of the category of people whose photographs may be disclosed would appear to be broad, including suspects and their accomplices or 'anyone else', provided the reasonableness test is met. The decision would also suggest that circulated photographic evidence can properly be used for the prevention of crime to 'ban' known or suspected troublemakers from stores, and not used simply for the purposes of arrest and prosecution. And it certainly follows that the retailers themselves could be more active in asking their local police for 'mug shots' of suspected persons and in expecting these to be provided in the public interest.

Another initiative, which is of relevance to both town centre and shopping centres, is a plan in Manchester to set up a new day-care centre and all-night cafe for beggars. The plan is the joint idea of retailers, who think that beggars are 'bad for business', and the charity Crisis, which seeks to help the homeless (Ward, 1995). The centre would offer food, warmth and medical help in non-judgemental surroundings – and keep beggars and vagrants off the streets during trading hours. It is not clear, however, how the £500,000 annual costs would be provided. There was a suggestion that members of the public, instead of giving cash to beggars, should be encouraged to give 'charity vouchers' which could only be redeemed at the centre. This proposal has the merit of avoiding using either conventional police or private security guards in policing part of the retail environment.

The critical difference between security in town centres and shopping centres is that the latter have become dependent on private security. This option may be open to town centres but it is already a fact of life for contemporary shopping centres. All the evidence points to the continued growth of the private security industry, of which manned services in shopping malls is but one part. The new-style security may have an unstoppable momentum and it certainly has some intriguing features – for example, the banning of known or suspected troublemakers. The growth of the industry and the exercise of this type of authority has recently generated substantial interest in the possible need for formal regulation, an aspect which is examined in the next chapter.

6 Regulating the Private Security Industry

The 'rise and rise' of private security, of which security guards in shopping centres is but one manifestation, has prompted the House of Commons (1995a and 1995b) Home Affairs Committee to establish an inquiry into the regulation of the private security industry. This question merits an extended discussion because of its implications for risk and security management in the retail sector generally, as well as because it raises specific points about guarding services in town centres and shopping centres.

Sir John Smith, as Deputy Commissioner of the Metropolitan Police, argued that although private security offers much the same sort of service as public policing (the reassuring presence of an 'officer' in uniform, with deterrent potential and powers of detention) there is one significant difference (see Campbell, 1994). Traditional policing is grounded on two principles – that it stems from the community it serves and that it is democratically accountable. The use of private security guards in retailing appears to meet the former criterion in that it offers a service which the shoppers deem to be effective and acceptable, but it certainly fails to meet the latter. Democratic accountability in conventional policing is replaced by accountability largely to those who pay for the security services; and power is being exercised with little responsibility. As the Deputy Commissioner put it – Who controls them? and Who decides their operational policies and priorities? And, if they overstep the mark, to whom should the public complain? There are no obvious answers to these questions except when it is clear that security officers have stepped well outside the boundaries of legal behaviour. In general, actions which affect the lives of ordinary citizens are being taken with little or no public scrutiny or accountability. This may be considered an example of a democratic deficit.

There is a series of interrelated issues here. Current efforts to establish nationally recognised standards of training for security operatives are seen to be inadequate; and in any case, these may not impact on the policies and procedures of those who control the security guards – and who were recently described as 'private security barons' (Blair, 1994). As one senior police officer has put it, all that is required to set up as a security company is 'a mobile phone, a van and a dog' (see Campbell, 1994). Finally, there is no guarantee that the purchaser of manned services will require a level of performance which meets the minimum standards of public policing; and there may be strong arguments against his or her doing so. These misgivings were summarised by Diane Reardon, vice-chairman of the constables' section of the Police Federation, at the 1995 annual conference, who said of the 'civil patrollers':

> They might be dressed to look like regular officers but in fact they would be untrained, badly equipped and poorly paid. In short they will be little more than a mixture of bully boys, concerned with completing the shift with a minimum of disruption.
>
> (quoted in Tendler, 1995c: *The Times*, 17th May)

Security industry perspectives

Attempts at self-regulation in the private security industry are seen not to be working. The Inspectorate of the Security Industry (ISI) was established in 1992, jointly by the British Security Industry Association (BSIA) and the International Professional Security Association (IPSA), as an independent, third party certification body to inspect guarding companies and cash-in-transit companies against British Standard 7499, British Standard 5750 and industry codes of practice. The inspectorate was accredited by the National Accreditation Council for Certification Bodies (NACCB) in September 1994 and the certificate was signed by the President of the Board of Trade. The board of management includes representatives of industry, other trade associations, insurers, customers, the police and government departments (British Security Industry Association, 1994b; Inspectorate of the Security Industry, 1994). Since October 1992 only 20 companies have met the highest standard under the Assessed Companies Scheme (BS 5750); only 50 companies have achieved certification through the Inspected Companies Scheme (the lesser BS 7499); and only eight out of 37 applications have been successful in obtaining registration under the Enrolled Companies Scheme (aspiring to broad compliance with BS 7499). One possible reason for the lack of progress is that there is no 'muscle' behind the schemes.

In this respect the ISI stands in contrast to the National Approval Council for Security Systems (NACOSS), the sister organisation for regulation and certification for companies involved in the installation of intruder alarms, access control systems and CCTV systems. The Council estimates that it covers 60 per cent of all installations and up to 90 per cent of those in the commercial sector (NACOSS, 1994). It operates under the aegis of the Loss Prevention Council and its success is attributed to the support of insurance companies who specify that for certain classes of risk the installing firm must have been assessed by a non-partisan third party organisation. Although NACOSS is confident that it offers a successful example of self-regulation, it would like access to any criminal records there may be of those working in the industry, together with the removal of obstacles placed by the Rehabilitation of Offenders Act 1974.

The same level of confidence is not to be found within the manned security industry. On the contrary, both large and small firms offered evidence which points to the need for controls. Although all BSIA member companies are subject to ISI independent inspection, IPSA has withdrawn from the scheme (20,000 employees and £250 million turnover) and non-affiliated companies (also with 20,000 employees and £250 million turnover) were never party to it. In effect, self-regulation only applies to about one-half of the guarding industry – BSIA companies (40,000 employees and £530 million turnover). The British Security Industry Association now takes the view that self-regulation is not working because the buyers of security tend to base their decisions 'purely on price', with too little regard to the quality of service they are purchasing. The Association is pressing government for statutory regulation to ensure that guarding companies meet minimum standards which are established, controlled and monitored by an independent inspectorate reporting to the licensing body (British Security Industry Association, 1994b). This is something of an about-face for the BSIA which has been in general, but with some inconsistency over time, rather sceptical of various proposals for licensing measures – certainly through the 1980s (South, 1988). The new view is strongly articulated by Mr Jim Harrower, BSIA chairman and managing director of Group 4, who has said:

> Self regulation has run its course. We need a regulatory body.
>
> (quoted in Gibbons, 1994: 17)

The British Security Industry Association is well aware that the whole of the private security industry has had something of a bad press. It attributes this tarnished image to the reckless and irresponsible actions of non-affiliated, unregulated companies (1994b). There are anxieties that private security patrols may increase the fear of crime. There are concerns that firms employ persons with criminal records (including people who have served terms of imprisonment) and they have no means of checking for previous convictions. And there are fears that private guards may act outside the law.

The International Professional Security Association also points out that, although there has been a National Vocational Qualification (NVQ) Level II in existence for two years to cover the requirements of security guards, the uptake by the industry has been disappointing. Employers are faced with two disincentives to assess an employee's competence – the direct costs of the £78 fee and the indirect costs of the length of time involved. They are also reluctant because the high staff turnover in the guarding industry means that the benefit is unlikely to accrue to the present employer (IPSA, 1994). The Association is also pressing government for the statutory control of security guards, or at least for a register of persons employed in the industry.

Small security firms have joined the chorus calling for regulation. One company, which chose to remain outside both the BSIA and the IPSA, argued to the Home Affairs Committee that the bodies, particularly the BSIA, were dominated by the 'major' companies. This meant that, although both purport to defend high standards of pay and training, they fail to achieve this because of the pressure to remain competitive. Simple commercial interests prevent either from being 'a serious governing, regulatory or advisory body' (Casson, 1994).

For rather different reasons, one of the largest security companies, Securicor Security Services, has put its weight behind the demand for regulation. Securicor thinks that the ISI is something of a lame duck – with 'no tangible endorsement' from the Home Office, the police or the insurers. The breakdown of merger talks between the BSIA and the IPSA and the latter's withdrawal from the ISI have only made matters worse. Most importantly, Securicor's long-standing commitment to the careful selection and screening of staff has meant that its manned guarding services cost roughly 10 per cent more than those offered by competitors. In the current climate this price disadvantage is not sustainable and these terms will no longer be offered. The immediate consequence of this is likely to be an increase in the rate of turnover of staff – something which is negatively correlated with 'quality of service'; and the only way out of the impasse is regulation. Securicor advocates an independent, self-financing agency to be responsible for vetting, together with security guard licensing (a 'fit and proper person' requirement) and exceptions under the Rehabilitation of Offenders Act (Securicor Security Services, 1994).

Police perspectives

The House of Commons Home Affairs Committee also received police evidence in favour of regulation. The Association of Chief Police Officers cited a police study conducted in Lancashire in 1993–94. The private security industry employed some 4,500 persons compared with 3,200 police officers in the same area. During the course of the study 130 private security employees committed 249 criminal offences. On the assumption that this offending rate is typical for the industry nationally, it was estimated that some 2,600 offences are committed annually by employees within the private security industry. It was suggested that the reported offending rate in the private security industry was 21 times greater than that for the police service and six times greater than that for the postal service. It was argued that these figures gave grounds for 'considerable concern'. The data were used to support the view that some form of statutory regulation was necessary in order to ensure accountability. The Association pointed out that under current arrangements private operators faced neither the disciplinary controls imposed on police officers nor the obligations placed on police forces to answer to elected police authorities. It saw registration and regulation, with vetting, as the key to quality of membership and quality of service in the industry (Association of Chief Police Officers, 1994). An ACPO spokesman summarised these misgivings as follows:

> We found examples of employees with what can only be described as horrendous previous convictions ... Real and potential abuses of private security status are much higher than previously envisaged ... In every area we looked there was evidence of criminal behaviour. A lot of companies say they are police approved but that's a myth. No companies are approved or vetted by us and we are very concerned about the quality of people touting for business ... The gravity of some of the offences is frightening and the public need some reassurances ... The relationship between customers and businesses in the security industry is, of necessity, one of trust ... Without safeguards, such a relationship is open to abuse.
>
> (quoted in Gibbons, 1994: 17)

Tellingly, while there were such demands for regulation, the president of the Association of Chief Police Officers, John Hoddinott, was keen to debate and clarify the role of policing at the turn of the century, including its relation to the private security industry – the role of which was firmly acknowledged. This was a welcome breath of realism. Late in 1994 Hoddinott accepted that policing was increasingly subject to the rules of the market-place and, with regard to private security, added:

> It is no good simply saying we will have nothing to do with them because we already do and there has also historically always been a private security industry. We need to be clear about our relationship.
>
> (quoted in Weeks, 1994: 14)

The Police Superintendents' Association of England and Wales took the same line, arguing for a licensed private security industry with a regulatory body, to be responsible for the vetting of all staff (Police Superintendents' Association, 1994). The Police Federation of England and Wales agreed, pointing to the need for legislation to establish the registration, licensing and inspection of all companies offering a security service, together with a Private Security Industry Authority to control and oversee matters (Police Federation, 1994a). The Federation argued that every other organisation which was even loosely concerned with crime control was subject to statutory regulation and public accountability; and added that the enormous profits of the industry could easily be used to finance control, without additional costs being passed on to customers (Police Federation, 1994b). Both organisations conjured up distasteful images of rogue or 'cowboy' operators offering fraudulent, exaggerated or inefficient services to the public, sometimes by persons with a known criminal record. The 'one man and his dog and a van' profile was prominent.

Towards regulation?

The Home Affairs Committee also received evidence in favour of regulation from the pressure group Liberty which offered details of 14 cases where members of the public had been injured in clashes with private security guards, mostly in connection with public demonstrations against motorway building or hunting. The group argued that an unregulated industry was incompatible with the observance of internationally recognised rights of freedom of assembly and privacy (Cohen, 1994). The Association of District Councils (1994) and the Association of Metropolitan Authorities (1994) agreed on the need for regulation. Concern centred on the potential for the employment of people with criminal records, poor training, poor health and safety policies and inadequate or uncertain insurance cover. And there was a strong feeling that police-related functions, especially patrol work, should be undertaken only by sworn officers or under very firm regulation. This issue has, of course, not just come to the fore.

Bruce George MP has crusaded long and hard for the statutory regulation of the industry by introducing bills in the House of Commons in 1977, 1988, 1990, 1992 and 1994; and in so doing has articulated most of the arguments cited above (George and Button, 1994; and see Button and George, 1994). The ground swell of opinion in favour of regulation is considerable – and it is interesting to note that the major players in the industry itself, the various groups representing the interests of policing and other groups are using much the same sorts of arguments.

In May 1995 serious allegations were made about the criminal infiltration of local Labour councils by 'organised gangsters', and there were calls for a national police investigation. Party officials provided evidence to the police that leading criminals were employing hired thugs to work for so-called security firms and were then using intimidation to win council contracts for 'protecting' building sites and other local authority properties. Police inquiries seemed likely to concentrate on the activities of seven security companies that had tendered for work worth millions of pounds (Burrell and Levy, 1995). The charges against private security were moving beyond the mere employment of persons of dubious character with criminal records to active involvement in organised crime, extortion and protection.

In June 1995 the Home Affairs Committee reported, as expected, with a string of recommendations which would, if accepted by government, place the private security industry under some form of independent control (House of Commons, 1995a). The proposals included the establishment of a national vetting and licensing agency for manned security operators which would have direct access to police criminal records, the first such body to do so. This agency, which would be self-financing, would issue licences to all persons employed as contract security guards in the manned guarding sector. The committee recommended that companies wishing to operate in this sector should not be permitted to offer contract guarding services without themselves being subject to regulation. This would also require setting up another new agency, for which the committee did not offer a detailed blueprint, other than that it should be accountable through the Home Secretary to Parliament. If the double-barrelled proposal for the licensing of individuals and the regulation of companies were to be introduced, the legislation would make it a criminal offence for persons to operate in contract manned guarding without a licence and for contract guarding companies to employ a person as a guard who did not hold a licence; and companies would be subject to prosecution if security work was undertaken without meeting these requirements. Britain would then join the other members of the European Union, excluding the Republic of Ireland, in exercising some form of supervision over the private security industry (Burrell and Levy, 1995). It is, however, important to note that these recommendations apply only to the provision of contract guarding services and not to the provision of in-house security.

The proposal for the introduction of a vetting and licensing system with a new regulatory agency reflects government thinking as expressed in a Home Office (1993b) discussion paper on the disclosure of criminal records for employment vetting purposes. By early 1995 ministers were considering the option of setting up a commercial criminal inquiries agency with the authority to sell details of criminal records to potential employers, including the security industry, who want to vet job applicants. This is one way of accommodating the growing demands for regulation and doing so at minimum cost (Travis, 1995c). It appears to meet some of the government's fears about the practical consequences of regulation, especially the need to invent and finance regulatory bodies with sufficient powers to dictate and apply standards (South, 1988). The new police national computer, named Phoenix and holding some four million criminal records, would make this possible. The recommendation from the Home Affairs Committee would not be subject to the constraints of the Rehabilitation of Offenders Act 1974, which allows the records of people sentenced to jail for between six months and two-and-a-half-years to be 'wiped clean' after ten years, but would not give information about acquittals or police intelligence reports. This proposal was backed by the British Retail Consortium which argued that retailers needed a licensing authority, with its own inspectorate, with access to the police national computer (British Retail Consortium, 1995). As regards the second proposal, the committee was clear that any regulatory body would have to be accountable to Parliament through the Home Secretary, while having strong links with the police and with industry and commerce but being independent of the security industry itself. Apart from authorising applicant companies to operate in the manned security sector, the body would take responsibility for setting minimum standards for training, working conditions (pay and working hours) and insurance cover.

The committee recognised that the private security industry had grown significantly in recent years and that the dividing line between activities undertaken by the police and private security companies had become 'increasingly blurred' and 'increasingly uncertain'. Although the committee did not attempt to answer the question of whether particular tasks should be transferred from conventional policing to private security, the critical point was the need for the citizen to be assured that he or she was 'no more under threat from private security personnel ... than if they were police officers'. As private security takes on some of the roles of the police, it becomes all the more sensible to think in terms of its 'structure, powers and conduct' being subject to formal controls – such as those which apply, for example, to the security industry's involvement in the management of prison and court escort duties. The new roles for private security, the committee concluded, called for safeguards to guarantee the development of a 'disciplined, honest and effective' private sector industry. Intervention would therefore be justified as being in the interests of protecting the public. Alongside this, the committee found – in line with the massive weight of evidence presented to it (see above) – that the current system of voluntary self-regulation was demonstrably inadequate as far as manned services were concerned, primarily because a large number of smaller guarding companies elected not to become involved – perhaps over 80 per cent of the total number of companies. The committee took the general view that the imposition of minimum standards by means of statutory regulation, with the costs being borne by the manned security sector itself, would lead to some loss of freedom for companies to enter or stay in the market-place, but that this was an 'acceptable price' to pay for securing standards of service in which the public would have greater confidence. Such a body would go a long way to raising the 'pitiful' levels of training and 'gross levels of under-performance'.

At present it is unclear how the government will respond to these recommendations. Despite the near-unanimous demand for regulation it does not appear to be wholly persuaded of the need for statutory controls. During the passage of the Police and Magistrates' Courts Bill through the House of Commons in 1994 an opposition amendment calling for the regulation of the private security industry was defeated. And the Home Secretary was adamant that no regulation was required:

> We have no reason to believe that the level of offending by private security firms is so substantial as to warrant the introduction of a statutory licensing system ... We risk adding unnecessary bureaucracy and costs to industry if we go for statutory controls.
> (Public Eye, 'Out of Order', BBC2, 21st October 1994)

And the Home Office minister, David Maclean, told the select committee that there was no need for a statutory licensing body or controls because there was no demand from the industry for self-regulation to be abandoned (Cohen, 1994). In the absence of overwhelming demand, the cost of regulation would not be justified by the benefits. The government's view on regulation was clearly spelled out in its *Memorandum of Evidence* to the select committee:

> The Government has not been persuaded so far that the balance of argument lies in favour of its intervention in the regulation of the private security industry. However it does not rule out action in the future if substantial problems are identified in the industry as a whole, or within specific areas of it. It is naturally concerned that, in this field as in others, excessive interference in regulating recruitment practice and other employment conditions could lead to higher costs on employers, thereby damaging businesses and job opportunities.
>
> (Home Office, 1994d: 13)

The document went on to report a six month monitoring exercise conducted by ACPO in 1990 (1st April – 30th September) which indicated a rate of offending within the security industry of 336 per 100,000 employees compared with over 8,000 per 100,000 for the general male population aged 17–50 years. The conclusion drawn was that the criminal presence in the security industry, when placed in the context of the levels of offending in the general population, 'would not by itself justify the introduction of an expensive and bureaucratic licensing system'.

The chairman of the Home Affairs Committee, Sir Ivan Lawrence, was optimistic, however, that government would acknowledge the problem and be 'prepared to act upon it' (Bennetto, 1995). On this assumption, the most likely outcome is that there will be some form of limited initiative to 'weed out cowboy security firms', with legislation requiring would-be guards to declare criminal convictions and to be licensed and regulators checking up on would-be employees through police files (*The Times*, 6th June, 1995). It is less likely that the second proposal for a new body to regulate companies will be accepted. The government already has some sort of model in mind for the former and it would be self-financing, whilst the structure and funding of the latter are much less well defined in the report. It is possible that the committee thought that if they divided their proposals into two parts they would stand a better chance of securing acceptance of the idea of a vetting and licensing agency for manned guards, even if the government remained unconvinced of the need to license companies. Such an outcome would certainly appear to meet most of the demands for regulation, but its impact could well be limited.

Both the vetting of prospective guards and the licensing of manned guarding companies would only set minimum standards at the point of entry to the guarding industry. This should prevent the stereotypical muscle-bound ex-con with a van and a dog from setting up as a private security consultant – a euphemism often found to cover for a lack of expertise or previous criminal convictions. This is rightly seen as a necessary pre-condition for good private security practice. What it would be less likely to secure, however, is minimum standards of service or performance, let alone the conditions under which private security could be sought or offered.

The committee certainly claims far too much for its vetting proposals. For example, it is unclear how the vetting of prospective staff would guarantee that the private security industry became 'disciplined, honest and effective', any more than it would ensure that its 'structure, powers and conduct' would be similar to those found in conventional policing. Minimum standards at the point of entry to the industry would not necessarily have an impact on quality of service: vetting and licensing may be a necessary condition for 'good practice' but they are certainly not a sufficient condition. As was made clear to the committee in evidence, it is one thing to control *who* may be employed, but it is another matter to determine *what* standard of service is then provided. And even a regulatory agency accountable to Parliament through the Home Secretary would scarcely provide the transparency and accountability which are built into the structure of conventional policing.

The committee appears to have taken the view that market forces by themselves have not proved to be effective in providing adequate protection against rogue operators, so what is required is to graft some additional safeguards onto market mechanisms. The United States model of a tough regulatory regime and the operation of the free market is quoted with approval. In effect, the report favours a 'free market plus some controls' approach, and the recommendation for the imposition of controls at the point of entry to the industry may be seen as a modest first step in regulation. There then arise much larger issues about the relationship between demand, supply and quality of service. These aspects need to be explored. The committee also failed to recognise properly the 'unstoppable momentum' apparent in the expansion in private security services, and the extent to which manned guards are now to be regarded as 'primary protectors' in many public places. The deployment of security guards in shopping centres is a graphic illustration of the substitution of the 'bobby on the beat' by the 'guard in the mall'. And it is interesting to note that the committee makes but one reference to the use of private security firms in the retail sector – and then simply by acknowledging the 'new role' of guards in shopping centres, without any discussion of what security functions they perform, how they carry them out and to whom they are accountable, and in what ways. The case for some form of regulation is relatively straight-forward; but the committee does not address the wider issues of the nature and content of private security provision, not least in the retail environment – including town centres and shopping centres.

Market forces and commercial justice

Most of the current arguments against regulation by government are essentially utilitarian in that the costs of controls are seen to be out of proportion to the scale of the problems. But there is also an underlying ideological argument for rejecting regulation – and this is much stronger. Although it remains largely unstated by government at the present time, it has a much longer pedigree. As far back as the green paper *The Private Security Industry*, which was published in 1979, there were firm statements that crime control was not and ought not to be the exclusive concern of the state:

> There is no modern society in which a government can provide total protection against crime ... It is inconceivable that the police should be expected to meet *all* demands for protective services and to do so at the expense of taxpayer and ratepayer.
>
> (Home Office, 1979: 10-11, emphasis in original)

And if private forms of security have an existence independent of public policing, then it follows that the conventional mechanisms for control and accountability simply do not apply. They are not two versions of the same thing but different services. Private security means 'commercial policing'. It is perfectly possible to assert that traditional forms of 'police' accountability are simply irrelevant even when quasi-police functions are being performed. One commentator holds that this has been the government's view since the late 1970s (South, 1988).

This implies that there is simply no need to seek or to impose regulation. The retailer will choose to buy-in private security in order to counteract the threat posed by crime to retail profits. When the costs of crime are high it becomes prudent to purchase security – at least to the point where the benefits of minimising losses exceed the costs of buying-in private protection. This offers a solution in strict accord with free-market principles. The retailer will purchase security to a level which balances benefits and quality of service against costs. The security company which fails to deliver effective security at a reasonable price will not remain in the market-place. The 'market forces' solution is certainly plausible and it may be sensible.

First, it would appear to offer the consumer-shopper additional protection, over and above that provided by conventional policing in and around the shopping environment. Customers would receive the benefit of existing police services and shopping-specific private security protection. Secondly, it may well offer the purchaser of these services, and in turn the shopper, a genuine feeling of improved safety and security. This may be a real benefit (less fear of crime) even if there is no demonstrable impact on crime and nuisance levels. Thirdly, it would follow that there was no need for the security industry to feel under an obligation to contribute to wider crime prevention in the community beyond what was required to meet its clients' loss-prevention needs in the market-place (Williams et al, 1984).

There are strong countervailing arguments. There is some danger that if private security is seen to be 'doing the job', there will be less and less reason for conventional policing to seek a role for itself in those areas which have begun to use private security – such as shopping centres. This would reinforce the view that the policing of retail environments is at best an ancillary task for the police. At this point private security becomes alternative security rather than additional security. This may be undesirable in itself and would certainly tend to widen the gulf between public policing in town centres and private security in shopping centres. As ACPO argued in its submission to the Home Affairs Committee, public policing operates within a clear framework of standards, constraints and sanctions – not least because it has a national responsibility to society at large and to all of its members. It is a linchpin of social stability in the body politic. In contrast, the private security industry mostly protects organisations and only those which can afford and are willing to purchase its services. This means that, by definition, it protects interests rather than rights (Association of Chief Police Officers, 1994).

Without taking the argument any further, what this means is that private security becomes 'partial' security – something which operates only in the interests of those who can purchase the service and then only in the way, and to the extent, that the purchaser of the service requires. Sir John Smith, as Deputy Commissioner of the Metropolitan Police, pointed out that the so-called market forces solution would lead to a bifurcation in the provision of security services. Whatever the level of need, those most able to afford private security would be most able to secure it. And those least able to afford it, even where their need was great, would not be in a position to purchase services. Where the theory of public policing points in principle towards an even-handed and universal service, the reality of private security is that of a service tailored to the requirements of the purchaser. South (1988) has summarised these misgivings in a single, memorable sentence:

> Private security is not in the business to serve the general public good; it is in business to serve the needs of its paying clients.

> (South, 1988: 152)

Sir John Smith condemned this free-market philosophy because the net effect of a creeping privatisation of traditional police functions would be a two-tier system. Affluent individuals and businesses would be willing and able to pay for their own protection, whilst the less wealthy members of society would remain largely unprotected and, relative to the others, that much more vulnerable:

> Who in the market place would decide? Would it be the most powerful – those with the loudest voices? Would the weaker and more marginalised be left out, even though their needs are as great?

> (quoted in Campbell, 1994: *The Guardian*, 10th January)

If this two-tier view of the development of security services is correct, there are retail-specific consequences. It would probably follow that the more organised and purposeful offenders would simply redirect their efforts away from privately patrolled and protected areas to places with less protection because their owners could not afford security guards. It will certainly be the case that the retail 'giants' (shopping centres and larger town-centre stores) are best placed to purchase their own security, whilst smaller singleton outlets are less able to afford these services. Private policing then means selective and unequal protection because it is premised on the ability to pay for services. This is a well-established trend and it is probably irreversible. The private security guard in the shopping centre is a conspicuous example of a well-funded, comprehensive security service – protecting both retailers and shoppers. The less affluent store in the town centre is unable to buy-in a similar level of protection. They are at opposite ends of the private security spectrum.

There are two caveats. First, where private security services are provided on a mall-wide or retail park-wide scale, the smaller retailer in the same location will receive the same benefit as the larger retailer, although it is arguable that even this will not affect the smallest retailer, who is unlikely to trade in this type of environment. Secondly, in spite of the progressive displacement of conventional policing by private security services, it will remain the case that the police will (rightly) be primarily responsible for dealing with serious crimes – such as burglary, robbery and large-scale disorder. These offences, however, make up only a tiny proportion of shopping-centre 'crime', which largely falls under the headings of nuisance-type behaviour and incivilities.

Finally, although the market forces solution can be made true by definition, there is some danger that if the market will only pay the so-called 'real guardians' a pittance (on average a take-home wage of less than £120 for a 50-hour week), there will be negative consequences as far as the quality of service is concerned. Private security may not be an adequate substitute for public policing if it fails to deliver a near-equivalent service. Bob Shearsmith, executive director of Care Security Services, a major provider of uniformed staff in shopping centres, has summed up this problem:

> The security officer does not feel adequately rewarded, experiences little or no job satisfaction and ends up seeking other more financially rewarding employment. The effect on the customer is one of an unstable workforce and permanent lack of experience in the team.
>
> (quoted in Young, D., 1995: *The Times*, 25th January).

Symbols of security

One of the major concerns in the 'regulation' debate is whether a security guard can command the same degree of respect from members of the public as do police officers. This leads to an ironic postscript. In December 1994 a review of police clothing undertaken by the Metropolitan Police decided that the traditional policeman's helmet – dating back to 1863 – would continue to be worn (Tendler, 1994b). Significant changes were made in other areas – for example, the tunic jacket was to be superseded by pullovers and anoraks. The decision to retain the Victorian helmet was perfectly rational and not an exercise in misplaced nostalgia. It remains an effective means of protection; but Sir Paul Condon, the Metropolitan Police Commissioner, also believed that it was desirable to retain this distinctive symbol in order to prevent the public from becoming confused by the increasing number of security guards who wear police-style uniforms!

It is also interesting to note that section 52(1) of the Police Act 1964 makes it an offence for any person to impersonate a member of a police force with intent to deceive. This prevents private individuals from wearing a uniform or badges which might mislead the public into believing they are, or carry the authority of, police officers. But if imitation is the sincerest form of flattery, then retaining the unique policemen's helmet may be a prudent way of asserting a police identity which is increasingly threat-ened by the rise of uniformed private security guards. Notwithstanding the legislation, one commentator has argued that, with varying degrees of subtlety, the private security industry – simply by opting for uniforms – has always sought to gain authority and respect and, by implication, police-type powers (South, 1988).

It would be unwise to underestimate the symbolic importance of uniforms – for both police officers and private security guards. Policing studies show consistently that the public have a marked preference for police officers walking the beat in uniform, not least as a form of reassurance to the community that their expectations are being met (Shapland and Vagg, 1988; Bennett, 1994). A recent MORI poll found that 87 per cent of a national sample wanted to see more officers on the beat (Ford, 1994a). And a major crime prevention survey found that there was significant support for recruiting more police (35%) but even greater support for more officers being deployed on the beat (50%). It was the walking, talking bobby in uniform who commanded the greatest support (Willis, 1992). Research by the police found that 70 per cent of members of the public thought that there were too few police in their area; but that when they were asked to choose between 'PC Smith' who arrests and deters offenders and 'PC Jones' who works with local people to solve crime problems, three-quarters chose the latter (Joint Consultative Committee, 1990). The influential Shopfront Security Group (1994) agrees:

> A policeman on the beat is still the most reassuring form of surveillance to members of the public. That reassurance is important if people are to feel that it is safe to visit town and city centres.
>
> (Shopfront Security Group, 1994: 12)

There are probably two reasons for this preference. First, the officer on patrol is by definition closer to the public than is a colleague in a control room or a motor vehicle. This means that they have a physical presence and close proximity to the public. This is reassuring. Secondly, the officer in uniform is a symbolic affirmation that 'all is well' – a visible sign that crime is under control. This is possibly even more reassuring (Reiner, 1992). The same could be true for security guards on patrol in uniform. The Police Foundation and Policy Studies Institute (1994) review of polic-ing is clear about the general impact of the security officer in uniform:

> It is known that most citizens are deferential to figures in uniform whether or not they have legal powers.
>
> (Police Foundation and Policy Studies Institute, 1994: 20)

Part of the public's confidence in crime control may reflect little more than an underlying belief that where protection is seen to be offered by a special and distinct agency, then that protection is real – irrespective of whether the belief is well founded or not. Police officers and security guards on patrol can have a real impact on reducing the fear of crime even where they have a marginal or negligible impact on crime itself. Given that public policing is under budgetary constraints, the private security guard in the shopping centre may be taking over this symbolic function of affirming a state of public order. To the extent that this is important, and the studies of fear of crime suggest that it is, the security guard may prove to be an enduring and expanding feature of both the town-centre and the shopping-centre retail environments. The demand for police-like protection, even where this means little more than symbolic reassurance, is not to be underestimated. In shopping centres, the symbols of security are private security guards, providing a service which is now taken for granted in this part of the retail environment. This presence will be maintained with or without regulation of the private security industry. Although some form of regulation may help to introduce minimum standards, regulation per se does not address the fundamental difficulties of 'unequal protection', when private security is provided solely in response to market forces.

7 Management Priorities and Security

Complementary to the audit of existing security measures (Chapter 5) was an exploration of the self-reported priorities accorded to security by both town-centre and shopping-centre managers. The assumption was that managers were able to describe the ways in which security formed part of their job descriptions and how this was reflected in their day-to-day activities, including the prominence given to specific measures to preserve and protect the safety of shoppers. It was also thought that there could be a strong correlation between identified crime and nuisance problems and the priority given to measures designed to minimise them. Town-centre and shopping-centre managers were therefore asked to rank their range of responsibilities in order of priority, including the security of shoppers. This can be seen as a parallel enquiry to the earlier exploration of security cover, but one where the emphasis switches from the extent of provision and its effectiveness to its perceived importance – and the way in which security is given prominence relative to other aspects of managers' responsibilities.

Security priorities for managers

Town-centre and shopping-centre managers were asked to rank a range of their responsibilities in order of priority. The findings are summarised in Tables 7.1 and 7.2. Town-centre managers gave the highest priority to tasks which fell under the general heading of facilitating the commercial well-being of the town centre – its development (68%), its promotion (63%) and the co-ordination of inter-agency activities, such as liaison between the local authority and the town-centre retailers (66%). Security-related measures were given a lower priority – town-centre security (44%), the security of shoppers (22%) and the security of private premises (7%).

Table 7.1 High, medium and low priorities for town-centre managers by areas of responsibility

Areas of responsibility	High priority	Medium priority	Low priority
		Per cent	
Development of town centre	68.0	11.0	21.0
Co-ordination of agencies	65.7	18.7	15.6
Promoting the town centre	62.6	25.1	12.3
Security of town centre	43.8	46.8	9.4
Ensuring cleanliness	43.7	43.8	12.5
Security of shoppers	22.0	50.0	28.0
Security of private premises	6.7	–	93.3

Shopping-centre managers gave the highest priority to tasks which involved making the shopping environment a safe place for shoppers – most notably the security of shoppers (54%) and the general security of the shopping centre itself (44%). They ranked the protection of retail units very much lower. There was little evidence that the promotion (35%) and development (22%) of the shopping centre itself had a high priority.

Table 7.2 High, medium and low priorities for shopping-centre managers by areas of responsibility

Areas of responsibility	High priority	Medium priority	Low priority
		Per cent	
Security of shoppers	54.0	34.5	11.5
Security of shopping centre	44.8	44.8	10.3
Ensuring cleanliness	36.3	52.0	11.6
Promoting the shopping centre	34.3	34.6	31.1
Development of shopping centre	24.3	24.3	51.5
Relationships with tenants	19.3	62.8	17.9
Security of retail units	13.0	29.8	57.2

The emphasis given by shopping-centre managers to protecting the shopping public and the centre itself was reinforced by more detailed information on the types and level of shopping-centre security measures (Table 7.3). Over one in three shopping-centre managers employed a full-time security manager (38%) and over four in five centres had a security control room (84%) which was mostly manned 24 hours a day (81%).

Table 7.3 Security presence in shopping centres

Security presence	Number	Per cent
Full-time security manager		
Yes	56	38.1
No	91	61.9
Total	147	100.0
Security control room		
Yes	124	84.4
No	23	15.6
Total	147	100.0
Security control room manned		
12 hours a day	23	18.7
24 hours a day	100	81.3
Total	123	100.0

Security versus commercial development

One of the more striking and important findings of the survey was the difference in the emphasis placed by town-centre and shopping-centre managers on the safety and security of shoppers. Town-centre managers saw their role primarily in terms of the development of the town in commercial terms and in promoting this end. The security of shoppers was given much less importance. In contrast, the shopping-centre managers gave priority to the security of their customers and of the shopping centre; and there was also an emphasis on shopping-centre cleanliness. The critical differences are summarised in Table 7.4. It is worth emphasising that the basis for these findings was an assessment by the managers themselves of their priorities in meeting their day-to-day responsibilities.

Table 7.4 Percentage of town-centre and shopping-centre managers giving 'security' and 'commercial development' a high priority

Responsibilities	Town-centre managers	Shopping-centre managers
	Per cent	
Security of shoppers	22.0	54.0
Development of town centre/ shopping centre	68.0	24.3

The summary data show the clear inverse relationship across the two sectors between the priority accorded to the security of shoppers and the emphasis placed on developing the retail environment. The irony here is that the problems of crime and nuisance were far greater in town centres than in shopping centres (Chapters 3 and 4) whilst security was given a much higher priority in shopping centres than in town centres. The areas with the worst problems of crime and nuisance were the areas which placed the least emphasis on the security of shoppers. The lower levels of crime and nuisance in shopping centres may be due to the fact that they are less susceptible to crime or more easy to police than town centres; but it could also reflect the very high priority given by shopping-centre managers to the safety and security of shoppers. Conversely, the higher levels of crime and nuisance in town centres may be attributable to the fact that they are more susceptible to crime or less easy to police than shopping centres, but it could also be a function of the relative lack of emphasis given by town-centre managers to the safety and security of shoppers. Whatever the explanation, town-centre managers would be wise to consider giving security a greater emphasis in their work.

Raising the profile of town centre management

The Association of Town Centre Management is well placed to play a lead role in the reassessment of the security priorities of town-centre managers, which could then be included in the job specifications of its members. What may be lacking is the political will to raise the security profile because there can be no argument about the need. Quite apart from the findings in this study, the Association's own research points to a chasm between the demand for security and its provision (Donaldsons and Healey & Baker, 1994). The ATCM report offers illuminating data on the unmet need for security in town centres and the lack of emphasis given to security by town-centre managers. There were three key findings.

First, the shoppers themselves were aware of a security deficit. As many as four in five respondents (79%) rated safety and security as a 'very important' consideration in making town centres more attractive places for visitors. At the same time there was a perceived shortfall in security cover. More than one-half of the visitors were not satisfied with safety measures (55%) and one-third (34%) pointed to a deterioration in standards relating to crime and violence in recent years.

Secondly, there was evidence that those who had a professional interest in the well-being of town centres also gave security a high priority. Informal discussion groups were held in the eight case-study towns, each of up to three hours and involving between seven and 23 persons concerned with and involved in town-centre issues. The majority of participants were local authority officers, police officers and retailers – and every meeting included a representative from a major retailer such as Marks & Spencer or Boots. These groups expressed concern about safety and security in the town centres, together with an interest in specific security action such as the use of closed circuit television.

Thirdly, telephone interviews were conducted with 145 regional or area managers from multiple retailers and businesses in order to explore their awareness of town centre management (TCM). Nearly two-thirds of the sample knew about the concept, although only one in ten respondents had had any experience of an initiative in their area. They were then asked to define TCM's broad aims. All of the respondents saw TCM as representing the interests of the private and public sectors in co-ordinating activities to improve town centres. None suggested that it was in any way concerned with maintaining or promoting the safety or security of the shopping public.

The Association will be pleased that it has a relatively high profile in the wider retail and commercial communities, but it may be less pleased that these interested parties do not see security as falling within the TCM sphere of influence. This finding mirrors the town-centre managers' assessment of their priorities in the current study. Whatever else the

Association may offer, security for shoppers is not at the top of its agenda. And all of this stands in marked contrast to what the town-centre users and what the providers of town-centre services highlight as an important requirement – a safe and secure shopping environment.

It is incongruous that the ATCM is so out of touch with the expressed wishes of both town-centre shoppers and town-centre retailers in relation to town-centre security. There is an overdue requirement for an urgent reappraisal of the priority given to safe shopping by the Association. The Nottingham crime audit offers some useful pointers. Any effective response to the problems of crime and nuisance will need to be predicated on the establishment of local control and influence over initiatives. The question of the 'ownership' of problems and solutions is critical. Highlighting local concerns, particularly those of the shopping public, is one thing; but someone somewhere has then to accept that these are their concerns and be prepared to act on them (KPMG Peat Marwick, 1991). Jointly developed initiatives rarely work at all, let alone thrive, unless somebody is prepared to take the lead role and then orchestrate a collaborative effort. The ATCM is one of the best placed organisations to shoulder this responsibility. Action in this can be seen as good in itself, but there are also prudential considerations. Improvements in safety and security are a necessary condition for developing and promoting town centres. In addition, if the Association fails to make an explicit commitment to security it could face some unwelcome consequences. It will run the risk of forfeiting the confidence of its members; and it may inadvertently contribute to the migration of town-centre shoppers to more congenial and risk-free shopping environments.

The Association of Town Centre Management and its work received a strong vote of confidence from the House of Commons Environment Committee, although there were two important reservations. The first was that town-centre managers might not be being remunerated at a level commensurate with their responsibilities. The second was that town-centre managers were generally not regarded as having sufficient status to liaise successfully with the chief executives of local authorities and major retailers (House of Commons, 1994). The committee recommended that managers be given the status and authority which would enable them to exert more influence in developing town-centre management strategies – and that the Department of the Environment should advocate this in its guidance to local authorities. The environment secretary has accepted this recommendation (Brown, 1995). Were this change to occur, town-centre managers would be better placed to articulate the need for improved security – as well as to play a major role in devising, implementing and evaluating strategies.

Although the initial impetus for the role of town-centre managers came from the model offered by shopping-centre managers (British Council of Shopping Centres, 1987), the differences outweigh the similarities. The former is less well placed than the latter to co-ordinate a security strategy – mainly because of the difficulty of securing the co-operation of all the parties with interests in the town centre, including the retail sector. The role of the shopping-centre manager reflects the estate practices used by the owners who have legal title with the right to recover management fees, maintenance costs and promotional expenditure. The shopping centre is a largely self-contained unit where the responsibilities of the owner are as clear as the obligations of the tenant. This gives the manager a focused role. The position of the town-centre manager is very different: he or she has to deal with multiple ownership and tenancies, as well as the juxtaposition of private property and public places. This leads to a complex web of loyalties and affiliations, compounded by a three-way obligation to serve the needs of the retailers and businesses, the local authority and the wider community of town-centre users. For example, it is not uncommon to see a wide range of interests represented in TCM – the Chamber of Trade, the Chamber of Commerce, the Town Centre Forum, City Challenge, the Police Community Forum, the Market Traders Association, the Retailers Association, as well as major, multiple stores and the local authority. This may look like a 'basket' of valuable resources, but it can also be seen as a 'porridge' of competing and conflicting interests.

During the course of the research informal discussions with town-centre and shopping-centre managers revealed interesting and instructive differences in the vocabularies used to describe their roles and functions. Town-centre managers tended to talk in rather general terms of their role, mostly as being the development, co-ordination and promotion of the town centre. This is reflected in the ATCM's published literature and the Donaldsons and Healey & Baker (1994) research report. For example, two managers saw their priorities as:

> It's a complicated role – part diplomat and part businessman, but I suppose what I really do is orchestrate a partnership of effort.

> Building up the town and its image ... and it's very much about working at the interface of the public and private sectors.

The language of the shopping-centre managers was rather different. They tended to speak in more specific and concrete terms – mostly seeing their role as being to keep the centre clean, to ban known troublemakers and to make sure that security guards were on duty. One shopping-centre manager was very blunt:

> Security is a major part of my job ... and we take it seriously. We want to welcome everyone. The shoppers can stay ... because that's what gives me my salary. The layabouts and the weirdos – they get moved on.

Town-centre managers used aspirational language whilst shopping-centre managers spoke more in terms of practical tasks. These vocabularies reflect different realities as well as different priorities. The clear physical boundaries and the equally clear legal framework make it easier for shopping-centre managers to be specific about their role than it is for town-centre managers with their more diffuse responsibilities. More importantly, to the extent that town-centre managers give priority to the rather nebulous goal of 'promoting' the town centre, the ways in which their operational responsibilities are described will also tend to be rather vague and abstract. Where the aim is to promote a general good, it is all too easy to remain unfocused about what precisely needs to be done. Conversely, because a high priority for shopping-centre managers is the elimination of crime and nuisance, the job-specific comments will tend to be both practical and clear. Where the aim is to reduce a specific threat, the nature of the target must already have been clarified.

As far as the town-centre manager is concerned, what is called for are more substantial efforts to articulate clear and practical objectives, including priorities for the safety and security of shoppers. While the Association of Town Centre Management may continue to rehearse only the generalised themes of TCM, this does not absolve the Association from its responsibility to meet the security needs of its membership. The rhetoric of 'promoting and developing' town centres is no substitute for detailed crime protection and crime prevention aims and objectives, including those related to the safety and security of shoppers. The data from retailers and shoppers alike, in this study and the ATCM's own research, clearly show a demonstrable deficit. Belatedly, this has been recognised by the Association's chairman, Alan Tallentire, who has (just about) conceded that there could be a problem:

> Without any doubt there is a level of fear in the urban environment. Whether that is a reality or simply a perception, it has to be addressed.
> (quoted in Grigsby, 1995a: The Times, 27th June)

Funding town centre management

Increased emphasis on the security of shoppers on the part of town-centre managers will also require a commensurate level of funding in order to operationalise any new security imperatives. This is the core problem for town centre management. The House of Commons Environment Committee recognised that TCM is best led by the local authority because of its statutory responsibilities, but noted the difficulties in harnessing freeholder and other institutional funding for it (House of Commons, 1994). At present there is widespread support for TCM in principle but little evidence of a readiness to provide funds for initiatives (Donaldsons and Healey & Baker, 1994). Indeed support and funding are inversely related.

For example, the ATCM private sector user survey of area and regional business managers found a clear majority in favour of a partnership of effort – of town-centre managers acting as brokers between private and public interests in the town centre in order to promote its best interests. There was much less agreement on how this should be financed. One-half or more of the area and regional managers were committed to releasing staff to become involved in a TCM management group (64%) or to take on an advisory role (50%). The private sector appeared to be prepared to fund TCM, but only at a low and occasional level by financing some of the revenue costs by seconding staff. There was much less readiness to finance TCM directly or to fund its initiatives. Only one in ten respondents said that their companies would support regional funding and just 3 per cent thought that central or core funding would be forthcoming. The local authority was seen as the 'natural provider' of project-specific capital resources. The Environment Committee also found that TCM was being supported by the same few generous retailers or property owners; and it warned that the practice of seconding senior officers from leading retailers was only justified if those officers had the ability to think strategically about all the activities and uses of the town centre, not simply retailing (House of Commons, 1994). Town centre management in Maidstone, Kent, has 14 sponsors, with the borough and county paying 40 per cent of core costs, whilst the private sector provides the remaining 60 per cent; and in Romford, Essex, the TCM initiative (up against the formidable Lakeside development) is jointly funded by Boots, Debenhams, Marks & Spencer and Havering Borough Council (Grigsby, 1995b). These arrangements are typical.

In the ATCM survey the private sector appeared reluctant to commit resources unless there was clear control over their use and a specific commitment to limited and measurable goals (Donaldsons and Healey & Baker, 1994). The latter point is particularly important because it stands in contrast to the ATCM's rather general objectives. The business community's image of a town-centre manager was that of a successful 'business manager' who takes the initiative and makes decisions. The 'management' component of TCM was defined in terms of a high-status, high-profile decision-maker who exercises executive authority. This may be somewhat at odds with the notion of a partnership of effort, especially in view of the democratic accountability of the local authority; and it may be even more of a threat to the broader notion of community involvement. Hardly surprisingly, the persons who were prepared to pay the piper also wanted to call the tune.

This tension points towards something of a funding crisis, but there may be grounds for optimism as far as the securing of private investment or joint funding for initiatives with the limited and focused goals of improving town-centre security for shoppers is concerned. On the one hand, the shopping public's anxiety is high and with reason and the effects of crime and nuisance impact on the whole of the town-centre retail environment. This means that the private and public sectors and the community, including its shoppers, have a legitimate stake in dealing with the problems of crime and nuisance. There is a genuine convergence of interests so that 'security' may be fully incorporated into the aims and objectives of the Association of Town Centre Management.

On the other hand, strategies against crime and nuisance can be broken down into limited and measurable objectives. These would include a reduction in the number of incidents in a given period of time, or a move towards less serious types of incident. Police figures or in-house data would provide some useful indicators, and surveys of shoppers now offer a reliable guide to the level of fear of crime and perceptions of risk. There are readily available measures of town-centre crime problems, and straightforward indicators of success or failure which can be used to assess the value of investing in a particular remedy. The town-centre manager is in a position to orchestrate efforts to resolve a common problem and to evaluate the outcomes. This would appear to offer potential investors a focused approach with measurable goals.

Less optimistically, the ATCM research confirmed that there was a big difference between the attitudes of town-centre and shopping-centre managers towards how any TCM money should be spent. The former wanted to maximise across-the-board investment in town-centre-wide initiatives. The latter had a much narrower focus on what was needed within the physical boundaries of the shopping centres (Donaldsons and Healey & Baker, 1994). Many retail companies located in shopping centres expressed concern about making a general funding commitment to town centres. They were already paying their own service charges and the uniform business rate (UBR) and were decidedly reluctant to commit themselves to a third-level investment in the town centre generally, especially where there were no immediate and quantifiable returns. There is also a near-universal complaint that the UBR is not spent in the area in which it is collected, but simply disappears into the national 'pot'. The British Property Federation has suggested that town centre management could be funded in part if a small proportion of the rate was set aside and used only for improvements in the local area from which it was collected (Grigsby, 1995a).

The House of Commons Environment Committee failed to offer a feasible and realistic solution to the funding problem. It recognised that indecision over how to fund town centre management initiatives had hindered the development of TCM in Britain and asserted that it must be resolved as a matter of 'urgency' (House of Commons, 1994). The committee was less forthcoming about how this should be done, although it put forward two interesting recommendations. First, it endorsed the view that a City Challenge-type scheme could be instituted to encourage local authorities working in partnership with the private sector to put forward commercially viable proposals on a competitive basis. The government should consider such a scheme, to be funded from the Single Regeneration Budget (SRB) – possibly to the tune of £20 million a year for 20 such initiatives over a five-year period. Government money would have to be 'more than matched' by private sector investment which would be 'levered in' as part of the rules of the competition. Secondly, the committee recommended that the government should consider extending tax relief on contributions made by private companies to approved town-centre initiatives.

The problem with the SRB-funded scheme is that it would only apply to 20 towns or cities, and then only to those which put forward 'commercially viable' proposals. This begs the question of whether the private sector would be prepared to finance such schemes at the 50 per cent level or more. This is unlikely because the private sector is not able to gauge with any precision what return, if any, there would be on general town-centre investment; and even if there were benefits, to whom they would accrue.

The problem with the tax relief idea is that this would only apply to 'approved' schemes; and there is no indication of how these would be chosen. Finally, the tone of both recommendations is cautious in that government is invited to 'consider' these options, and both fall well short of urging a firm commitment to large-scale public expenditure. The committee may have been genuinely concerned for the 'vitality and viability' of all forms of town-centre shopping, but it was seemingly more reticent in making proposals about how best to fund it. The same ambivalence has since been shown by the environment secretary, who has endorsed the principle of local authorities and private enterprise entering into partnerships to finance new town-centre developments, but failed to offer direct financial support (Brown, 1995). In the present study one town-centre manager summed up the various difficulties:

> The problem is not in not knowing what to do, but in finding the investment to do it ... and in overcoming the difficulties in working out who pays for what.

And another manager pointed to the need for some public sector funding:

> For successful town-centre management, there must be public sector funding to pump prime investment by the private sector.

It is difficult not to reach the conclusion that there is a general and genuine belief in the importance of town-centre management, but that the central question Who pays? has remained unanswered. This is probably because government and its advisers take the view that town centres are predominantly private places, to be funded and managed by the owners and occupiers of the shops and businesses in them. The local authority is seen as an adjunct – something which binds things together by providing an infrastructure and support services. Members of the public and town-centre users figure even less prominently. And government has little or no role to play in funding. All this seems to be near to the view of the Environment Committee, not least given its assertion that the most important element of any town centre – its 'life blood' – are its shops. One can hardly fail to conclude that town-centre shopping is increasingly seen as falling under the umbrella of 'private responsibility'. The opposite view is that town centres are first and foremost 'of and for' the public – the commercial, cultural and community focal points for the local population. The very use of the word 'centre' implies this sense of community. On this view, members of the public and town-centre users must take the highest priority. And it is the retailers and businesses who provide the services for them, while the local authority creates a coherent environment. This points in the direction of town-centre funding from government.

To the extent that the government is inclined to the former view, public sector funding obligations are being passed on to the private sector. This explains why some of the larger retail companies are having to fund town-centre management. They may feel that they have no option because government has abrogated its responsibilities. But they will do so unwillingly because they do not see this as their responsibility; and nor can it be justified in terms of offering a clear dividend to the individual contributors. In many respects the continued support for TCM from major retailers, such as Boots and Marks & Spencer, can be seen increasingly as a genuine 'public service' for town centres from the private sector, as well as in terms of protecting their own commercial interests. The latter is far from unimportant. The major multiple stores are most likely to own their high-street premises rather than to rent outlets. If they are to avoid the baleful consequences of the doughnut syndrome and maintain a profitable presence in the town centres, then they may have little option but to support TCM initiatives. As town-centre property owners they are locked as equally into the potential for a spiral of decline as they may be party to any upward curve in profitability.

To conclude, there are first-order problems relating to the ways in which town-centre managers can give the security of shoppers a higher profile; and then there are second-order problems of how to fund subsequent initiatives. With regard to the former, the lesson from shopping-centre managers appears to be that profits and the stated ATCM goal of 'commercial well-being' are intimately linked to the safety of shoppers. Safety and security are necessary conditions for shoppers to shop in comfort and so for profitable trading. Protecting shoppers is one part of protecting profit. The Association of Town Centre Management would be well advised to conceive of security as an integral part of commercial development. With regard to the latter, the future funding of town-centre management is far from clear. The pessimist will conclude that ad hoc funding, primarily by the occasional secondment of staff from multiple retailers, is a less than satisfactory solution to the financial problem. The optimist may conclude that because there is some evidence of some coherence in the funding of TCM, which has been achieved against the odds, there are modest grounds for believing that a decent enough beginning has been made – something which invites potential partners to re-double their efforts.

8   The Use of Closed Circuit Television

Although preliminary data relating to the use and effectiveness of CCTV were presented in Chapter 5, the findings were not discussed in detail because the major theme which emerged was the contrast between public policing in town centres and private security in shopping centres – with CCTV a major factor in both town-centre and shopping-centre security, but rather at the margin of the 'public policing' and 'private security' debate. The growing number of CCTV installations, however, require that this security option be reviewed thoroughly in its own right. Few would doubt that CCTV has caught the imagination of both the government and those responsible for security in public and semi-public places, but these new-found enthusiasms do not reflect a considered assessment of its contribution to security in the shopping environment in general, or its impact in town centres and shopping centres.

The audit of existing security measures included an evaluation of CCTV from four viewpoints. First, managers were asked whether CCTV was being used in their town centre or shopping centre and, if so, to what extent. This was a broad indicator of the extent of its use. Secondly, people shopping in places where CCTV was being used were asked whether they were aware of it. This was important because its effectiveness as a deterrent is predicated on its visibility to would-be offenders. Thirdly, town-centre and shopping-centre managers were asked to rate the effectiveness of closed circuit television. This question was put to all managers, whether or not CCTV was in use, in order to assess perceived effectiveness on the basis of as large a sample as possible. Finally, members of the public were asked about the acceptability of closed circuit television. This question was put to all shoppers, whether or not CCTV was in use, in order to assess acceptability on the basis of as large a sample as possible.

Use and awareness of CCTV

Closed circuit television was found to be being used in a high proportion of both shopping environments (Table 8.1); where it was in use, managers reported that it was deployed extensively (Table 8.2); and the public generally showed a high level of awareness of it (Table 8.3). Over three-quarters of town-centre managers (77%) and nearly nine in ten shopping-centre managers (89%) said that CCTV was currently in use in their areas of responsibility. Some data were collected on the number of cameras and the cost of installations but it was not possible to use these figures in a way which took account of the size and character of the town centres and shopping centres, but managers did give their impression on the extent of CCTV coverage. Where it was being used, two-thirds of town-centre managers (65%) and slightly more shopping-centre managers (70%) thought that it was used extensively. Only one in ten town-centre managers (10%) and even fewer shopping-centre managers (3%) thought that CCTV coverage was low.

Table 8.1 Use of CCTV in town centres and shopping centres

Usage	Town centres	Shopping centres
	Per cent	
In use	76.9	88.7
Not in use	23.1	11.3
Total	100.0	100.0

Table 8.2 Extent of CCTV use in town centres and shopping centres

Coverage	Town centres	Shopping centres
	Per cent	
High	65.0	69.6
Medium	25.0	27.1
Low	10.0	3.4
Total	100.0	100.0

In those areas where CCTV was being used 50 per cent or more members of the shopping public were aware of its existence. One-half of the town-centre shoppers (50%) had noticed CCTV compared with six in ten customers in shopping centres (60%).

Table 8.3 Public awareness of CCTV in town centres and shopping centres

Awareness	Town centres	Shopping centres
	Per cent	
Aware	49.6	60.2
Not aware	50.4	39.8
Total	100.0	100.0

Effectiveness and acceptability of CCTV

Both town-centre and shopping-centre managers were of the opinion that CCTV contributed to the control of crime and nuisance problems in their shopping environments (Table 8.4). The figures for the two sets of managers were nearly identical. Over four in five managers thought that CCTV was effective – 82 per cent of town-centre managers and 85 per cent of shopping-centre managers. Very few managers took the view that CCTV made only a poor contribution to shopping-related security – 6 per cent in town centres and 2 per cent in shopping centres.

Table 8.4 The perceived effectiveness of CCTV in town centres and shopping centres

Effectiveness	Town-centre managers	Shopping-centre managers
	Per cent	
Excellent/Good	82.3	84.6
Average	11.8	13.5
Poor	5.9	1.8
Total	100.0	100.0

The shoppers in both town centres and shopping centres were highly accommodating to the use of CCTV in their shopping environments – on a scale from 'very acceptable' to 'very unacceptable' (Table 8.5). Again there were near-identical figures in the two shopping areas. In town centres an overwhelming majority of 91 per cent of the shopping public found CCTV acceptable – 53 per cent very acceptable and 37 per cent acceptable. A minority of 9 per cent or one in eleven of the town-centre shoppers thought that CCTV was unacceptable – 6 per cent unacceptable and 3 per cent very unacceptable. In shopping centres an overwhelming majority of 96 per cent of the shopping public found CCTV acceptable – 61 per cent very acceptable and 35 per cent acceptable. Only 4 per cent or one in twenty five of the shopping-centre visitors thought that CCTV was unacceptable (2%) or very unacceptable (2%).

Table 8.5 The acceptability of CCTV in town centres and shopping centres

Acceptability	Town centres	Shopping centres
	Per cent	
Very acceptable	53.2	60.7
Acceptable	37.4	35.3
Unacceptable	6.4	2.2
Very unacceptable	3.0	1.8
Total	100.0	100.0

Endorsement of CCTV

When the data are aggregated there would appear to be a ringing endorsement of the use of closed circuit television. The views of both town-centre and shopping-centre managers were much the same and these coincided with the opinions of the shoppers. There was little difference across the two retail environments. All parties in both settings tended to offer similar views. This striking congruence is summarised in Table 8.6.

Closed circuit television was being used in more than three-quarters of the shopping environments – 77 per cent of town centres and 89 per cent of shopping centres. Where it was in operation two-thirds of the town-centre managers (65%) and two-thirds of the shopping-centre managers (70%) judged that it was being used extensively. Between 50 and 60 per cent of the public were aware of its presence. Rather more than eight in ten managers deemed CCTV to be effective – 82 per cent in town centres and 85 per cent in shopping centres. Finally, more than nine in ten members of the shopping public took the view that surveillance cameras in the shopping environment were acceptable – 91 per cent in town centres and 96 per cent in shopping centres.

Table 8.6 Use, awareness, effectiveness and acceptability of CCTV in town centres and shopping centres

Closed circuit television	Town centres	Shopping centres
	Per cent	
CCTV in use	76.9	88.7
High-level of coverage	65.0	69.6
Awareness of CCTV	49.6	60.2
High-level of perceived effectiveness	82.3	84.6
High-level of perceived acceptability	90.6	96.0

These findings mirror those of the Birmingham study where nearly all shoppers (98%) said that CCTV helped to reduce crime and was to be welcomed (Poole, 1991). They also roughly mirror those of the recent Home Office study which found public awareness levels of 35 per cent on the high streets and 62 per cent in shopping centres. Closed circuit television was also thought to be acceptable by 89 per cent of the 'street' public and 85 per cent of the shopping-centre public. Finally, over one-half of all shoppers (53%) thought that CCTV contributed to making people feel more safe, 62 per cent saw it as contributing to crime prevention and 74 per cent thought it to be an aid to the detection of crime (Honess and Charman, 1992).

Taken at face value the various findings are strongly supportive of the use of CCTV in the retail environment. It is already being used widely and is thought to be effective by town-centre and shopping-centre managers and is deemed to be acceptable by members of the shopping public. Nobody with a professional interest in ensuring safe shopping and the protection of customers can afford to ignore the potential of closed circuit television. Those concerned include local authorities and the police, as well as the retailers (who frequently contribute to the costs of installing and running CCTV systems) and both town-centre and shopping-centre managers.

There are, however, a number of issues which are obscured by the apparent general endorsement of its value. Closed circuit television is certainly becoming an ever more prominent feature of the retail environment; but it would be naive to assume that its deployment is unproblematic.

The rise and rise of CCTV

A recent Home Office study on public attitudes towards CCTV took as its starting point the fact that systems are now to be found in a 'bewildering variety' of settings, apart from town centres and shopping centres, including airports and ports and railway stations, schools and hospitals, banks and building societies, industrial sites and car parks, as well as being used in the regulation of traffic. And that although the number of installations was unknown, 'cameras are now a common sight on public highways and in shopping malls and arcades' (Honess and Charman, 1992). The Home Secretary has added that 'television surveillance cameras are becoming a regular feature in an increasing number of towns and cities in response to public demand' (quoted in Edwards and Tilley, 1994). If anything this may be something of an understatement – surveillance cameras are now almost omnipresent in public areas. Some commentators have said that CCTV surveillance is 'running like wildfire' through society and 'no one is checking it' (Armstrong and Hobbs, 1994; Midgley, 1995). Although this last comment begs the question about the 'desirability' of widespread surveillance in public places, few would now doubt the near-universal deployment of closed circuit television.

Moreover, government is actively promoting this spread (Home Office Standing Conference on Crime Prevention, 1986; Property Services Agency, 1988; Department of Education, 1991; Tilley, 1993a). A recent Department of the Environment (1994) circular, *Planning Out Crime*, promises that government will amend the Town and Country Planning General Development Order 1988 so that even where cameras are seen as development it will not usually be necessary to submit a planning application, except in the case of listed or historic buildings where the fitting of cameras will still require listed building consent. The circular also points to the need for consultation between the police, community groups, business and the local authority prior to the installation of CCTV systems.

In late 1994 the Home Office launched a CCTV 'instruction manual' which was sent to all councils, large businesses and police forces (Edwards and Tilley, 1994; and see Davies, 1994). This offers advice on the need for systems, where CCTV may be useful, how it should be installed, together with technical details of system requirements, evaluation and elements of 'good practice'. And the Criminal Justice and Public Order Act 1994 (section 163) provides a statutory basis for local authorities to provide apparatus for recording visual events, together with appropriate telecommunications systems (without the need for a licence) if this is deemed to be in the interests of crime prevention. The Act also enables the Secretary of State to make discretionary payments or grants for the purpose of crime prevention (section 169) which could be used to promote the local authority use of closed circuit television.

It is estimated that over £300 million a year is spent on video surveillance equipment (Utley, 1993), that around 300,000 security cameras are sold annually and that more than a million may be in use (Watt, 1993; Beck and Willis, 1994b; Bulos, 1994). The British Security Industry Association puts the turnover on the installation and maintenance of CCTV systems at £168 million a year, with a further £174 million being spent on the manufacture of electronic security equipment; and the Association reports that there is 'very rapid growth' in the use of CCTV systems – with the market doubling since 1989 (British Security Industry Association, 1994b; Davies, 1994). There is a newly formed CCTV Manufacturers and Distributors Association (CCTV MDA) which held its inaugural meeting in May 1994. Its mission is to develop and regulate the infrastructure of the industry in the UK by promoting the advantages of CCTV through the implementation of quality standards in manufacture, installation and use. There is also a burgeoning professional literature – including the specialist journal *CCTV Today* and other publications such as *Security Industry* and *Security Management Today*.

The most complete estimate of the size of the CCTV market in the UK comes from Marketing Strategies for Industry, and may be summarised as follows:

Total CCTV market 1994	£338 million
Total CCTV market 1993	£297 million
Retail sector	£107 million
Industrial sector	£92 million
Commercial sector	£50 million
Public sector	£48 million
Annual growth 1993-94	14 per cent

It was estimated that there was growth of 12 per cent in 1993 to £297 million, together with a forecast of further growth of 14 per cent in 1994 to

£338 million and a suggestion that the market would rise to a peak in 1996 (Marketing Strategies for Industry, 1994). In 1993 the retail sector accounted for the largest proportion of the CCTV market (£107 million or 36 per cent), followed by the industrial sector (£92 million or 31 per cent), the commercial sector (£50 million or 17 per cent) and the public sector (£48 million or 16 per cent). Rentals of equipment rose to 51 per cent of the market and sales accounted for the rest. These are the current best estimates of the size of the market.

There is also some indication that current CCTV systems are only operating to a fraction of their potential. Most CCTV systems use only 'contributive' fibre transmission technology – many signals converging at one centre or control room. The first modest step in extending this is a London project to link 2,000 cameras in 120 locations to three security control centres and then on to a central monitoring point. Following an incident, this will permit the video 'back-tracking' of suspected persons using a London-wide database of images. However, security surveillance has yet to use 'distributive' technologies which make possible the relaying of information to interested parties elsewhere in the area or further afield – rather like cable television. The development of a passive optical network (PON), using sub carrier multiplexing (SCM) for contribution and time division multiplexing (TDM) for distribution, opens up the possibility of the unlimited transfer and re-routing of digitised video recordings (Smith, 1994). Authorised users will be able to access real-time video in any part of the network. The possibilities are endless. A security incident in a shop could be transmitted in the normal way to the local police and then on to other forces or to other retailers, although there could be implications as regards data protection (see Chapter 9).

The development and growth of security surveillance will continue to be driven by advances in technology, including thermal-imaging with low-light cameras (Stansell, 1994), heat measuring devices combined with video images which can 'see' temperature distributions (Glaskin, 1995) and 'active vision' cameras designed to follow and track certain pre-programmed things – for example, a person-like shape moving at a certain speed (Nuttall, 1993). And the miniaturisation of cameras will continue, with existing models designed for in-car security already down to the size of a 50 pence piece. And small units have been fitted to police dogs (Jabez, 1995; Tendler, 1995d). Both night-vision and active-vision cameras will eventually find a place in the high street and the shopping mall. There are also developments in video imaging processing where computer software is used to recognise properties of the video image itself, such as abnormal densities or disruptions in the flow of people, which can then be drawn automatically to the attention of the person exercising surveillance (Patel, 1994).

The 1990s enthusiasm for CCTV is buttressed by a number of recurring themes. It offers a technological equivalent to extensive police surveillance. As one senior police spokesman said in relation to the major scheme in Liverpool, the bobby on the beat is being replaced by an omnipresent, near-infallible robot eye in the sky – a 'camera policeman':

> This system is like 20 officers on duty 24 hours a day who make a note of everything, never take a holiday and are very rarely off sick.
>
> (quoted in Murray, 1994b: *The Times*, 6th July)

And an academic suggests that CCTV provides the urban equivalent of 'naturally defensible space' in villages and rural areas where villagers provide mutual surveillance of other people's property – and where strangers or incongruous activities stand out a mile (Reiner quoted in Kelly, 1993). The cameras, in effect, do the job of 'good neighbours' – a case of High-Tech Watch rather than Neighbourhood Watch. Moreover, such schemes are seen by the innocent to be benign while having terrifying law enforcement potential from the point of view of would-be or actual offenders. As the junior Home Office minister said at the launch of the Liverpool scheme:

> This is a friendly eye in the sky. There is nothing sinister about it and the innocent have nothing to fear. It will put criminals on the run and the evidence will be clear to see.
>
> (quoted in Murray, 1994b: *The Times*, 6th July)

Closed circuit television would appear to offer high-tech, day-and-night surveillance premised on a romantic appeal to an Arcadian vision of natural social control; and a wholly non-threatening use of technology for the innocent which offers an unparalleled capacity to deter or to detect the offender. It all adds up to a beguiling package and it is small wonder that CCTV is an increasingly common feature of everyday life.

Finally, such tragic events as the James Bulger abduction and murder lend an additional and almost irresistible impetus to the introduction of closed circuit television. In July 1994, less than a year after the Bulger case – and almost certainly in part as a response to it – a large-scale CCTV system 'went live', covering the whole of Liverpool city centre (Causer, 1994). The 'fuzzy images' on videotape which required computer enhancement to be of any value to the Bulger police inquiry, far from leading to criticism of CCTV, had the opposite effect. The case generated widespread public support for CCTV and strong demands for state-of-the-art technology to be introduced in the city centre as soon as possible. The James Bulger case is likely to be cited for many years in support of the development of CCTV in public places. The murder of the Woolworths assistant store manager, John Penfold, in November 1994 at the Broad Street store in Teddington is another example of crime leading to an extension of CCTV coverage; it prompted an immediate review of the use of surveillance cameras in the company's 788 outlets. The so-called 'Woolworths killer' had committed four previous attacks on different branches in west and south-west London in a little over two months. None of the Woolworths stores had security cameras, which led the police officer leading the inquiry to comment that perhaps the stores had been singled out as an 'easy hit' (Berrington and Ford, 1994).

The increasing use of CCTV on a national scale, and government strategies to promote its deployment even more widely and easily, appear to be validated by the across-the-board vote of confidence by managers and the public recorded in the current study. It is crucial to explore whether the belief in the effectiveness of CCTV which underlies this vote of confidence is warranted by the evidence. The argument to be developed below suggests that, all too frequently, the most readily available data point only to basic and limited information about the size and scale of the operation, sometimes including capital expenditure, but usually with little or no information about its effectiveness or the recurrent costs involved in running the system. This makes proper evaluation impossible. There is something of a disjunction between the way in which new systems are heralded as promising new and previously unattainable levels of crime control (the never blinking, never sleeping robot eye in the sky) and the paucity of information about operational effectiveness. It is almost as though the promise of all-embracing crime control is more important than what systems actually achieve. It is necessary to explore whether the 'rise and rise' of CCTV is premised more on well-meaning beliefs about its presumed effectiveness – something to be termed 'security wish fulfilment' – or whether there are more substantial grounds for its endorsement. The obvious starting point is to note some examples of recent installations.

CCTV in town centres and shopping centres

According to the Home Office, about 95 per cent of councils in Britain are considering setting up CCTV systems. About 80 towns have already installed surveillance systems to monitor public areas, including Blackpool, Swansea, Glasgow, Edinburgh, Hull, Torquay, Wolverhampton, Chester, Bath and Brighton; and more go on-line every week (Davies, 1994; Edwards and Tilley, 1994). And the British Retail Consortium has suggested that retailers have contributed over £1 million to help establish CCTV systems in the high street (Speed et al, 1995). A recent national survey of local authority use of CCTV in public places found that systems were in use in one-third of the London areas, 46 per cent of metropolitan areas and 48 per cent of non-metropolitan areas (Bulos, 1994). Nearly four in ten London authorities were planning installations, as were one-half of the metropolitan and 58 per cent of the non-metropolitan authorities. Surveillance systems were mostly installed to cover town centres, known trouble spots and car parks.

The Liverpool city centre scheme is one of the largest installations in Britain, covering two square miles. Liverpool City Council invested £360,000 – £196,920 on the supply and installation of the cameras, including three year maintenance, and £161,000 on the supply and installation of fibre optics (Davies, 1994; Ford, 1994; Liverpool City Centre Partnership, 1994). The 20-camera system is designed to provide colour pictures of 'court of law' evidential quality – incorporating electronic image enhancement, speed pan and tilt units with 15:1 zoom lenses, and micro lenses for improving low-light capability. The system, with a console room closed to all but security staff, is linked by fibre optic cable to Church Street police station and to the St Anne's Street police headquarters. The system offers 24-hour cover with one operator at non-peak times and two at peak times (Edwards and Tilley, 1994). The authorities are planning to expand the system to cover more of the city, using 65 cameras. It is expected to set a precedent for other towns and cities, especially in the use of high-definition colour cameras. The clarity of the images is startling – one can read a cigarette packet in colour at 100 metres, even in darkness. In nearby Kirby a 16-camera street surveillance system has recently been inaugurated. The system is monitored by shopping-centre management and is linked to the local police station (*CCTV Today*, July 1994).

Northampton Borough Council installed a 105-camera system covering three areas in the town centre in early 1993 – at a total cost of £300,000, mostly provided by the local authority. Sixty-two cameras monitor the four main multi-storey car parks 24 hours a day covering all access and exit points and the lifts. An additional eight cameras cover the British Rail station car park. And a further 17 cameras monitor the main shopping street and public thoroughfares. A fibre optic network connects all cameras to a central control room which is able to transmit recorded information directly to the divisional police control room. The system has 24-hour cover with two operators plus one relief operator per shift (Drury, 1993; *CCTV Today*, July 1994; Edwards and Tilley, 1994).

Another well-known example is the 1993 CCTV system in central Newcastle upon Tyne. There are 16 monochrome cameras with microwave transmission, linked to a police control room and monitored by civilians employed by the police. Various estimates put the cost at up to £400,000, jointly borne by city-centre retailers and the Department of the Environment (Drury, 1993; Watt, 1993). The cameras are capable of identifying a vehicle registration plate at 200 yards in the dark (Shopfront Security Group, 1994). The system offers 24-hour cover with one operator at all times (Edwards and Tilley, 1994).

The CityWatch system in Glasgow has 32-colour, 360-degree cameras continuously monitoring 30 streets from the city centre to the banks of the Clyde. The city invested £500,000 in the project. The pictures are monitored by civilians and scenes of crime and disorder are relayed instantly to senior police officers. A local poll, conducted immediately prior to the system going live in November 1994, found that 66 per cent of those interviewed believed that video surveillance would make the city centre a safer place, and about 40 per cent said that they would visit the centre more frequently if cameras were installed. An overwhelming 95 per cent approved of the introduction of cameras, whilst only a minority of 7 per cent thought that it infringed their civil liberties (Arlidge, 1994; Hennessey, 1994).

Bournemouth Borough Council spent £250,000 in 1992 on a 35-camera installation in shopping precincts and car parks. This was the third phase of a project, dating back to 1986, which started with 47 cameras along the seafront, to which were added eight more in the lower pleasure gardens. These cameras have infra-red capacity, allowing accurate night-time surveillance (Drury, 1993; Davies, 1994). And there are many more, less well-known examples. A major car park and high street system is planned for Croydon, at a cost of £300,000, which will include 30 cameras in five car parks, all linked and monitored centrally. Crewe has completed the first £80,000 phase of a system directed mainly against car thieves. Warrington, perhaps in part as a response to the terrorist bombings of 1993, completed a 20-camera town-centre system linked by BT cabling to a control room in a local police station in just eight weeks. Cheltenham Borough Council has installed an eight-camera system monitored by the local police. And Llanelli in South Wales has a modest five-camera system, even though the local council concedes that the town has a 'very low' crime rate (*CCTV Today*, July 1994).

The pace of CCTV development seems likely to be maintained. In October 1994 government plans were announced for small towns and housing estates to be targeted under a £5 million plan to spread the use of closed circuit television (Ford, 1994d). Local authorities and individual estates were invited to bid for grants for the installation of CCTV systems of up to £100,000 (provided the grant was matched by an equal amount from local authorities and the private sector). By the closing date in January 1995 some 500 applications had been made – prompting one commentator to suggest that CCTV was on the way to becoming as much a part of the British landscape as 'phone booths and postboxes' (Campbell, 1995). In the spring of 1995 the government allocated grants of £5 million for 100 CCTV systems to protect town centres, car parks, railway stations and community centres around the country (*The Times*, 28th March, 1995).

The City of London offers the most extensive and sophisticated example of the urban deployment of security surveillance systems, mainly against terrorist attacks. The detection of the 1993 'Harrods bombers' was in part due to videotape evidence from the 17 cameras located outside the Knightsbridge store. And the so-called 'ring of steel', erected in July 1993 in the aftermath of the IRA bomb attacks on the Baltic Exchange in 1992 and Bishopsgate a year later, is heavily dependent on video surveillance (Ashworth, 1994; Bulos, 1994). Remote-controlled cameras were installed in about 30 one-way streets and a bank of 36 screens can be monitored around the clock at Wood Street police station. Even in the wake of the so-called peace process, the City's head of security policy, Michael Cassidy, has confirmed that the corporation has approved an additional £1 million for a network of security cameras to monitor streets leading out of the City (Leppard, 1994c). And the existing cameras at police checkpoints have been upgraded to pan, tilt and zoom.

It is now possible to follow a car which enters the city through one of the eight access points, recording the number plates and the faces of drivers and passengers. The 'entry point' system is complemented by a 30-camera area traffic control network. And this is supported by 'CameraWatch' – a system for shared 24-hour monitoring of public places by pooling the resources of private systems which overlook public spaces (Edwards and Tilley, 1994). The cameras are seen not only as a deterrent and an aid to detection, but also as having 'a big role ... in intelligence gathering'

(Matthews, 1994). On the first two counts there is some evidence of success with reported crime falling by 10 per cent in 1992, following the introduction of high-profile policing and controlled access, and a further fall of 17 per cent in 1993 (Tendler, 1994c). The use of CCTV for intelligence purposes, however, adds a new dimension to the capabilities of electronic surveillance – one which would involve the purposeful recording of all the movements of a suspected person or the more indiscriminate recording of many people's movements in the hope that criminal or conspiracy patterns would emerge.

Much less data are available about the deployment and use of CCTV in shopping centres, although it is highly likely that the number of systems in them is far greater than in town centres. In a *Guidance Note*, the British Council of Shopping Centres sees a clear need for electronic surveillance to monitor the exterior and interior of a centre and the movement of people within it. The guidance offers advice on equipment, location, maintenance and operation, insurance and liability, and on responding to incidents. It is argued that CCTV:

> ... can make a significant contribution to the prevention and detection of all types of crime, including terrorism. The visible use of cameras can deter would-be criminals and vandals and offer reassurance to staff and public. The preservation of good quality recordings of activities can play an important role in the identification of criminals and miscreants.
>
> (British Council of Shopping Centres, 1993c: 1)

There are a number of recent installations which meet what might be termed the new minimum standard for shopping-centre installations. The Queens Arcade shopping centre in Cardiff, possibly the only centre to be built in 1994, has what might be regarded as a state-of-the-art CCTV system – a Baxall 7000 control system and a total of 22 cameras, with high and variable speed on all pan, tilt and zoom models. The Burlington Arcade in Mayfair – possibly Britain's oldest shopping mall, dating from 1819 – has a network of eight pan, tilt and zoom cameras covering the arcade's entrances and shops, with two further cameras positioned on the roof. The control room is equipped with monitors, multiplexer and time-lapse VCRs which record frames from all ten cameras (*CCTV Today*, July 1994). And Group 4 Systems installed a 34-camera, colour system in the Brent Cross shopping centre in north London in 1994 with a special tracking facility so that individuals or groups can be monitored as they move around inside the centre. The system augmented the existing equipment covering the exterior areas of the centre (Hobson, 1994).

These examples illustrate the way in which CCTV systems are increasingly seen as a normal part of the retail environment – in both town centres (the high street and associated parking facilities) and shopping centres. They are a near-universal sight in shopping centres and increasingly common in town centres (Honess and Charman, 1992; Edwards and Tilley, 1994). With government approval CCTV is likely to expand still further to an annual market of £338 million. But as one town-centre manager put it, the 'rise and rise' of CCTV is not accompanied by evidence of its effectiveness:

> I think my position reflects the national scene. This city has got the very best equipment ... but, in all honesty, I can't say anything very much about how well it works. Everyone will tell you that it is making a big difference – but they would wouldn't they? Perhaps you'll come back and tell me when you've finished your study.

The effectiveness of CCTV

Assessing the effectiveness of CCTV systems is highly problematic. By what measure is it possible to justify the introduction of a new CCTV system or the upgrading of an existing system? The belief that 'more' or 'better' equipment will necessarily mean less crime and nuisance comes up against a prudent concern to make sure that any investment in equipment offers value for money. Town-centre and shopping-centre managers are caught in the middle of this debate – impelled to invest heavily in equipment on the presumption that CCTV 'works' but under pressure to be cautious because of high start-up and recurrent costs. These issues are summarised in the latest British Retail Consortium's retail crime survey:

> ... retailers have been unsure as to whether [the] benefits are substantial enough to warrant financial investment ... There are similar uncertainties about whether there are any benefits to retailers in terms of crime prevention: schemes rarely target or report successes in tackling the many crimes that impose a direct financial burden on retailers.
>
> (Speed et al, 1995: 37)

What is lacking is a solid body of evidence on which to base informed judgements about the effectiveness of CCTV, as a first step to making sensible decisions about investing in it. There is little information available about the 'return' on this type of investment. The recent Home Office guide is unequivocal about the need for high-quality data which the authors emphasise is currently in 'short supply' (Edwards and Tilley, 1994).

Extravagant claims

Despite these caveats from authoritative sources, some quite extravagant claims have been made for the success of CCTV, although in rather general terms. In evidence to the House of Commons Home Affairs Committee, for example, the British Security Industry Association claimed that CCTV was widely used to monitor public areas and that its:

> ... effectiveness in the prevention and detection of crime has been proved. These include places such as town centres, shopping malls and car parks.
>
> (British Security Industry Association, 1994b: 11)

A designer and supplier of systems was just as confident:

> CCTV has proved itself to be a flexible, efficient and effective means of deterring, detecting and monitoring criminal activity in a wide variety of applications.
>
> (Carr, 1992: 20)

The leading insurer, General Accident (1994; and see Hearnden, 1994), estimated that in 1993 a retail business stood a 45 per cent chance of being burgled, but where CCTV schemes were operating this figure could drop as low as 5 per cent. Northampton Borough Council found that 200 cars a year were being stolen from the four town-centre car parks prior to the installation of CCTV, dropping by 80 per cent since installation in 1987, and then by a further 24 per cent in 1993 (*CCTV Today*, July, 1994). Following the introduction of an eight-camera CCTV system in Bathgate town centre, West Lothian, actual and attempted break-ins fell by 69 per cent and vandalism to shops and offices was reduced by 63 per cent – without evidence of any increase in other areas of the town (*CCTV Today*, July 1994).

A street surveillance system installed in the town centre of North Shields, Northumbria, cut crime by 37 per cent overall in its first year, according to the consortium of local traders set up to manage it. There was an increase in detected crime from 47 to 60 per cent, and a reduction in town-centre burglary of 65 per cent (*CCTV Today*, July, 1994). Also in the North East, the Newcastle 16-camera system was credited with a 13 per cent reduction in crime in the first two months of operation. The Hexham scheme of just two cameras is thought to be responsible for a 17 per cent reduction in crime within three months, with a 12 per cent rise being recorded elsewhere in the town. The Wolverhampton system is said to have reduced crime by 15 per cent and retailers' stock losses by 38 per cent since its introduction in 1992 (Drury, 1993; Preston, C., 1995). A 10-camera installation in Airdrie, Strathclyde, is said to have been responsible for a 75 per cent reduction in crime within five months of its installation in November 1992, together with a doubling of detection rates from 36 per cent to 70 per cent (Drury, 1993; Watt, 1993). And a scheme in Birmingham brought a 9 per cent reduction in crime within three months, although there was a 16 per cent rise in crime in areas not covered by the cameras (Drury, 1993).

The first two phases of the Bournemouth scheme were said to have led to 'dramatic' crime reductions, with £180,000 savings through reduced vandalism being claimed in the first year of phase one alone, and the whole system paying for itself in under two years. The Norfolk town of King's Lynn has a 45-camera system which provides continuous monitoring at an annual cost of £215,000 – of which £150,000 or 70 per cent is attributable to 19 cameras in 17 car parks. The system is almost self-financing because 10 pence has been added to the cost of each ticket and those companies with a camera on their property contribute £1,000 a year. The benefits have been a 91 per cent reduction in thefts of vehicles and a 97 per cent drop in thefts from cars (Drury, 1993; Kelly, 1993). Around-the-clock surveillance in Coventry city centre is credited with an 8 per cent drop in crime overall and up to a 40 per cent reduction in auto crime. Additionally, the city-centre manager claims that the cameras have provided a 'greater sense of well-being for people who use the city centre', and the bonus of being able to spot lost children or get help quickly to people who have collapsed (Hobson, 1994). The Newcastle system has been given part of the credit for a 30 per cent reduction in crime (from 9,850 offences in the last nine months of 1993 down to 6,750 offences in the first nine months of 1994), but other initiatives taken at the same time (proactive policing, including a door supervisors' registration scheme and a pubwatch scheme) are believed to have contributed to the success (Edwards and Tilley, 1994).

Notes of caution

There are a number of problems with these claims. All too frequently the 'success' of CCTV is proclaimed in grandiose statements but mostly in terms of a distinctly general nature, and frequently by persons who were party to the decision to install the system. The poor quality of the data and lack of detail make it impossible to assess the schemes properly and with independence of judgement. Even the latest Home Office guide to the use of CCTV in town centres contains but a single paragraph on its effectiveness – and even this falls into the same trap. The sole contribution to a considered assessment of its effectiveness, in what is intended to be an authoritative guide, is an unsupported but sweeping assertion:

> Independent research has shown that CCTV can be effective in car parks – most notably theft of cars. Where CCTV has been installed in town and city centres, dramatic improvements in terms both of crime prevention and crime detection are often reported by system users.
>
> (Edwards and Tilley, 1994: 9)

No further details are given and no further data are presented. The claim, right at the beginning of the guide, is as unequivocal as it is lacking in substance. It does not fit well with the statement that evaluative data on CCTV's effectiveness are in 'short supply'. Other commentators are more cautious. For example, the British Council of Shopping Centres (1993c) suggests that CCTV 'can' make a contribution to crime prevention through deterrence or detection and that it 'can' operate so as to reassure staff and customers. This may be less exciting but the more cautious tone is decidedly more appropriate.

It is also interesting to note that where so-called successes are reported with figures, the effectiveness of systems is almost invariably expressed in percentage terms and only rarely are the raw figures provided. When they are, the findings appear much less dramatic because the level of crime is frequently already low in the pre-installation phase (Hobson, 1994). For example, in Workington in Cumbria the introduction of a modest three-camera system led to thefts from cars dropping from 48 a year to just six a year. This was seen as a sufficient justification for investing £80,000 in a round-the-clock system. Following the introduction of a £40,000 CCTV system in Kirkcaldy in Fife, the number of crimes in a three-month period dropped from 38 to 20 (compared with the same period a year before) and the detection rate improved from nine to thirteen cases. In percentage terms the Workington initiative could claim an 88 per cent reduction in crime; and the Kirkcaldy scheme would point to a 47 per cent reduction in crime, together with a 44 per cent increase in the detection rate.

In addition, the percentage fall in crime is often not precisely related to the time-frame of the CCTV installation or to the area which is covered by it. For example, one commentary on the Newcastle scheme points to substantial falls in crime – thefts from vehicles (40%), thefts of vehicles (56%) and criminal damage (56%) – between 1991 and 1994; but the CCTV system only became fully operational in March 1993. And the cameras do not cover existing police beats which 'hampered comparison', although it is then blithely asserted that there is 'statistical ... and ... anecdotal evidence' to show the impact of the system – leading to the conclusion that CCTV is 'formidable' at targeting offenders (Durham, 1995).

Equally, account has to be taken of the reluctance of the CCTV literature (which is mainly provided by manufacturers, distributors and installers and is found in the trade journals) to acknowledge the recurrent costs of manning, servicing and maintaining the equipment once it has been installed. CCTV is expensive to install, expensive to monitor and expensive to maintain. The Home Office guide to the use of CCTV sensibly suggests in any business plan it will be necessary to identify the financial implications of a scheme, including the costs of the initial installation, premises, annual staffing, operating (tapes, phone lines, equipment rentals), maintenance and equipment upgrades (Edwards and Tilley, 1994). What is surprising, given that some 12 schemes are reviewed in detail (and 80 schemes cited overall), is that no information on capital or recurrent expenditure is offered, although possible sources of funding (local authority, business sector, the police, the Single Regeneration Budget) are mentioned. This is a major omission because the effectiveness of a system can only be properly judged in relation to its costs. Only very limited data are available.

For example, the much-vaunted Liverpool scheme required capital funding of £357,920. The only detail on recurrent expenditure is an 'additional' £13,000 a year for staffing the control centre and about £1,500 a year for rental and maintenance payments to BT for the fibre optic communication lines, although the document does not specify whether these additional figures are all or part of the running costs (Liverpool City Centre Partnership, 1994). This means that the total operating costs remain obscure. Another estimate suggests that the running costs are of the order of £15,000 a year (Cooper, 1994). The scheme in King's Lynn, however, is estimated to have annual operating costs of £180,000 (Kelly, 1993). The proposed scheme for Leicester city centre would cost £250,000 to install a 20-camera system and then £90,000 a year to run it – to be divided equally between the city council and the private sector (Morris, 1994). These figures are less than helpful.

There is a marked contrast between the level of detail (and publicity) which is given to the capital costs of CCTV systems and the lack of information about recurrent expenditure. The former probably reflects the political benefit to those concerned of large-scale investment as an indicator of their resolve and commitment to be seen to be doing something about town-centre crime. The public impact of investing in CCTV (the high-tech crime-stopper) is largely positive. The scrappy information about the running costs may reflect a lack of confidence on the part of installers and operators that the crime control dividend is really as great as is claimed. Rather more charitably, the information deficit may reflect the methodological problems of assessing the impact of CCTV on crime.

In order to assess the effectiveness of any CCTV system in crime control, what is clearly needed and long overdue are three sets of figures: the capital costs of installation; the full recurrent costs; and the raw figures on numbers and types of crime (not simply percentage changes) in the pre-CCTV and post-CCTV phases. In most cases the latter two sets of figures are either not available or only available in truncated form, which makes a proper assessment impossible. Continued failure to provide the three sets of figures can only lead to the sombre conclusion that the effectiveness of CCTV is being taken for granted and not subject to the normal standards of performance measurement – the relationship between inputs or costs (capital and ongoing) and outputs or benefits, measured in terms of crime reduction. In addition, formal evaluation would require a 'before and after' research design or one which compares areas with and like areas without closed circuit television.

It is the clear view of the West Midlands Police (1994) on the basis of an area-wide study that assessments of CCTV systems tend to be 'subjective' and 'undertaken by those who had commissioned and/or installed' the equipment. Not surprisingly, assessment and system reviews then provide statistics which indicate that the objectives are being achieved. The study also found that little work had been undertaken to estimate the long-term impact of CCTV on community safety. Another commentary pointed to the 'powerful commercial and political interests' behind the promotion of CCTV and the absence of consideration of the three 'Es' – efficiency, effectiveness and economy (Groombridge and Murji, 1994). And this review concluded that insufficient attention was being paid to the three 'pillars' of evaluation – setting objectives, developing appropriate measures and collecting data. These notes of caution are entirely justified. The seemingly exponential growth in CCTV systems has not been matched by parallel investment in assessing their effectiveness. The next chapter attempts to redress this imbalance by exploring in detail the contours of sound evaluation in relation to the use of CCTV in the retail environment. The above-mentioned Home Office guide, although it fails to present relevant data, does point to the need for evaluation, particularly by setting costs against benefits:

A comprehensive and honest evaluation and monitoring process should be built into the costs and must be designed around *your* specific identified problems ... Without rigorous, independent evaluation, it will not be possible to make decisions other than on hunches.

(Edwards and Tilley, 1994: 31, emphasis in original)

Against this, there is a rather less informed but more prevalent view, summarised by one town-centre manager:

CCTV is relatively new but there are few studies available to prove or disprove its effectiveness and to be honest the public want it, retailers want it and we cannot hang around for too long waiting for more academic research to be produced.

There are grounds for concluding that the 'rise and rise' of CCTV has been largely predicated on little more than a presumption of benefits which do not need to be made the subject of formal enquiry. When large sums of both public and private money are being spent with no attention being paid to the return on the investment, this is clearly unsatisfactory. Given that the retail community knows only too well that its profits are not premised on mere 'wish fulfilment', it is surprising that CCTV has not been subject to more rigorous scrutiny. If the present chapter has shown that there is an unmet need, the next chapter outlines some of the major issues which have to be addressed.

9   CCTV and the 'High-Tech Fix': Some Unanswered Questions

While there is a lack of reliable information to confirm the effectiveness of CCTV there is an over-abundance of data to show that the shopping public and others are strongly supportive of it. In the current study over nine in ten shoppers thought that CCTV was very acceptable or acceptable and over four in five managers thought it to be effective. These findings confirm the results of earlier studies. The general public is strongly in favour of the use of CCTV in shops to counter the threat of terrorism – at the 80 per cent level (Beck and Willis, 1993a, 1993b and 1994a); and there is as much or more support for CCTV as a general crime control measure in the retail sector (Beck and Willis, 1992, 1994b and 1995; Honess and Charman, 1992). Closed circuit television is decidedly not resented as an unwarranted, 'big brother' infringement of civil liberties.

A study in Bathgate, West Lothian, showed that 94 per cent of shoppers who were questioned were 'in favour' of the newly-installed town-centre system (*CCTV Today*, July 1994). Public confidence has also been found to be high in Liverpool (Davies, 1994). The Home Office guide states that there is 'no evidence' that the public regard CCTV as a threat to civil liberties, citing studies which show that on average only 6 per cent of the public are worried about its presence. A Glasgow survey found that 95 per cent of respondents were in favour of CCTV with just 7 per cent thinking that it posed a threat to civil liberties (Edwards and Tilley, 1994). The BRC retail crime survey found that a significant proportion of retailers thought that CCTV brought genuine crime control benefits, although only 20 per cent of the sample offered an opinion (Speed et al, 1995). More than one-half of those who offered an opinion (55%) took the view that the primary benefits were in terms of improved staff perceptions of safety. And over one-third of the retailers (38%) thought that there were benefits in terms of a reduction in the costs of crime.

One possible reason for this widespread support is the way CCTV promises comprehensive crime control in a neat, high-technology package – an off-the-shelf, state-of-the-art, electronic panacea for crime. This seductive appeal is something which might be called the 'high-tech fix'. Commitment to CCTV on the part of town-centre and shopping-centre managers and the shopping public may be more a matter of 'security wish fulfilment' than a judgement based on hard evidence (Beck and Willis, 1994b). Closed circuit television may be receiving a vote of confidence primarily because everyone wants to believe that it is effective, not because it has been proved to be effective. There is a danger that it is easier and more convenient to have faith in its effectiveness than it is to assess properly its contribution to crime control. Perhaps the 'hunches' which inform decisions to install CCTV systems are largely a product of a needs-led belief that at long last a techno-fix solution guarantees real-life crime control benefits, but a measured assessment would need to take into account a number of interrelated considerations.

Deterrence, detection and displacement

Deterrence, detection and displacement are different ways in which CCTV could have a measurable impact on crime. They are crucial concepts because they focus attention on the purposes for which systems are installed and on unintended consequences. The available data are not encouraging. In a survey of 135 small businesses (up to 100 staff) with CCTV, of which 59 per cent were retail outlets, the sombre conclusion was that the stated aims of installation were not being consistently met; and this was associated with a decline in the businessman's satisfaction with the technology (Hearnden, 1994). The study also found that although two-thirds or more of the companies had installed systems because of general concerns about security or to provide an anti-theft deterrent, 17 per cent took no advice whatsoever before installation, over one-third relied on a single source and one in six took advice solely from a CCTV supplier. Perhaps it is not surprising that with such generalised expectations and little, if any, independent advice, there was not much correlation between expectations and performance. The need for pre-installation advice was also stressed in the Home Office guide (Edwards and Tilley, 1994).

A major question is the extent to which CCTV helps to prevent crime through deterrence – that is, the extent to which it frightens off would-be offenders by making them think that there is a high prospect of their being identified, caught and punished. In the general criminological literature (Zimring and Hawkins, 1973; Beyleveld, 1979; Walker, 1991), there are numerous discussions about whether penalties set at a sufficiently high level will operate so as to outweigh the likely benefits of offending and related empirical studies. These do not refer either to the retail environment or to the use of closed circuit television. There are only a few relevant studies. In one, which focused on retail store staff attitudes to CCTV surveillance, the data suggested that staff had more confidence in the potential of CCTV to act as a deterrent (54%) than in its ability to help detect offenders (40%) (Beck and Willis, 1992). And a survey of 1,000 youngsters aged between 13 and 17 years, undertaken for General Accident, found that more than one-half of the respondents listed video cameras in public places as an important crime deterrent, second only to more police on the street (see Hearnden, 1994). Deterrence is an appealing concept but it is notoriously difficult to measure. It is all too easy to claim that CCTV systems are having a generalised deterrent impact on crime. This is indeed an irrefutable assertion: whatever the current level of crime, without CCTV it would have been higher – so its use is justified. The only sensible way to measure deterrent effects is either to conduct 'before and after' research or to compare like environments with and without surveillance equipment.

Some findings are decidedly less than impressive. The Liverpool police were confident that the CCTV system installed in 1994 would help to deter would-be street offenders intent on muggings and other thefts from the person, but they also conceded that these accounted for less than 3 per cent of all city-centre crimes. They also thought that thefts from shops, which comprised 13 per cent of city-centre offences, would remain largely immune to the new system simply because it only operated in the streets and not within the shops (Foster, 1994a). Police in the West Midlands (1994) have pointed out that if cameras are positioned close to the ground, and even more if they are painted in bright colours and marked with notices stating that they are in use, the deterrent effects may be maximised. But the cameras then become much more accessible targets for vandals and the line of sight is more likely to be compromised by obstructions such as trees or canopies.

There is also the related question of the extent to which CCTV is an aid to the detection of offenders. This directs attention to the ways in which

CCTV can be used to 'track' offences in progress in real time so as to generate an instant response. There is also a need to assess the ability of systems to record images which can then be used to identify offenders after the event. Closed circuit television images must be of sufficient quality and clarity so as to become the first step in a process which runs through identification, apprehension and prosecution to eventual conviction – and does so in a way which meets with the approval of the courts. The first time that videotape was admitted as evidence in court was in 1976. In 1982 it was established that it was admissible on the same principle as eye witness testimony (*R* v *Grimer*, 1982). The decision in this case held that there was no distinction between the evidence of a person looking at a tape and that of a bystander observing the event – provided that there was no challenge to the validity of the tape, which must be the original or an authenticated copy and have no signs of editing or unexplained breaks (Doran, 1992; Sharpe, 1989).

However, a more recent ruling by Judge Mitchell in the Old Bailey in 1991 has made matters more complex. He ruled that he was not going to allow expert evidence as to whether the defendant was 'possibly, probably or very probably the same man' as the suspect recorded on videotape because of a lack of statistical data and a scientific basis for recognising a combination of features on tape and matching them with a particular person (Burne, 1994). Expert evidence of a match between photograph and suspect was seen to be no more than a matter of opinion, with no measure of the probability that one or more features would be similar. This has prompted extensive work on what is known as the Video Identity Assessment System (VIAS) which matches parts of known profiles held on a computer database to those of the suspected person – giving a statistical likelihood of a match occurring on a range of features. Even though progress has been made on this front, roughly parallel to the use of DNA fingerprinting for evidential purposes, the legal question remains open as to how such evidence should be related to the 'prior probability' of guilt implied by other evidence.

A recent Court of Appeal decision in *R* v *Clare* and *R* v *Peach* (*The Times*, 7th April, 1995), however, gives considerable impetus to the use of videotaped evidence. The defendants were convicted of violent disorder following a football match. A rather fuzzy black and white video recording was available but, because the incident was brief and other members of the public were milling about and creating a confused scene, the prosecution had a police constable study the film closely and analytically, who then presented his identification evidence as an expert. The court upheld this on the grounds that the evidence was 'no more secondary ... than any other oral identification made from a photograph'; and added that as technology advanced it was necessary for the courts to evolve evidential practice so as to gain full assistance from the technology. But the use to date of video images to secure convictions has been limited. One police spokesman estimated that his force's technical support unit was being asked to process 800 surveillance videotapes a year, of which no more than six were used subsequently to secure a conviction. He commented that cameras were 'almost useless' when it came to identifying criminals (Burne, 1994).

A study of a trial of security equipment for a national retailer found that the use of CCTV in general, the introduction of more cameras and the use of CCTV linked to electronic article surveillance (EAS) were not associated with increased rates of detection of crime (Beck and Willis, 1995). More positively, the Merseyside police are confident that when offenders know that they have been caught offending on videotape, they admit the offence immediately. This is likely to improve the detection rate and certainly saves time and money at trials. The Newcastle system is also credited with a 100 per cent success rate in inducing CCTV-identified offenders to plead guilty to the offence (Edwards and Tilley, 1994). The police in Airdrie point to the opposite side of the coin, emphasising the fact that video evidence can help to eliminate wrongly suspected persons (Davies, 1994).

The case of *Hellewell* v *Chief Constable of Derbyshire* (*The Times*, 13th January, 1995; Whitaker, 1995; and see Chapter 5) confirmed that police 'mug shots' could be given to shopkeepers and then circulated for the purpose of identifying known troublemakers in order to ban them from local stores. This decision has two possible implications with regard to the use of video-recorded images. Although the case related to the distribution of a photograph taken of somebody in police custody, it raises the possibility that the same rather wide public interest considerations would apply with regard to the circulation of photographs from CCTV recordings. The critical variable would seem to be the reasonable purpose for which the photograph is to be used, rather than the circumstances under which it was initially taken. This would appear to underwrite the use of electronically derived images for crime control purposes. The decision also raises the possibility that retailers themselves could legitimately record and circulate their own photographic material in the general interest of preventing and detecting crime – provided they had only these purposes in mind and made no more than reasonable use of the photographs.

If recorded images were circulated in this way the primary benefits would probably not be in terms of either deterrence or detection. The identification of known troublemakers in this way would allow retailers and their security staff to ban suspected persons with a significant degree of confidence.

In the current study managers in the two locations strongly endorsed CCTV as an effective crime control option, although they were only asked to comment in general terms and not specifically in relation to its potential for deterrence and detection. Within this broad support, however, there were marked differences. At one extreme some managers said that a very sophisticated and expensive configuration would be justified if it led to the detection, arrest and conviction of just one terrorist bomber or a single offender guilty of a James Bulger-type abduction and killing. High-cost options would be worthwhile if they contributed to the detection of even very small numbers of serious offences. At the other extreme some managers offered the view that dummy cameras were the best way to maximise deterrence at minimum cost. Large-scale, across-the-board investment in high-tech equipment was too high a price to pay when much the same sort of dividends could be secured by low-cost dummy equipment which would 'frighten off' the majority of opportunistic thieves. This points to the need for clarity of purpose when an installation is being considered.

To the extent that CCTV is effective either as an aid to detection or as a deterrent, there is a clear risk that its use in one area will displace the problems of crime and nuisance to other, unprotected areas without surveillance. The Home Office guide points to this unintended outcome:

> It is possible that there will be some displacement of crime to another town or to another area of your town but it is likely that much opportunistic crime will not be displaced.
>
> (Edwards and Tilley, 1994: 9)

No guidance is offered on when displacement occurs and under what circumstances, although to the extent that the criminal actor is capable of rational choice, involving strategic thinking and decision-making, the potential clearly exists (see Cornish and Clarke, 1986); and there is limited indirect evidence of its occurring.

Although some studies have not found anything approaching a mirror-image change in crime rates, with the reduction in protected areas being matched by the increase in unprotected areas nearby (Forrester et al,

1988), Neighbourhood Watch and crime prevention studies have shown that crime control benefits may be obtained at the cost of moving the problems around the corner (Heal and Laycock, 1988; Bulos, 1994). There was concern that the Coventry experiment in banning public drinking would simply drive the problem outwards away from the city centre (Ramsay, 1990). A study of CCTV and crime on the London Underground found positive anti-crime effects, but there was some suggestion of displacement rather than prevention (Burrows, 1980). And in the current study one shopping-centre manager commented that the 'banning' of troublemakers had had the effect of moving offenders on to 'somebody else's area of responsibility'. To the extent that displacement does take place, shopping centres could be re-locating crime to town centres, and town centres could be relocating crime to their outer margins. It is also possible that there could be another form of adaptation as offenders change their behaviour to defeat the CCTV cameras – like, for example, football hooligans or robbers wearing hooded clothes or masks so as to avoid identification.

There are also shopping-specific examples. In July 1994, following decisions by Stirling and Dundee to install CCTV, Perth, which had a low crime rate decided that it too should have a system, not least to avoid crime from the other two places being displaced to its area (Hennessey, 1994). The police in Liverpool were confident when the city-centre CCTV system became operational in mid-1994, that it would act as a deterrent to street crime; but they were also fearful that the network would turn criminals away from the largely pedestrianised shopping and recreational centre to peripheral car parks, most of which were not under camera surveillance (Foster, 1994a). In the first five months of 1994 a total of 5,954 offences were recorded in the division covering the city centre, compared with 7,131 offences in the north Liverpool division, in which there were no public security systems. In the period leading up to the installation of CCTV in the city centre, the latter division recorded a 20 per cent increase in crime – and there were concerns that this could worsen as more crime moved out from the centre. An Autoglass crime survey pointed to a similar conclusion. In 1992 only one in twenty acts of vandalism and thefts from cars took place in shopping centre car parks and one-half of all incidents took place on the street. By 1994 seven out of twenty attacks were taking place in car parks, and less than one-quarter on the street (Langley, 1994). It was argued that the change was in part a consequence of much improved street surveillance through the installation of town-centre and city-centre CCTV during this period in some areas. Motor vehicle crime figures tended to go down in streets and car parks protected by CCTV installations; but up in unprotected adjacent streets and car parks. Protecting one group of motorist successfully may have placed other car owners relatively more at risk.

Operating the system

A conspicuous area of neglect in assessing the effectiveness of CCTV is the distinction between 'live' CCTV and images which are retained on a video recorder. Most modern systems have an extraordinary capacity to retain and store visual data on tape, and it is normal if not routine for CCTV to be used in this way. It is by no means certain, however, that retaining miles and miles of images on tape makes a major contribution to security. In the occasional newsworthy case, such as that of James Bulger or Abbie Humphreys, the retained images may be useful for purposes of identification. They may also be of evidential quality. One of the most important factors is the amount of time which can be made available to re-run tapes. In general the average store manager or CCTV operator will not be in a position to review most of what has been recorded. Another factor is the quality of the image on a tape which has been used many times before.

Alternatively, the use of CCTV may involve on-line monitoring of events in real time. This appears to be implicit in the advice offered by the British Council of Shopping Centres (1993c). Incidents requiring 'clarification' should be brought promptly to the attention of patrolling security staff or management or the police by the operators; and communication between centre management and retail outlets in the centre should be secured by radio links, with easy telephone communication being provided between control rooms. There is an underlying assumption here that security operators are manning the system and watching the monitors because this is the only way in which it is possible to respond to an event 'promptly'. What is not discussed, however, is the cost implications of providing a manned surveillance system. These costs are far from insignificant; they may be of the order of £15,000 a year for around-the-clock supervision of monitors by a single operator, although other estimates suggest that the figure for a typical city-centre installation will be as much as £100,000 a year, or even twice this amount. A further factor is that some of the more established schemes provide evidence that as local authorities and traders become more attached to CCTV, the local police wind down some of their direct funding and manpower support (Preston, C., 1995). This would be entirely consistent with the general tendency of the police to offer 'core' services only and it would impose a heavier burden of recurrent expenditure on those operating CCTV systems.

In addition, if real-time monitoring is deemed to be essential – usually by using pan, tilt and zoom cameras which can focus on and follow an unfolding incident – then this zooming-in on one incident means that other areas are unmonitored for some time (West Midlands Police, 1994). One solution is capital expenditure on equipment which offers overlapping facilities. There are no national data on manned and unmanned systems, nor are there studies to date on whether real-time CCTV offers advantages over recorded images. There is clearly a prima facie case for believing that continuous viewing and instant responses offer more benefits than after-the-event monitoring, but this is unproved; and any assessment would need to set the benefits of crime control against the costs of manned systems.

More generally, there is a complex relationship between the sophistication of the equipment and the appropriate manning level. There is no point in installing state-of-the-art equipment if there are no funds available to support recurrent expenditure on staffing. To the extent that live images are thought to be important, live staff need to be in front of the monitors. There is no evidence in the literature that this balance is being addressed. It may, for example, be more prudent to spend less on hardware and to reserve funds for manning the system than to have first-class equipment which remains unmanned. It would be unrealistic to expect CCTV manufacturers to do anything other than try to sell the most sophisticated (and most expensive) systems, which puts the onus of deciding the trade-off between capital and recurrent costs on local authorities, retailers and town-centre and shopping-centre managers.

For example, in the Home Office guide to CCTV (Edwards and Tilley, 1994), of nine schemes reviewed in detail where there was information on operator cover over a 24-hour period, six installations had a single person monitoring the equipment (Airdrie, Birmingham, Bournemouth, Coventry, King's Lynn and Newport), and three others had up to two persons at peak times (Liverpool, Newcastle and Northampton). Between them these nine schemes had 395 cameras in operation. This means that for most of the time, when there was only a single operator on duty, each installation had on average one person watching as many as 44 cameras. Almost no attention has been paid to the capacity of operators to 'take in and understand' an enormous quantity of images from many monitors simultaneously. It is highly probable that some incidents are being recorded but not spotted at the time. The recently opened Broadway Centre in Hammersmith, west London, has 56 cameras – and the controller admits the problem:

> Obviously you can't watch all 56 cameras all the time. You miss some things ... It's difficult to stare at multiple pictures.
>
> (Matthews, 1994: *The Independent*, 29th August)

In the case of a modest system of 32 units connected to one control room, each camera will throw out an astonishing 4.3 million pictures in a 24-hour period; and in the course of a week each camera will produce over 30 million images. The 32-camera system as a whole will generate over 960 million pictures each week. Comprehensive recording would require 32 tape recorders and nearly 1,800 three-hour tapes a week (Morse, 1994). The critical variable is not the electronics (which already offer enough, if not too much, material) but the way in which the picture output is handled, especially the operators' performance in monitoring dynamic scenes. The so-called 'camera policeman' offers exceptional service in recording events, but unless there is someone available to monitor what the cameras are picking up, and then to take decisions based on those images, there is no possibility of responding to an incident. The operator is a critical link between observation and action.

There are unanswered questions about so-called 'video blindness' and the extent to which operators can take in information from a number of screens; and whether they can do so in a way which allows them to analyse and to react to images which give grounds for concern. Operators need to take decisions about where to focus cameras and then how best to respond to what is being seen in real-time. The Home Office guide is clear on this point:

> It may seem odd, but we really do not know how long someone can concentrate on what they are seeing on a bank of screens showing scenes from a variety of cameras.
>
> (Edwards and Tilley, 1994: 27)

Evidence from the West Midlands Police (1994) suggests that an operator's effective span of attention is no greater than 20 minutes, after which a rest period of equal length is necessary. Experiments were conducted where a man wearing a white suit walked across a black background. Even when CCTV viewers had been on duty for only a short period before being presented with a single picture on one monitor, in many cases the 'suspect' went unnoticed. Whilst the camera may see everything within its field of view, the operator does not. This problem is compounded when operators watch multiple screens or multiple images (of inferior size, quality and resolution) on a single screen. Although CCTV is a contemporary phenomenon, the general problem of attention span and short-term memory is one which has engaged psychologists since the second world war when concerns were first expressed about the capacity of radar screen operators to function at a high level of efficiency on a continuous basis. The accepted view, backed by numerous experiments, is that short-term memory retention is not a passive activity. It requires some kind of continuing effort which restricts the ability to engage meanwhile in other tasks; and it also means that short-term retention is liable to disruption by other distractions (see Broadbent, 1958 for a classic summary). These findings confirm the view of the CCTV operator quoted above, namely that in concentrating on one screen images from another screen will simply not be observed, let alone remembered and acted upon.

In addition, at present no-one knows how an operator selects particular displays on screen and constructs his or her reasoned interpretation of what is taking place. Progress may be possible through 'cued' monitoring – for example, critical event monitoring and the use of alarms; and the introduction of 'intelligent scene monitoring' is around the corner where the operator has his or her attention directed by the technology to a significant feature – for example, an abandoned suitcase in an otherwise busy street scene. At present the operator is left alone with over 1.4 million images in the course of an average eight-hour shift. The Shopfront Security Group (1994), a pressure group formed by retailers, is rather misguided on this point. The group argues that 'cameras are relatively cheap' because they obviate the need for extra (and expensive) staff. In fact CCTV creates the need for additional staff because unless there is someone on duty to monitor events continuously, there is no means of responding to them. And the staffing costs go up not down when comprehensive real-time monitoring is provided, especially when operators are given the regular relief they need from the burdensome activity of concentrating on small-screen images over extended periods of time.

Impact on staff and customers

Alongside the obvious indicators of performance such as the impact on crime, there are also concerns about the way in which CCTV may affect retail staff and customers in both town centres and shopping centres. If staff and guards uncritically accept the crime control benefits attributed to CCTV, this could lead to a relaxation in staff vigilance. Staff may too readily assume that CCTV is making a major contribution to the detection or deterrence of offenders – an example of the mistaken belief that it offers a technological panacea for the problem of crime. And if they believe that security hardware is a primary factor in store crime control, this could result in an over-reliance on an impersonal, 'high-tech' approach to security. There is then a danger that staff could come to see themselves as absolved from security responsibilities. Closed circuit television may be a double-edged sword where any crime control benefits need to be set against the possible costs of lower levels of staff vigilance (Beck and Willis, 1994b). The Home Office guide is alert to the risk of both members of the public and shop staff feeling that they no longer need to be vigilant about crime simply because CCTV is in use:

> Take care that the installation of CCTV will not reduce the vigilance of otherwise active citizens. There is some evidence that this has happened in shops, where assistants come to believe that security cameras make their attention to suspicious behaviour unnecessary ... Be careful that the installation of CCTV will not produce an *exaggerated sense of security* amongst vulnerable members of the community.
>
> (Edwards and Tilley, 1994: 15, emphasis in original)

As noted above, the British Retail Consortium's (BRC) retail crime survey identified staff perceptions of enhanced safety as the primary benefit to retailers from the introduction of closed circuit television. More than one-half of the retailers (55%) took this view. This finding points to the possibility that CCTV may cause feelings of security to go up but in the process cause feelings of responsibility to go down (Speed et al, 1995).

With regard to customers, there is some strength in the point that it does not matter a great deal whether CCTV is genuinely effective or whether members of the public merely believe that it offers real crime control benefits, even though this belief is mistaken and unfounded. It is quite possible that the presence of CCTV has the real effect of alleviating fear and anxiety about crime. This could be considered a good thing in itself, especially in the light of the finding that shoppers' anxieties about crime far outstrip the chances of actual victimisation. For the majority of shoppers and for most of the time, the fear of crime is greater than the actual risk – so dealing with the fear alone becomes entirely appropriate. This could be seen as a sufficient justification for CCTV in the retail environment; something which definitely acts as a symbolic and reassuring presence and which possibly operates to control crime.

There was certainly no evidence in the current study that the presence of CCTV made shoppers in town centres or shopping centres more anxious because it confirmed or heightened their awareness of the problems of crime and nuisance. The 'reassurance' factor should not be underestimated. On the contrary, the findings point to widespread public endorsement of CCTV in public places. More than nine in ten members of the public held the view that surveillance cameras in the shopping environment were acceptable – 91 per cent in town centres and 96 per cent in shopping centres. And a survey in Hexham, Northumbria, found that 83 per cent of women and 45 per cent of men felt safer with CCTV in the town centre. They were of the view that cameras were 'no different' from uniformed police officers located at the same sites (Drury, 1993). The authorities in Liverpool justified the expansion of the 20-camera system to a 65-camera system on the grounds of almost universal approval by the public (Davies, 1994). The Shopfront Security Group (1994) commends the advertisement of the presence of CCTV on street furniture. It refers approvingly to the practice of the Toronto subway system which has designated 'zones' where CCTV is guaranteed to be constantly in use. These zones may also be created informally. Reports from Birmingham suggest that at night young women choose to wait for their boyfriends or for their escorts home within range of the cameras – and that they wave to operators, 'acknowledging the comfort they derive from this protection' (West Midlands Police, 1994). This is anecdotal but powerful evidence that CCTV is a reassuring and comforting presence.

Whatever faith the general public may have in CCTV, town-centre and city-centre managers and retail staff need to be altogether more pragmatic. They must not be lulled into a sense of false security by over-optimistically believing that CCTV is effective. It would be unwise to equate a general belief in its effectiveness with factual proof of its crime control capabilities (Beck and Willis, 1994b). Indeed, for retailers and those with responsibilities for managing the retail environment, it may not be sensible to presume too much. If CCTV is assumed to offer genuine crime control benefits and this is associated with lower staff vigilance, the net effect is less, not more, protection. Closed circuit television would not be fulfilling expectations and existing, more informal, mechanisms would not be being utilised as much as before.

CCTV and possible abuse

In the town centres and shopping centres studied in this enquiry, CCTV surveillance was carried out by private security companies on behalf of either the local authorities or the owners of the shopping centres. The Environment Committee reported the same feature (House of Commons, 1994). Given the widespread use of CCTV in both environments it is clear that private companies have a major role in shopping-related security. Rather like the findings presented in Chapter 5 on the use of security guards in shopping centres, the debate about video surveillance has been resolved in both town centres and shopping centres in favour of the use of private companies to operate the systems. The House of Commons Home Affairs Committee is currently exploring the need for codes of practice to regulate the use of CCTV installations. The Home Office Crime Prevention Unit is keen to encourage operational procedures which will maximise effectiveness and minimise any threat to civil liberties which could 'arise from either sloppy practice or the deliberate misuse' of such systems (Reinhard, 1992).

A fresh analysis of Home Office data on the public's attitudes towards CCTV (Honess and Charman, 1992) by the Information Protection & Management Consultants (1994–95) found an undercurrent of anxiety about possible abuse. In the general survey, nearly three-quarters of respondents (72%) agreed with the statement that cameras could be 'used by the wrong people' and 38 per cent thought that the people in control could not be trusted always to use them for the public good. A similar proportion (41%) supposed that cameras were sometimes used 'to spy on people', whilst one-third expressed the view that they 'invaded people's privacy'. The higher levels of support for CCTV emerged in the responses to questions which clearly related to its use in the context of crime and crime prevention. There would appear to be at least four possible ways in which CCTV could be mismanaged in the retail environment: covert surveillance; abuse by management; personal misuse by operators; and an absence of regulation.

Although the present study did not explore retail staff perceptions of CCTV, data from other studies suggest that between three-quarters and nine in ten store staff welcome the use of in-store cameras (Beck and Willis, 1992; Beck and Willis, 1995). The latter study also found that 35 per cent of sales staff in a major fashion retailer would be reassured by the deployment of covert CCTV in their working environment and that a further one in three staff were indifferent to its use. A minority of 18 per cent thought that it would be intrusive. In effect, nearly three-quarters of staff welcomed or did not mind covert surveillance. The 'big brother' syndrome was mostly absent. The value of CCTV was seen as deriving from its ability to record incidents and to identify troublemakers. No staff offered the view that it might be used to witness dishonest acts by staff or to monitor staff compliance with company procedures. This may be surprising but staff views appeared to be in line with the general finding from the current study that CCTV has widespread endorsement.

But clearly CCTV can be used by management to monitor staff. Store managers involved in other studies have volunteered information about CCTV being used initially to target staff suspected of dishonesty, but then unexpectedly proving to be more valuable in checking whether staff were meeting company requirements – for example, compliance with till procedures or rules relating to refunds and exchanges (Beck and Willis, 1992). The next step could be to use CCTV primarily for these purposes. Employees will tend to assume that CCTV is directed mainly against dishonest customers and to some extent against 'rotten apple' staff who steal. In both cases the underlying purpose is protection of the business against dishonesty. If CCTV is subsequently used mainly as a management tool then there is a clear discrepancy between the stated and the real purpose. This is not to suggest that monitoring-for-management is necessarily wrong; but it is arguable that it should be done only when staff are aware that it is being used in this way. The high level of staff confidence in CCTV could evaporate if they felt they were being misled in this way.

The report from Marketing Strategies for Industry suggested that 77 per cent of CCTV applications or end-uses were for general security surveillance, 9 per cent were for specific access control and the remaining 8 per cent were for 'process' control – that is, to ensure the smooth running of the area under surveillance in accordance with company procedures. In a market worth some £300 million a year, this means that about £24 million a year is being spent on CCTV for what can be termed management purposes (Marketing Strategies for Industry, 1994). Although there is an undoubted potential for abuse, when there is a discrepancy between the stated and actual use of CCTV, there can also be benefits. For example, it was unexpectedly found in Liverpool that police resources could be managed more efficiently by using video pictures to determine the appropriate level of response to an incident (Davies, 1994).

There is also a danger that CCTV cameras could be trained on unsuspecting members of the public or staff for reasons other than those of security or efficient management. The ease with which the cameras can pan, tilt and zoom, as well as the high resolution of the images, allows them to be used to focus on anyone, pretty well anywhere and at any time. And those in control will ordinarily not be subject to supervision, especially if the 'record' facility is turned off. The operator will be free to indulge private and possibly salacious interests – even fantasies. There is no guarantee against the 'peeping Tom'. The potential for abuse is possibly greatest in circumstances where the CCTV operators are mostly male and where the majority of sales staff or customers are female. There is also the possibility of unauthorised use being made of recorded material by operators, which could take the form of feeding local gossip, harassment or intimidation, or even blackmail (Reinhard, 1992; Utley, 1993). For example, as part of a £10 million security programme to combat theft from telephone kiosks BT has hidden micro-cameras (no bigger than a fingertip) and microphones in 40 boxes in Basingstoke and Alton, Hampshire (*The Times*, 23rd April, 1994). A company spokesman said that offences against protected boxes had fallen by about two-thirds, and that the experiment would be extended to a further 500 boxes. The assurance has been given that the cameras are only triggered when the sensors detect attempted theft from the cash boxes. But how confident can the public be that there is 'no question' of taking pictures or listening to people using the phone normally?

Whatever the benefits of CCTV there are residual concerns that the cameras may be pointed at the wrong people and for the wrong reasons. Whether they are or not is a matter for conjecture. What is certain is that the potential for abuse exists. Liberty, the campaign group, has generally welcomed the use of video cameras in public places, but it is concerned about the absence of statutory controls, particularly with regard to who watches the screens, who has access to the tapes and when the tapes are erased (Watt, 1993). The Washington-based watchdog group, Privacy International, is concerned that the creation of a surveillance infrastructure will eventually lead to the monitoring of public morals as well as criminal behaviour. At this point the use of the technology moves beyond crime control to social control (Davies, 1994).

Part of the solution to these incipient problems, which hinge around the balance between the protection of an individual's privacy against the need to watch people in a given area, lies in the introduction of codes of practice. One such code, developed by the West Midlands Police (1994) provides for random spot checks on operators, tapes and systems, backed by employers' disciplinary codes or criminal sanctions. Factual data on the number of cameras, their location and information on the system's effectiveness are publicly available. Most important, in order to retain the confidence of the public, is respect for individual privacy. To this end, under the West Midlands code all cameras are sited in a fixed and prominent position and, except when wide-angle or distance shots are used, domestic and office premises are not included within a camera's field of vision. No facility for recording sound is permitted or contemplated. Similarly, under normal circumstances the recording of drunk and disorderly behaviour and other relatively minor offences for court purposes is precluded in the Newcastle scheme (Edwards and Tilley, 1994), although this may have more to do with a wish to concentrate on serious offences than concern for the civil liberties of the minor offender.

These sorts of rules would appear to go some way to answering the most obvious objections to the use of CCTV in public places, although it is interesting to note that the current study has uncovered few examples of attempts to regulate the use of CCTV so that civil liberties are not infringed. If there are others, they have not been readily available. This is a pity because the transparency of the controls, as much as the controls themselves, is crucial to the reassurance which is required. The Home Office guide points only to the need to develop codes of conduct to safeguard privacy and civil liberties, together with the need for breaches to be identified and to lead to disciplinary action (Edwards and Tilley, 1994). The proposal for a 'typical' statement of purpose for CCTV is not helpful:

> To provide a secure and safe centre for the benefit of those who visit, work or live in the town and to allow full enjoyment of the facilities of the town.
> (Edwards and Tilley, 1994: 35)

This is at such a level of generality that is does not state what the CCTV system would do, let alone the boundaries beyond which it would not be used. Similarly, the declaration of CCTV policy from the Association of Chief Police Officers (quoted in Edwards and Tilley, 1994) is prefaced by a benign acknowledgement of the 'individual's right of privacy' but there is no recognition of the tension (or indeed the contradiction) between this and any form of surveillance which places an unsuspecting member of the public under scrutiny without his or her permission. A supposed safeguard which is so superficial and bland may not offer any protection at all – however well intentioned.

Finally, advice from the Office of the Data Protection Registrar which is briefly summarised by Edwards and Tilley (1994) suggests that there are conditions under which CCTV video tapes would fall within the scope of the Data Protection Act 1984. Section 1(2) defines data as 'information recorded in a form in which it can be processed by equipment operating automatically in response to instructions given for that purpose'. Section 1(3) applies to personal data where an individual can be identified from that information. Quite apart from the obvious parallels between information stored on video tape and on magnetic tape, the technological advances in CCTV systems mean that the cameras are increasingly subject to pre-programmed instructions – which enable them to identify certain events (for example, changes in the density of moving populations). If the same sort of techniques were to be used to interrogate video recordings automatically so as to process data by reference to the video subject (a particular individual), then the provisions of the Act would apply. There is no objection to extracting information about a person by viewing his or her recorded activities, but there would be if this were to be done automatically. Simple video recordings of unknown persons would not present a problem; and this would cover a great deal of anonymous and generalised CCTV surveillance. But where a video image is of an individual whose identity could be worked out from the recorded image, or from other information held by the data user, the Act could apply (Pounder, 1995).

More generally, the Information Protection & Management Consultants (1994–95) take the view that CCTV operators could be in breach of the 'first principle' of the legislation if they failed to provide reasonably clear and accessible notices identifying the data user; used the system covertly; used it for purposes other than the stated quasi-policing purposes; used it 'to harass' an individual without good cause – for example, because someone was 'hanging around' or seen to be a potential 'troublemaker'; or failed to get planning permission for the installation. Images recorded by the CCTV system require registration under the Act and the purposes for which the equipment was being used would need to be made public; and were personal data to be used or disclosed in contravention of the register entry, then prosecution could follow. Finally, given that there is specific Home Office advice about 'codes of conduct' for the use of CCTV, if compensation to an individual became an issue, then a 'reasonable care' defence under section 23 would scarcely apply if that advice had not been followed. The critical variables are clarity of purpose and publicity, together with scrupulous adherence to Home Office codes of conduct.

Making the most of CCTV

Drawing the threads together from this and the previous chapter, all that can be said with certainty about the effectiveness of CCTV in town centres and shopping centres is that there is a limited amount of information, mostly of a rather general nature and relating to town centres, indicating that there is some impact on crime; but there is a widespread belief on the part of managers and shoppers alike that it has a considerable impact on crime. The situation, as one town-centre manager put it, is that:

> CCTV is here to stay – but we simply don't know what contribution it's making to crime prevention.

One of the most important issues is to decide just what a CCTV system is designed to achieve. This is rarely obvious. The Shopfront Security Group emphasises the point:

> If a system is being considered, the critical question which must be asked, is why is it being proposed. A clear set of policy objectives must be drawn which is capable of being monitored.
>
> (Shopfront Security Group, 1994: 13)

The Home Office guide also highlights the importance of having clear objectives:

> You need to think through how it [CCTV] is going to help reduce problems in your town ... You need to consider what ... is needed. You need to be clear that the potential crime prevention effectiveness of your CCTV system will relate to *your* town's particular problems.
>
> (Edwards and Tilley, 1994: 14, emphasis in original)

Closed circuit television may work in a number of different ways: more effective deployment of security guards or police; deterring would-be offenders; identifying offenders and obtaining photographic evidence; reassuring town-centre users; warning those whose behaviour is suspicious; highlighting crime problems; tracking offenders on the move; and increasing the efficiency of town-centre and shopping-centre management. A necessary condition for the successful deployment of cameras is being clear about the purpose for which they are being used. If the overriding objective is to direct attention to incidents as they occur, this points to a real-time system with skilled operators. If an important function is to provide good-quality pictures for evidential purposes there are implications for the siting of cameras and their capacity to provide high-resolution images, as well as implications for the use, retrieval and storage of tapes. If CCTV is mainly intended as a deterrent, then dummy cameras may be as useful and a great deal cheaper than genuine equipment.

In practice it is unlikely that any one of these aims will be highlighted to the exclusion of the others, and the choice will almost invariably involve some form of trade-off between competing claims on the system. What is important is the clarity with which these conflicting objectives are defined and the priority they are given. It is particularly necessary that the contribution of CCTV to crime control and crime prevention be assessed thoroughly and independently. Unless these two conditions are met (explicit operational requirements and effectiveness assessed against clear objectives) the danger will remain that investment in CCTV is as much a matter of 'security wish fulfilment' as it is a considered response to crime or to the threat of crime. This would play into the hands of the manufacturers of CCTV and their sales teams who will continue to exploit the lay person's belief that camera technology offers a panacea to crime and nuisance. It would mean that both private and public money was being squandered. And worst of all, it would mean that the public was not receiving the protection it wants and deserves.

Finally, it would be naive to presume that in the search for effective security there is a choice to be made between the use of security personnel, such as police officers on patrol or private security guards (Chapter 5) and closed circuit television (Chapter 7). It is highly probable that there is a complex relationship between these measures – where security effectiveness is greater than the sum of its individual components. For example, in the present study and with regard to existing security measures in shopping centres, three security options were identified as being in current use by nine in ten or more managers – the use of private security guards (90%), CCTV (89%) and staff radio link-up (96%). This same combination was also credited by the vast majority of managers as offering the most effective response to crime and nuisance – with private security guards (85%) being directed by means of a radio link-up (88%), frequently with the benefit of on-line CCTV pictures (85%).

The British Council of Shopping Centres (1993c) appears to endorse this integrated approach. Televised incidents requiring 'clarification' should be brought promptly to the attention of patrolling security staff or management or the police by the operators; communication between centre management and retail outlets in the centre should be reinforced by radio links and there should be easy telephone communication between control rooms. This was reflected in a comment by one shopping-centre manager:

> The high presence of security personnel and cameras has made the centre an extremely safe place for shoppers. The small number of incidents needs to be taken against a background of eight million visitors per annum.

There was an interesting parallel here with town centres where there was also an emphasis on using both security personnel and closed circuit television. Town-centre managers believed that existing security measures reflected a two-way combination of police officers on patrol (96%) or dedicated police squads (93%) and closed circuit television (77%). A similar combination was seen to offer the most effective response to crime and nuisance – when CCTV (82%) was used in conjunction with dedicated police squads (70%). The Home Office guide to CCTV in public places commends the use of small two-way radios (radio link) as a means of linking video evidence of incidents to remedial action by the police or security staff, especially when the movements of shop thieves are being tracked (Edwards and Tilley, 1994). Such schemes are currently in use in Coventry, Leicester, Northampton and Wolverhampton.

It would appear that the preferred security strategies in the two shopping environments were not that dissimilar and that managers in both locations saw security as a function of personnel plus CCTV equipment, but there were important differences. In shopping centres there was seemingly a preference for a triple-barrelled approach combining security guards, radios and closed circuit television. In town centres there appeared to be a double-barrelled strategy combining police on patrol or dedicated police squads and closed circuit television. These findings confirm the importance of CCTV but they also suggest that one should be cautious about seeing the 'eye in the sky' as the only solution to the problems of safe shopping.

10 Security Shutters: Designing Out Crime or Designing In Anxiety?

The final area of enquiry was the use of security shutters in town centres, concentrating on their perceived effectiveness and acceptability to town-centre managers and to town-centre shoppers. It is a useful case study because it explores the complex relationship between the perceived effectiveness of a security measure and any unwanted and unwelcome side effects. The research shows that there is a balance to be struck between obtaining crime prevention benefits and causing an unintended and detrimental impact on the look and character of the town centre. The findings are important in their own right because they add an empirical dimension to a longstanding debate about the relative importance which should be attached to the benefits of improved security against the costs of environmental degradation. The subsequent discussion is extended to include a review of the safety and security implications of urban regeneration and renewal.

Use and effectiveness of security shutters

Town-centre managers were first asked to estimate the proportion of retail outlets which had and used security shutters (Table 10.1). Four in ten managers thought that more than one-quarter of outlets had shutters (41%) and nearly one in three managers estimated that more than one-half of the outlets had shutters (30%). Even allowing for the fact that managers could only be expected to offer a rough approximation of their use, security shutters would appear to be a widely-used town-centre security option.

Table 10.1 Managers' estimates of shops with shutters in town centres

Percentage of shops with shutters	Number	Per cent
0–25	16	59.3
26–50	3	11.1
51–75	4	14.8
76–100	4	14.8
Total	27	100.0

No doubt the best judges of the effectiveness of security shutters would be the retailers who use them, but it is also reasonable to suppose that town-centre managers are in a position to offer an informed view. They were asked to estimate how effective security shutters were in preventing attacks against retail outlets (Table 10.2). Although a minority of one in five managers thought that they were ineffective (20%) and nearly as many supposed that they were neither effective nor ineffective (17%), a majority of six in ten managers thought that they were very effective or effective (63%). Of the town-centre managers who indicated that shutters were effective most held this view strongly:

> I know this seems old fashioned, but there's nothing like a good strong grille to give off the message 'You can't get in' ... which is true.

> Shutters are unlikely to put off the more professional burglar, but they do stop the late night attacks by opportunist thieves – people on their way home, often drunk.

Table 10.2 Managers' perceptions of the effectiveness of shutters in preventing attacks on shops

Effectiveness	Number	Per cent
Very effective/Effective	22	62.9
Neither effective nor ineffective	6	17.1
Ineffective/Very ineffective	7	20.0
Total	35	100.0

Images of security shutters

The shoppers and the managers agreed that security shutters had an adverse effect on the look or image of the shopping environment (Tables 10.3 and 10.4). Both sets of respondents were given an opportunity to comment in their own words.

Table 10.3 The public's views on security shutters in town centres

Views	Number	Per cent
Ugly but necessary	180	57.9
Look ugly	69	22.2
Bad for town's image	28	9.0
Don't notice	34	10.9
Total	311	100.0

Table 10.4 The managers' views on security shutters in town centres

Views	Number	Per cent
Unwelcoming appearance	13	54.2
Creates a climate of fear	7	29.2
Prevents window shopping	1	4.1
Combination of the above	3	12.5
Total	24	100.0

Among the nine in ten members of the public who noticed security shutters, there was a unanimous view that they detracted from the appearance of the town centre. They were deemed to be ugly (22%) or bad for the town's image (9%) or were seen as both an ugly feature of the town centre but a necessary one (58%). Town-centre managers also offered the very clear view that shutters had a detrimental effect on the look of the town centre. All the comments were negative. More specifically, over one-half criticised them on the grounds of their having an unwelcoming appearance (54%), whilst a further 29 per cent said that their presence created a climate of fear. As some town-centre managers put it:

Shutters give the impression it is a high crime risk area, not least because they present a dead frontage at night.

They reinforce negative feelings of desolation and fear of crime, leading almost to a siege mentality. Shutters seriously hinder attempts to provide a welcoming environment in the town centre out of shopping hours.

Shutters create the impression of a closed city with no vitality. They are oppressive and produce a culture of fear.

Solid external shutters give the town a fortress-like appearance which can be very threatening. Internal grilles allow light from the shop windows to spill onto the street and permit window shopping.

Solid steel shutters give a hostile appearance and ... encourage fly-posting and graffiti. The see-through type is preferable.

External shutters are visually unattractive and send out the wrong messages about levels of crime.

They drain life, colour and light from the city centre at night.

Aesthetics and security

There was considerable agreement between managers and the public with regard to both the effectiveness and the aesthetic impact of security shutters. The majority of managers thought that they were effective in preventing crime, but that they had a substantial negative effect on the appearance of the town centre. The majority of the public thought that shutters were necessary but ugly. The aesthetics of commercial premises in British high streets, including shopfronts and shutters, have a long history. The post-1960s trend in retail design in favour of large expanses of plate glass, together with an increase in standardised corporate images for multiple stores, has led retailers themselves to acknowledge that this contributes to 'the sense of indeterminate squalor in many British streets' (Shopfront Security Group, 1994). The Royal Fine Art Commission has also pointed to the:

> ... lack of relationship between most shopfronts and the buildings in which they are set ... The visual chaos caused by the insertion of shopfronts, unrelated both to the buildings which house them and the street to which they should contribute, is in every high street for all to see.
> (quoted in Shopfront Security Group, 1994: 7; see Mitchell, 1986)

It would appear that security shutters could only have the effect of making a bad situation worse. The earliest shopfront shutters were made of wood and were lifted into position and removed at the beginning and end of the trading period. Iron roller shutters date from about 1840. These were commonplace until the late nineteenth century when the spread of professional policing and street lighting gradually reduced the need for them. In recent years they have reappeared to meet the perceived need for improved shopfront physical security. Using British Retail Consortium (BRC) figures for 1992, the Shopfront Security Group (1994) found that over one-third of the shops surveyed (36%) had some form of shuttering. Of the outlets with shutters, roughly one-third had internal door or window shutters and two-thirds external door or window shutters. Of those premises with external door shutters, 80 per cent were of the roller shutter design and three-quarters of these were rollers with solid horizontal slats. Of those premises with external shutters on the windows, 78 per cent were of the roller shutter design and three-quarters of these were rollers with solid horizontal slats. Shutters were widely used and tended to be of the solid, roller shutter type.

The fitting of shutters appears to be fully justified. The same BRC survey found that there had been over 4,000 'frontal' attacks on premises in a 12-month period – giving a ratio of almost one attack for every three shops nationwide. The replacement of damaged or broken glass alone, excluding the costs of boarding-up and the consequential effects on trade, can cost around £500 for a single sheet window – a direct cost to the retailer (Shopfront Security Group, 1994). In addition, with a clear-up rate of only 20 per cent, those who attack shops in this way can expect to get away with it. This is the view within the retail industry:

> ... regrettably the experience of many retailers is that the police response is often slow; offenders are rarely caught; if they are, the sentences are not heavy enough to act as a deterrent.
> (David Sieff, BRC Security Conference, 26th October, 1992)

The present study would appear to suggest that the perceived need and the presumed effectiveness of shutters outweighs any aesthetic reservations. Shoppers seem to be fatalistically resigned to the use of security shutters. It was certainly the case that the public did not reject their use in principle. But it was equally clear that any adverse aesthetic impact on the shopping environment could be lessened by greater attention to design – so as to minimise any brutalisation of the high street. The town-centre managers were even more critical, but this may reflect the earlier finding that they accord a rather low priority to security. Overall, the managers tended to the view that, however effective shutters might be in preventing crime, they also blighted the retail environment by, ironically, making it appear more crime-prone. It is interesting to note, however, that the Design Council was advocating the use of shutters in the late 1970s, specifically of the lockable grille type, as a primary mechanism for combating vandalism to shops – with no comment about any adverse environmental impact (Sykes, 1979).

The views of the town-centre managers and the shopping public on security shutters are a mirror image of a critique made by the Shopfront Security Group (1994). One general criticism is that no matter how functional shutters may be, they are 'unattractive and intrusive'; and, when a number of solid shutters are installed in the same area, they can create a 'hostile environment' and can convey a 'message that the area is prone to crime'. This may have the effect of encouraging crime. It is even more likely that the siege-like presence of shutters will discourage the general public from entering such areas, and so any security benefits would be forfeited. There was a feeling among town-centre managers in the current study that a decidedly negative image could give rise to what has previously been called avoidance behaviour. Solid shutters also provide a blank surface which acts as an invitation to vandalism through graffiti – which, in turn, adds to the impression that an area is vulnerable. In September 1995 the shadow home secretary, Jack Straw, pointed to the need to reclaim the high streets for law-abiding citizens. A major part of the indictment related directly to the shopping public, security shutters and graffiti;

> Walking down a street should be the most straightforward of pleasures, for ... window shopping ... Yet ... physically, the street scene in many areas has been brutalised. Window shopping is no longer a possibility as many steel shutters have replaced windows. Graffiti ... 'adorns' much street furniture ... [and] it is often violent and uncontrolled in its ... image, and correctly gives the impression of a lack of order on the streets.
>
> (quoted in Travis, 1995b: *The Guardian*, 5th September)

The Shopfront Security Group (1994) also holds that in practice too many security shutters are 'wholly inappropriate' to the building in which they are installed. Many are out of character with the building as a whole and appear to be 'tacked-on afterthoughts' – which in many cases is just what they are. The scale of shutters is often inappropriate, particularly when they obliterate the whole of the ground floor facade. The texture and colour of many plain or highly polished metal finishes are frequently at odds with the more textured finishes of masonry and timber. And solid shutters have a 'deadening effect' in that they remove interest and visual stimulation at the pedestrian level. They prevent would-be shoppers from window shopping outside of business hours – which can have a detrimental impact on trade at a time when retailers are having to fight hard to increase custom.

Despite these reservations about shutters being unattractive and intrusive and creating a hostile environment, the near-unanimous view of both shoppers and managers in the present study was that their installation provides an effective defence against crime. There is empirical support for this view. In a small-scale study of 38 small businesses over a 12-month period prior to the installation of shutters the businesses suffered some 265 attacks or 6.9 incidents each on average. In a 12-month period following a security upgrade, including the installation of security shutters, there were only 80 attacks or 2.1 incidents on average per business. The introduction of security shutters brought a 70 per cent drop in the number of attacks (Tilley, 1993b). And a 1991–93 study of 130 electrical stores from three national chains, all of which traded in both high streets and out-of-town retail parks, found that there had been 123 ram-raid attacks between July 1991 and June 1993 – an average of nearly one attack per store in two years. The average cost was £4,500 – stock losses of £1,400 and repairs of structural damage costing £3,100 (Jacques, 1994). A more detailed investigation of six out-of-town superstores compared all burglary losses before and after the installation of security shutters. The six stores spent £50,700 on shutters or £8,400 per store on average. This compares with the Shopfront Security Group (1994) estimate that the average cost of installing shutters in 1992 was £4,000 per retail outlet. In the pre-installation phase (period not given) total losses were £125,400 or £20,900 per store on average. In the post-installation phase (six to 12 months afterwards) total losses were £57,700 or £9,600 per store. Jacques found that the introduction of security shutters reduced the average burglary loss by £11,300 or 54 per cent. Electrical stores are known to be at risk, particularly those in out-of-town locations (Burrows and Speed, 1994), but the introduction of security shutters would appear to reduce loss at around the 50 per cent level. The cost of installing shutters would be covered by the savings made within one year.

The 'mixed' findings suggest that there is a need to strike a balance between the security benefits derived from the use of shutters and any adverse effects of a more general kind. For example, a town centre which was shuttered and secured comprehensively (the Fort Knox approach to safe shopping through physical impregnability) would have undoubted crime control benefits, but these would be purchased at the expense of taking something important away from the ambience of the town centre. Such crime prevention measures would lead to certain retailers being safer, but shoppers would not necessarily end up feeling safer. The paradox here is that designing-out crime may mean designing-in anxiety; which, in extreme cases, could lead to an increase in town-centre crime.

Unintended consequences

Some studies suggest that a degradation of the physical environment is a cause of increased criminal activity (Ward, 1973; Kelling, 1986; Kinsey, Lea and Young, 1986; Maxfield, 1987). The more an area looks down-at-heel and unattractive, the more likely it is that nuisance-type offences will occur, possibly in the forms of litter, graffiti and other vandalism. An area can give the impression that no-one is exercising control or taking responsibility for it and this can lead to progressive damage (Wilson, 1979). A run-down environment may then attract the urban dispossessed, including drunks, beggars and vagrants. Street-scene offenders will also be attracted to urban blight and decay, including drug traffickers. And, to the extent that security shutters invite graffiti and other unlicensed use of shop-front surfaces, there is an increased possibility that the shadowy and often illegal business of fly-posting could increase (Brearley et al, undated; Foster, 1994b).

The use of security shutters falls clearly into the category of preventing crime by means of 'target hardening' – that is, by raising the coefficient of physical security and by making premises as impregnable as possible. The placing of barriers between prospective offenders and their targets is seen as a deterrent, especially to the more opportunistic offender, but this may not operate in the way that is intended. One possibility is that the physical fortification of shop fronts displaces crime from protected premises to unprotected targets. This would make the retailer who could not afford protection that much more vulnerable.

There is also circumstantial evidence of displacement in terms of type of crime rather than from one area to another. One of the six electrical superstores studied in detail by Jacques (1994) offers strong evidence of this. In the pre-installation phase the store suffered losses of over £33,000, rising to nearly £57,000 after installation. This rise was accounted for by a single burglary to the value of £50,000 where the roof of the building was penetrated. Protecting one part of a store may make another more likely to be attacked. Although the evidence of displacement occurring is limited, the potential is clear. An attractive retail target which is secured at the front by means of a grille or shutter will remain tempting and the committed criminal may simply seek entry at the point of next least resistance. Another possibility is that the installation of shutters could precipitate even more violent attacks on the property. Stanley Kalms, chairman of the Dixons Group, has warned of the 'increasing violence' associated with ram-raids against retail outlets as opposed to 'smash and grab' intrusions (Chairman's Report, Dixons AGM, 1993). As the coefficient of physical security increases, so too could the propensity of the offender to use ever-increasing violence.

The BRC retail crime survey estimated that ram-raids comprised 3 per cent of retail burglaries in 1992–93 – a total of nearly 18,000 such attacks in the year (Burrows and Speed, 1994). Such attacks are now seen as serious offences. The Court of Appeal has recently likened ram-raiding to a kind of military operation, a new-style robbery involving the breaking down of part of a building. The case of *R* v *Rothery and Others* involved a stolen JCB being driven into the wall of a bank in order to enable an automated telling machine to be stolen and the court held that such an attack was 'an affront to a civilised society and an outrageous offence' (*The Times*, 19th May, 1994). The gravity of the offence was seen to lie in its composite character – the theft of vehicles prior to the attack; the planning and purposefulness of the operation; the way in which it was aimed to defeat even the best security; the amount of damage done; and the element of breach of the peace, where honest people were both woken up and frightened.

It is also the case that the more brutally direct the attack on property, the more likely it is that shopkeepers, sales staff, security guards and innocent bystanders will be caught up in the incident and exposed to danger (Macdonald, 1994). Increasing attention is being paid to the problem of violent attacks on staff in the retail sector, including services for victims (Thompson, 1995). One recent study conducted for a major fashion retailer with multiple town-centre and shopping-centre outlets found that the one-year prevalence rate for physical assault was 11 per cent or that one in nine staff could expect to be attacked during the course of a working year. Two-thirds of the victims were attacked by an offender in a group of two or more, and one in three suffered some form of physical injury. The majority of incidents were related to shop theft (Beck et al, 1994). It is possible that some offenders who had been deterred from breaking into stores at night (possibly because of the level of physical protection, including shutters) had subsequently adapted their modus operandi, entering stores by day, when there were no physical barriers, in order to steal in a blatantly uncouth, predatory and intimidating manner – and ready to resort to violence if discovered and challenged. This puts sales staff even more at risk because previous research has shown that, in general, where workers handle money and where they have frequent contacts with the public the risks to them are substantial (Mayhew et al, 1989).

Engineered solutions

The crucial question is whether it is possible to have effective physical security without any of the aesthetic or displacement-type drawbacks. The current study provides some evidence that fortress-like shutters can be avoided; planning regulations can be used to prevent the use of shutters altogether, or to stipulate that they must conform to certain specifications (for example, be open-mesh and transparent) in certain locations – for example, historic town centres and conservation areas. Here a delicate balance of interests has to be struck between the retailers' need for maximum physical protection and the justifiable concern of the planning authorities to prevent the character of the area being blighted. Informal comments from town-centre managers indicated a substantial gulf between the two parties. They felt that the planning authorities were all too ready to see all shutters as being of the fortress type which led to restrictions that the managers condemned as 'bureaucratic interference'. This polarisation of views is not helpful.

The way forward is to recognise that there is a balance to be struck between the right of retailers and town-centre managers to improve physical security and the planners' responsibility to preserve the social and architectural character of an area – such as the historic towns of Poole and Cheltenham which have placed restrictions on the use of solid shutters and external grilles (Blackman, 1991). Both parties must recognise the other's legitimate interests. There is also a need to accept the retailers' commitment to floor-to-ceiling glazing as crucial to maximising sales. Stallrisers (which can reduce the window area by as much as 20 percent), vertical mullions and horizontal glazing bars all reduce the visibility of goods on display. This points towards the need for shutters. The next step is to recognise that ugly, solid curtain shutters of galvanised steel epitomise all that is wrong with physical security:

> Such shutters are a blot on the character of a town. They prevent light being transmitted from shop windows. They hinder police surveillance. They destroy the visual appeal of buildings.
>
> (Harris, 1992: 24)

The present study confirms and corroborates this indictment. There is little that can be said in defence of what one town-centre manager referred to as the 'Alcatraz shutter' – the heavy galvanised version. Other managers pointed out that more often than not this type of shutter can be levered from the wall easily or pushed into a window by a ram-raider; that shutters were difficult to operate manually and prone to operational faults; that they acted as something of a magnet to graffiti 'artists'; and that they prevented goods from remaining on display when stores were shut.

The final step is to acknowledge that engineered solutions can offer the highest level of physical protection together with an acceptable and aesthetically pleasing appearance. The way forward is through the use of lighter-weight aluminium roller shutters, with brickbond designs that allow through visibility with or without glazing to the punched apertures in each lath section. Bespoke installations are possible so as not to spoil the historic features of a listed building or the profile of a parade of shops. Nothing is sacrificed in terms of strength of protection. It is possible to insert stainless steel stranded cables with a breaking load of two tonnes through the hollow bodies of selected laths. These are particularly effective against ram-raids because they extend and absorb the force of impact so bringing the vehicle to a halt progressively. They are also resistant to sawing and levering. Such products are available and can ease or eliminate the conflict between the environmental aspirations of planning authorities and the retailers' need for physical security (Harris, 1992).

The solid flat lath shutter and the industrial solid curved lath shutter, usually to be found in galvanised steel or mill-finished aluminium, have probably had their day – and need to be replaced by the punched lath shutter (with a series of slots to allow some visibility), the perforated lath shutter (which creates the illusion that there is no physical barrier, if there is sufficient backlighting) and the polycarbonate panel shutter (which offers excellent vision). Progress has been made in setting performance standards for shutters in the European CEN Technical Committee (TC33). Its draft standards, which can be used as a proxy until the final decisions are made, were adopted in October 1993 by the Loss Prevention Certification Board as the basis for its scheme for testing, approving and classifying the resistance of doors, windows, shutters and grilles to attack by burglars (Shopfront Security Group, 1994). And for internal security in shops armoured glass screens are now available which can be made to go blank and opaque at the touch of a button – a huge security version of the liquid crystal screens used in pocket calculators (Partridge, 1995). This conjures up the possibility that the shutters of the future could be made of attack-proof glass which allow goods on the inside of the store to be seen and may even show product images to the passing public. The scope for technological development which combines security with marketing is enormous.

The critical variable in moving towards engineered solutions is not likely to be technical because the planner-friendly options are increasingly available; it is more likely to lie in changing the culture of antipathy – even hostility – between the retailers (and town-centre managers) and the planners. Conflict is wasteful and time-consuming. Both parties will have to accept that there is a trade-off between improved physical security and aesthetic factors. It is not a question of one or the other, but of finding an appropriate balance between competing and conflicting (but not irreconcilable) demands. The onus is on the manufacturers to find the technological answers to the planners' misgivings, but there is an equal obligation on the planners to accept what is feasible and realistic. There is a certain elasticity built into the concept of 'material alteration' to a shop front and room for latitude in its application. This is less so in conservation areas where local planners are required in law to have special regard to the preservation or enhancement of such areas. And it is even less true where a shop is contained within a building which is listed as being of architectural or historic interest, where listed building consent is required in addition to planning permission. If some sort of compromise or balance is not found, there is always the chance that the retailer who cannot protect his stock and premises will take the business to an area where adequate physical protection can be achieved – which is scarcely in the best interests of the local community and its economy.

A 1994 circular from the Department of the Environment, *Planning and Crime Prevention*, acknowledges that these tensions exist and suggests practical ways to find an acceptable trade-off between competing demands. One of its most important features is the presumption that crime prevention efforts can be seen as material considerations in planning applications. This puts security considerably higher on the planners' list of priorities. The circular also accepts that planning can make a contribution to crime control, especially when local authorities take the lead in co-ordinating area-based crime initiatives, with financial support from retailers. In effect, local planners are encouraged to incorporate crime prevention policies in their planning, and to do so on a multi-agency basis – which includes taking the security priorities of retailers into account. The section on security shutters urges local authorities to adopt a sympathetic approach to the needs of applicants and to seek mutually acceptable solutions; and then suggests that shutters which would let light through to the street outside of trading hours, and which would be relatively unobtrusive at other times, may be a material consideration in determining a planning application. The circular is very much in line with the thinking of the Shopfront Security Group (1994) which recognises that local authorities are in an ideal position to take the lead in confronting the problems of creating town centres with attractive retail facilities without ignoring the legitimate interests of the retailers in proper physical security for their stores. The group also acknowledges the role of town centre management in promoting the twin interests of the town and retailers' security.

Reclaiming town centres and natural surveillance

The British Urban Regeneration Association (BURA), with over 500 members from central and local government, private sector companies and voluntary organisations, takes a lead role in promoting town and city centres, as does the Association of Town Centre Management. Both are concerned to reverse what has been called the 'erosion of civic culture' by the brutalisation of the high street (Gardner and Sheppard, 1989). The Department of the Environment's Urban and Economic Development Group is also taking an interest with a recent report on regeneration which places a significant part of the blame on institutional planning inertia (1994; and see McKie, 1995). Striking a balance between protecting shops and other commercial premises adequately and meeting the aesthetic aspirations of the planning authorities is clearly relevant to the broader issue of town-centre regeneration. The concentration of effort on ground-level physical protection is only a small part of town-centre security which, in turn, is only one component of the town-centre environment. Other factors, seemingly not directly related to shop security, may prove to be important – not to the point of obviating the need for security shutters, but as supplementing physical protection to the advantage of both the retailers and the community as a whole.

The Shopfront Security Group (1994), backed by retailers, insurers and MPs and launched in January 1994 with the support of the Home Secretary, in part campaigns to stimulate interest in the crime control benefits of helping to re-populate town centres by persuading retailers to let empty flats above their shops (Travis, 1994c). Flats over shops, many built 50 to 100 years ago, have become empty because retailers prefer to live away from their business or because they were taken over by retail chains whose managers tended to have their own homes. Modern retail premises are rarely used for storage since retailers carry less and less stock but have it delivered as and when required from central or regional distribution centres. The campaign suggests that there are 'tens of thousands of empty flats above shops' and that were these to be occupied, there would be benefits both to the retailers and to the wider town-centre community. There are also indications that many town-centre office blocks, the 'dinosaurs' of post-war urban planning, are becoming redundant as companies seek relocation to purpose-built accommodation rather than face the enormous costs of on-site redevelopment. It is estimated that there are over two million sq ft of empty commercial premises in London alone; and with the introduction of favourable planning regulations and the abolition of VAT on refurbishing buildings, many of these could be converted for residential use. The conversion of offices for so-called 'loft living' (Bellos, 1995) is seen as a major factor in urban renewal.

A government-sponsored Living Over the Shops (LOTS) scheme is designed to make use of empty office space above shops and offices in town centres. Since 1990, more than £45 million of public funding from the Department of the Environment, housing associations and local authorities has been made available to LOTS schemes (Greenwood, 1995). For example, Newcastle city council identified over 1.7 million sq ft of empty office space in the city centre suitable for regeneration and refurbishment, and the council was awarded £1.5 million over three years to provide residential accommodation. Property is made available through a two-tier leasing arrangement: a commercial lease between the owner and an intermediary (eg a housing association), together with an assured shorthold tenancy agreement between the housing association and the ultimate tenant. Various LOTS schemes are to be found in Brixham, Cardiff, Fleetwood, Halifax, Hartlepool, Leicester and Newcastle – each one showing that there can be a common interest between commercial property owners and those concerned to provide social housing.

Retailers and others benefit from such development because the additional people in and around the town centre offer a degree of 'natural surveillance' over the area, particularly at night when shoppers have left. As residents they overlook commercial premises, and move around the area. Their presence helps to create a feeling of activity not emptiness, and there are grounds for supposing that this in itself leads to increased public confidence in the area (Atkins, 1989). There are three interrelated crime control benefits. First, there is an element of deterrence because would-be offenders know that they might be heard and seen. Secondly, surveillance can increase the chances of crimes being witnessed and then reported rapidly (rather than being discovered the next morning at shop opening times). Thirdly, there is evidence that the less run-down and desolate an area looks, the less likely it is to suffer vandalism and graffiti.

The wider community benefits because tens of thousands of empty flats above shops could provide new and low-cost homes. At a time when there is something of a crisis in public sector housing and little capital investment, any move to increase the total available housing stock would be welcomed by local authorities. This would also go some way to meeting the concerns of the government and the Environment Committee about town-centre population decline. And it could also act as an incentive for inward investment in town centres to cater for the needs of the new residents, especially in the field of leisure activities, which might in turn attract the town-centre commuter back in the evenings.

Street lighting may also have a significant impact on crime in town centres, although most of the published literature deals with lighting on council housing estates. Recent research by a University of Cambridge team found that crime was reduced on a council estate in Staffordshire by as much as one-quarter simply by improving the quality of the street lighting (*The Times*, 1st December, 1994). Better lighting gave muggers, burglars and vandals fewer places to hide; and it also increased the confidence of residents. The same logic could be applied to town centres. The image of crime is strongly associated with murky and shadowy places and it is not unreasonable to suppose that 'lighting up' may drive crime down. Interestingly, the most significant reductions were in those types of crime with which town centres seem most afflicted – vehicle crime (-37%), vandalism (-39%), disorderly behaviour (-48%) and violent crime (-65%). To the extent that the town centres become re-populated the residents will demand and get decent lighting to meet their needs as citizens – so the additional benefits in crime control will come as a bonus. One recent commentary, relating to city-centre management in Nottingham, enthusiastically endorses the benefits of lighting for urban renewal:

> Changes in ... street lighting ... can increase people's sense of 'defensible space', increase the range of surveillance and affect 'territoriality'. All of these factors can influence the ... immediate environment, enhance security and deter offenders.
>
> (Brearley et al, undated: 6)

Earlier evidence on the effects of improved street lighting on crime rates and the fear of crime is more equivocal. Studies carried out in London by Painter (1988, 1989a, 1989b and 1991) generally reported dramatic reductions in criminal victimisation. Five research studies, organised by the

British Parliamentary Lighting Group and carried out simultaneously in 1990 and 1991 (Glasgow Crime Survey Team, 1991; Barr and Lawes, 1991; Herbert and Moore, 1991; Davidson and Goodey, 1991; Burden and Murphy, 1991) all showed that improved lighting reduced fear amongst the affected population, particularly for women and the elderly. In contrast, a major study by Atkins et al (1991) in Wandsworth, on the relighting of the whole borough, found no evidence of reduced crime and little evidence of a general abatement of fear, except among women walking alone after dark. Even where there have been positive results, the studies have been criticised for the very short follow-up periods (usually six weeks), which allowed the immediate impact to be registered but not the so-called 'taper-off' effect over time (Ramsay, 1991). A Glasgow study, with a 12-month interval before and after street lighting improvements, found that there was little or no behavioural change (Nair et al, 1993). Indeed, more respondents felt a bit or very unsafe at home – a rise from 11 per cent to 18 per cent. Local feelings of safety failed to respond to a significant investment in improved lighting. The evidence does not unequivocally endorse the effectiveness of the 'pure white light' solution to town-centre crime in the long term, although it could be the case that in conjunction with other measures it helps to improve users' perceptions of an area and to lessen the fear of crime (Ramsay, 1991).

Another significant factor could be the December 1994 decision to abolish the legal restrictions on high-street opening hours. Under legislation dating from 1950 shops were required to close by 8.00 pm with an option to stay open until 9.00 pm on one weekday evening. All shopkeepers are now able to set their own opening hours. To the extent that they extend them this can only prolong the period when shoppers themselves can offer natural surveillance over town-centre stores. In the 1994 Christmas trading period at least one major supermarket (Asda) experimented with this option and others, like Tesco and J. Sainsbury, are likely to follow suit (Gilchrist, 1995d). Spar, the country's largest convenience store chain, has instituted 24-hour trading in 50 of its 2,200 outlets and expects the number to increase. This form of security is predicated on numbers of people simply being around who, at the same time as they are going about their lawful business (shopping or leisure, for example), are also in a position to notice anything untoward – and to report it as necessary. John Gummer, the environment secretary, is strongly supportive of these developments, primarily on the grounds of revitalising town centres rather than because of any collateral crime control benefits:

I have always advocated 24-hour town centres. They must be places to live, work and play – not just for shopping.

(quoted in Brown, 1994: *The Guardian*, 13th December)

The more that town centres are 'opened up' outside of normal trading hours and the greater the throughput of persons on an around-the-clock basis, the greater the bonus of a zero-cost contribution to security. In effect, the shopper becomes the 'eyes and ears' of both private security and public policing. However, the more security shutters retain their forbidding presence, the more reluctant the would-be late-night shopper or leisure maker will be to take advantage of the new opportunities. This offers another paradox. Although physical impregnability offers one solution to out-of-hours crime, the solution itself militates against another crime control option – the watchful presence of customers and service users late into the evening or through the night.

11   Conclusion

The purpose of this final chapter is to summarise the major findings of the study and to draw out the implications for retail security management. There is no intention to be heavily prescriptive, not least because the authors have no professional responsibilities for managing retail environments. But it has been emphasised throughout that a central objective of the study was to generate data which could have practical implications. Security professionals and town-centre and shopping-centre managers may choose not to accept the conclusions; but in any case they should be in a position to make more informed judgements about how best to promote safe shopping.

In order to make this final contribution as accessible as possible the summary data are pared to a minimum and the commentary makes no further reference to the available literature which is detailed in the earlier chapters. It can be read either as an end-piece which brings together the findings and analysis, or it can be seen as an introductory preview – something to be explored first as a means of directing attention to the substantive chapters.

Risk, fear and avoidance behaviour

The data on these three themes need to be looked at together. Each has implications for the others. It is important to note first that the rates of criminal victimisation were relatively low in both shopping environments – 6 per cent in town centres and one per cent in shopping centres. However, any rate of victimisation is unacceptable. Even though the small number of incidents makes comparisons difficult, there were six times as many victims in town centres as in shopping centres. There was also substantial evidence that shoppers were genuinely alarmed by the crime and nuisance threats to safe shopping. One-quarter or more were worried or concerned about possible criminal victimisation whilst shopping in either location but more so in town centres (28%) than in shopping centres (22%). The same differential between the two shopping environments was apparent with regard to shoppers' perceptions of the seriousness of the crime and nuisance problems likely to be encountered. Taking all categories of crime, nuisance and pollution, three times as many town-centre shoppers as shopping-centre visitors rated the problems very serious or serious. The only crime or nuisance problem of significance for shopping-centre visitors was that of kids hanging around (24%).

As with most previous studies which relate fear of crime to the risk of victimisation, the level of worry was far greater than the chances of becoming a victim. It would be most unwise, however, to ignore the degree of concern expressed because it does not mirror the real risk. Perceived risk is strongly associated with what has been termed 'avoidance behaviour' – changes in the pattern of shopping behaviour as customers elect not to visit those areas they deem to be unsafe. Nearly three times as many shoppers in town centres (13%) said that they 'avoided' certain places because of the fear of crime as in shopping centres (5%). This finding confirms that a perceived lack of security can have an adverse impact on shopping behaviour. Nearly one in seven town-centre shoppers said that they did not visit certain places, although fear of crime was not the only reason. Many respondents pointed to unwelcome behaviour, especially from persons in groups deemed to be troublemakers or from drunks.

Moreover, while it could be claimed that the two samples of shoppers were giving expression to standardised popular concepts of the crime and nuisance threats to shoppers, all their anxieties were reflected by town-centre and shopping-centre managers – persons clearly in a position to know with some degree of accuracy both the extent and the nature of the various threats. It seems prudent to take what the managers said at face value. Three times as many town-centre managers as shopping-centre managers thought that crime, nuisance and pollution were everyday occurrences. Six times as many town-centre managers (25%) as shopping-centre managers (4%) thought that crime was commonplace. And nearly two-thirds of the town-centre managers (64%) and one-half of the shopping-centre managers (47%) pointed to criminal behaviour as their most serious problem. The seriousness of motor vehicle crime was highlighted by both but there was a significant undercurrent of feeling about the gravity of physical assaults, drunkenness and drug-related criminality.

There was a striking congruence between the views of the shoppers and those of the managers. Shoppers and managers saw the problems of crime and nuisance in near-identical terms. With regard to 'all problems', more than three times more town-centre shoppers (37%) viewed crime and nuisance as a serious problem than did shopping-centre respondents (11%). And three times more town-centre managers (30%) viewed crime and nuisance as endemic than did shopping-centre managers (10%). From both perspectives, the crime and nuisance threats to safe shopping appeared to be far greater in town centres than in shopping centres. And in both environments the perceived risks were positively correlated with avoidance behaviour. Shoppers who had felt themselves to be at risk said that they had taken their custom elsewhere.

Implications

These findings have major implications for town-centre managers and shopping-centre managers. The former need to face the uncomfortable truth that a minority of their customers, like they themselves, perceive town centres to be blighted by both crime and nuisance. The latter can take some comfort from the finding that the only problem in shopping centres as compared with town centres was that of kids hanging around. On all the major indices the town centre was more troubled by crime and nuisance than the shopping centre. Although the study was focused on customers' and managers' perceptions of the various threats to safe shopping, there is substantial indirect evidence of real problems. These require further study.

One way to proceed would be to look in detail at the hard indicators of crime and nuisance, including offences reported to the police and those recorded by retailers and their security staff – and to do so on a comparative basis for the two retail environments. There are difficulties with this approach. They include the lack of correspondence between police sub-divisions and large retail areas such as town centres and even less of a 'fit' with smaller areas, such as a shopping centre. There are also problems with the quality of official retail crime figures, especially the way they are coded by the police. And they tend to be incomplete. Where there is a disinclination to report incidents on the part of the shopping public, or where there is a shortfall in the recording of reported incidents by managers, security staff or the police, the figures can only indicate the minimum extent of the problem. A great deal of the less serious crime and much of the nuisance-type behaviour would not find its way into formal crime figures – so the value of any such study would be limited. The best available indicators would probably be police data for town centres, and for shopping centres possibly information held by security staff.

Another option would be to conduct a victimisation survey of shoppers but, given the infrequency of serious crime, this would need to cover a large number of shoppers. The current data confirm the need to explore more thoroughly the extent to which shoppers are victims. Such studies would need to focus on the types of offence (crime, nuisance and pollution), where and when victimisation took place and the effects on the victims. Any future survey should also investigate further the relationship between the fear of crime and avoidance behaviour. Given the infrequency of actual victimisation and the direct impact of avoidance behaviour on sales and profits, the retail community may think that the fear of crime is a more important variable than the crime itself.

Motor-vehicle crime is an area of interest in its own right. It was highlighted by both groups of managers, but was seen as the single most serious crime problem by far more town-centre managers (39%) than shopping-centre managers (18%). More dramatically, where well over one-half of town-centre managers saw car crime as a daily occurrence, only 2 per cent of shopping-centre managers thought of it as an everyday event. Given the importance of the motor vehicle as the primary means by which shoppers put themselves in a position to shop, more attention needs to be given to crime directed against it. Many shopping-centre managers suggested that safe car parking should be looked upon as part of the overall service to shoppers and as something on a par with the retail environment itself. This seems eminently sensible.

A substantial and near-equal minority of town-centre managers (14%) and shopping-centre managers (12%) identified public drunkenness as their single most pressing problem; but there was a marked difference in its perceived frequency. Where only one in twenty shopping-centre managers considered that drunkenness was an everyday problem, as many as one-third of the town-centre managers thought that it was – a six-fold differential. The use of byelaws to restrict public drinking may offer one remedy, although the data on the Coventry experience are equivocal. The chronic skid-row drinker is unlikely to pay much attention to the law and the authorities may not give enforcement a high priority.

The same misgivings apply to the regulation of violent behaviour when it is drink-related. A small minority of managers took the view that violent crime was their most serious problem – 4 per cent of town-centre managers and 7 per cent of shopping-centre managers. Members of the shopping public were slightly more concerned in shopping centres (8%) and much more concerned in town centres (28%). These anxieties were reflected in the victimisation data. One-half or more of the incidents in town centres and shopping centres involved physical assault or robbery. Given the serious nature of these offences there is a need for proactive policing targeted on predatory street crimes. More work also needs to be done on the relationship between violent crime and the abuse of drug and other substances, about which there was a strong undercurrent of anxiety. A significant minority of town-centre managers (7%) and shopping-centre managers (11%) identified drug-related offences as their single most serious problem; and many more town-centre managers (12%) thought that these were an everyday occurrence than did shopping-centre managers (3%) – a four-fold differential. Further work is needed to explore the relationship between the use of drugs and other crimes. Does it lead to non-violent shop thefts or burglaries, or is it associated with predatory acts of violence? Or is the street-scene 'junkie' no more than an unsavoury eyesore?

Among all the crime and nuisance problems there was only one about which shopping-centre managers had a greater concern than town-centre managers. Over one-quarter of shopping-centre managers identified threatening youths as their single most serious problem, compared with just 4 per cent of town-centre managers. The most likely explanation for this is that the same features which attract shoppers to mall-type environments also act as a magnet for groups of youths who see 'hanging around' as a pleasurable end in itself. Shopping-centre managers have a clear legal right to refuse access to or to move on these groups, but it would be interesting to explore more fully the grounds on which they exercise a discretion and the criteria they use. The comments from managers suggest that they employ lay persons' stereotypes of 'undesirable' appearance and behaviour. And their decisions are not open to challenge. There are clear grounds for concern about the unfettered exercise of discretion in this area, even though banning is both legal and, in the eyes of shopping-centre managers, highly effective. No such remedy is available to town-centre managers.

Existing security measures: an audit

The investigation of existing security measures took the form of various comparisons between the two retail environments, including an assessment of the types and extent of measures in use (security personnel, including police officers and security guards on patrol; security equipment, such as CCTV; and involvement in Watch-type schemes). This was complemented by comments from managers on the effectiveness of the various measures. Customers were also asked which options they noticed and whether or not they found them to be acceptable. Nearly all town-centre managers pointed to police officers on patrol (97%) as the most prominent security measure. The majority of shoppers were aware of this feature of the retail environment (82%) and thought that it was highly acceptable (97%). Nearly all shopping-centre managers highlighted private security guards as the most prominent security option (90%) and saw them to be effective (85%). The majority of shoppers were aware of this feature of the retail environment (84%) and thought that this was highly acceptable (92%).

Implications

The most important finding to emerge from the audit of security measures in use was the contrast between the use of publicly-funded police officers in town centres and privately-funded security guards in shopping centres. Initially, this appeared to be only what might have been expected. It was assumed that there would be a stronger private security presence in shopping centres than in town centres, and that conventional policing would be more apparent in town centres. However, it was surprising to find that on all four variables (for the managers on use and effectiveness and for the public on awareness and acceptability) the distribution of responses was almost identical – the only difference being that the data referred to public policing in the case of town centres and to private security in the case of shopping centres. The findings indicate that in shopping centres a significant degree of privatisation of policing has already taken place, and that it commands the support of both the shopping-centre managers and the public. The bobby on the beat may still patrol the town centre but he or she has been superseded by the private security guard in the shopping mall; and both offer the presence of officers in uniform which the public finds reassuring.

There is a certain irony here. The Home Office is currently exploring the proper balance in policing between core and ancillary tasks, with the unstated underlying premise that the public may have to provide for themselves what has been a public service. And the House of Commons Select Committee on Home Affairs has opened a debate on the regulation of the private security industry. In both cases the intention is to explore options for the future, but what both must realise is that in one significant part of the national economy the debate has already been settled and private security has largely replaced public policing. The importance of this cannot be overstated. The retail sector employs nearly 10 per cent of the national workforce and has a turnover of around £150 billion a year. The private security industry is estimated to have a total turnover of nearly £3 billion a year, of which one-third is accounted for by some 80,000 security guards – about one-half the number of police officers. Major changes have taken place in one part of the retail environment – and done so without debate or scrutiny. The use of private security guards in shopping centres could be used as a case study in the privatisation of policing, and there could be wider implications for the more general balance between public policing and private security. What is not in doubt is that significant privatisation of policing in part of the retail sector has already taken place and has done so with the overwhelming approval of the interested parties.

The Select Committee on Home Affairs was concerned primarily with the regulation of the manned guarding sector of the private security industry. The discussion and evidence have tended to focus on the poor image of small companies employing rather untrustworthy personnel, sometimes with criminal records. The disparaging phrase 'one man, a dog and a van' recurs constantly. This is almost certainly unfair to the companies used for shopping-centre security, which are likely to come from the small number of big firms with established reputations. Further work is required on the size and activities of retail-oriented security firms, including the provision of in-house and contract guarding services. There is some danger that misgivings about security outfits of dubious standing could be unwarrantably applied to companies operating in the retail sector. The present study found no lack of confidence in private security companies operating in shopping centres. In fact private security guards in shopping malls received as strong a vote of confidence as did bobbies on the beat in town centres.

The bulk of submissions to the Home Affairs Committee were in favour of control – most often by way of some form of statutory licensing and inspection. The report duly recommended the establishment of an agency to vet and license potential employees in the contract manned guarding sector; together with a further recommendation for a national scheme to license security companies offering contract guarding services. It seems likely that the former will be accepted and implemented to allay fears about 'cowboy' operators, although the government is still inclined to the view that market forces alone could dictate the proper balance between need, provision and cost. It seems inevitable that manned security services will expand to around 150,000 employees by the turn of the century (equalling the number of police officers). And it seems highly likely that the provision of services will be determined by the ability of firms to minimise threats to profit at an acceptable cost, rather than by following public sector policing standards of responsibility and accountability.

A major consequence of expanding private security provision is that the larger and more prosperous retailers will be able to buy-in these services whilst smaller businesses will not. This will have the effect of increasing differentials in security cover. The critical variable will be the ability to pay for security rather than the need for protection. This gives some grounds for concern but, given that public sector policing has seemingly never been given a particularly high priority in the shopping environment (and that it looks certain to become an even more marginal or ancillary task), it can also be argued that 'some' private security provision is better than 'little or no' police protection.

The conspicuous and large-scale presence of uniformed security guards in shopping centres certainly requires more detailed investigation. The starting point would be to explore in greater depth the views of the shopping public about security guards in order to elicit precisely what they see as being beneficial – their deterrent and reassuring presence or their ability to detect and apprehend offenders or their role in dealing with incivilities. There is also a need to interview the guards themselves in order to discover how they see their role. The expectations of the public and the way guards see their job may not coincide. Thirdly, there is a need to undertake an analysis of what it is that guards actually do in the course of a working day, including liaison with the police, and to assess to what extent their activities contribute directly to the protection of the shopping public. Particular attention should be given to the exercise of discretion in banning known or suspected troublemakers.

Managers' priorities

The exploration of management's own priorities offered some of the strongest data of the whole study – and made possible a fascinating comparison between threats to safe shopping and the priority given to minimising those threats. In relation to all the major indicators of crime and nuisance, both the shopping public and managers agreed that town centres had substantially more problems than did shopping centres. Rather surprisingly, it was the shopping-centre managers who highlighted the importance of promoting a crime-free and nuisance-free shopping environment, whilst their colleagues in town centres accorded a higher priority to promoting business and trade. Town-centre managers saw their role principally in terms of the development of the town in commercial terms (68%), whilst the security of shoppers was much less emphasised. In shopping centres this position was reversed. Shopping-centre managers saw their role as giving priority to the security of their customers and to the security of the shopping centre (54%), with less emphasis being put on commercial development.

Implications

Town-centre managers had far more crime and nuisance problems than their counterparts in shopping centres and yet they gave security a low priority, whilst shopping-centre managers suffered from fewer problems but gave security a very high priority. The combination of 'high crime' and 'low security' for town-centre managers is an unfortunate conjunction and in need of remedy. The Association of Town Centre Management's own research into its performance made a bad situation worse by providing clear data on shoppers' and retailers' concerns about crime and violence in a major report, but then failing to take these findings into account in the overall conclusions. This is not good research practice and nor is it in the interests of developing TCM initiatives.

Town-centre managers will need to look carefully at the security-related components of their job specifications and to consider whether they should not be given a higher priority. The Association will need to accept that 'owning the problem' is the first step towards resolving their difficulties. The crime and nuisance findings in this study may assist in this process, as may the data on the low priority given to the shopping public's security by town-centre managers. The fundamental misconception would appear to be that security is somehow divorced from the commercial well-being of town centres. On the contrary, to the extent that shoppers avoid those environments which they perceive to be unsafe, security is a precondition for commercial success. One way to reverse the so-called 'spiral of decline' in town centres is to attract back those shoppers who have taken their custom to locations which appear less prone to crime and nuisance. This makes security a top priority rather than a secondary concern. The Association and its town-centre managers will also need to look at the ways in which action against crime and nuisance can be co-ordinated. Retailers as well as local authorities and others with commercial interests in town centres will have to be prepared to fund any new-style, safe-shopping strategies. It is unrealistic to expect town-centre managers to deal with a problem without an adequate budget.

The House of Commons Environment Committee acknowledged that the need was urgent, but there is little prospect of significant government funding for core ATCM activities. At least in the short term, TCM initiatives are likely to continue to rely on the generous support of a limited number of major companies. The Association would be well advised, however, to pay heed to its own research findings that there is a marked reluctance on the part of companies to commit resources unless there are clear goals and quantifiable performance indicators. Continued support from major retailers, such as Boots and Marks & Spencer, should not be seen as acts of altruism. These companies are investing so as to protect their own commercial interests in the high street, not least in avoiding the spiral of decline and the possible dereliction of their trading area. But they would be well advised to make clear that they are not ready to fund vague aspirations relating to town-centre development, but insist on focused initiatives where there is a return on their investment. If the ATCM elects not to give town-centre safety and security a higher priority then the major retailers may use their 'funding muscle' to compel them to do so. To some extent this would be a pity because it would confirm that the ATCM had rather abrogated its responsibilities in the area of town-centre safety. It would be more in line with the declared purposes of the Association if it recognised the need and then orchestrated the efforts to meet that need.

Closed circuit television

The use of CCTV received a ringing 'vote of confidence' in both locations from shoppers and managers. It was being used in more than three-quarters of the shopping environments; and where it was in operation, about two-thirds of the town-centre managers (65%) and of the shopping-centre managers (70%) agreed that it was being used extensively. Between 50 per cent and 60 per cent of the public were aware of its presence. Rather more than eight in ten managers in both shopping environments deemed CCTV to be effective. Finally, more than 90 per cent of the shopping public found surveillance cameras in the shopping environment acceptable. The national picture reflects this confidence. The 'rise and rise' of CCTV has resulted in a market of around £300 million a year and annual growth of up to 14 per cent. The government is keen to promote its use; it has eased planning requirements, issued guidelines for the use of CCTV and is providing 50 per cent of the cost of some installations. Television surveillance now takes place in one-third of public places in London and in nearly one-half of metropolitan and non-metropolitan areas outside London. Many of these systems are located in high streets and therefore relate directly to the security of the shopping public. A 20-camera system with pan, tilt and zoom units connected to a central control room, such as the one in Liverpool, can cost in excess of £300,000 to install; and the annual cost of manning such systems will be anything between £15,000 and £200,000, although the figures for operating costs seem far from reliable.

Implications

The installation of CCTV systems is frequently accompanied by hyper-bolic claims for its capacity to 'cut crime'. Most of these claims do not reflect proper standards of evaluation; all too often they are made by people with an interest in the success of the project in question. They are mostly based on percentage changes, often derived from very low base rates, and they rarely include the raw figures. Little or no attempt is made to acquire the statistical data needed for a reliable 'before and after' comparison. And only limited information is made available on the capital costs of installations, and less still on recurrent expenditure. At present it is not possible to make informed judgements about the effectiveness of CCTV; even the Home Office guide recognises that high-quality data are in 'short supply', although it is determinedly optimistic about the potential of closed circuit television.

The explanation for this state of affairs is simply that almost everyone has been seduced by CCTV's 'promise' of comprehensive crime control in a neat, high-technology package – an off-the-shelf, state-of-the-art, electronic panacea for crime. It receives such ringing endorsements primarily because people wish to believe that it offers unparalleled crime control benefits, a phenomenon which has been termed 'security wish fulfilment'. However genuinely these beliefs may be held, they are no substitute for rigorous and independent evaluation. This will have to take into account a number of factors. Simplistic assertions such as that 'CCTV cuts car crime by 60 per cent' are not acceptable.

First, it is necessary to distinguish between the capability of CCTV to help in the detection of offenders and its capacity to deter would-be offenders. Rarely are these purposes made explicit. If the emphasis is on detection this points to the use of manned CCTV systems which monitor events in real time so as to permit an immediate response; or the use of video images to confront apprehended suspects and facilitate confessions. If the emphasis is on deterrence this points to minimal systems, possibly using only dummy cameras, but with prominent signs so as to maximise their impact. Detection and deterrence are not mutually exclusive goals, although in both cases any measurable crime control benefits would need to be set against the possibility of displacing crime away from CCTV-covered areas to unprotected areas.

Secondly, and paradoxically, the technological sophistication of CCTV systems generates difficulties. A standard 32-camera system will put out nearly one billion images in a week. Quite apart from the quality of these images, it is inconceivable that shop staff (including hard-pressed managers) or security personnel can review such a staggering amount of data. Even in cases where they know what they are looking for and are aware of the date and approximate time of an incident, there are enormous logistical problems in trawling through 'miles and miles' of tape. Problems arise too if operators are used to monitor video images in real time, especially if a single member of staff has responsibility for watching between 30 and 40 screens simultaneously, as is not uncommon. Almost nothing is known about the nature of the cues which lead operators to decide that something may be amiss, and there are uncertainties about how long operators can concentrate on a screen or screens before so-called 'video blindness' occurs. Manned systems are expensive enough to start with, but they are all the more costly if operators fail to notice significant events.

Thirdly, to the extent that CCTV does provide a 'high-tech fix' for the problems of crime and nuisance, there are very different implications for shop staff and for customers. If sales staff believe that protection is being provided by the cameras, there is less incentive for them to see themselves as having a security function. There is a danger that the more the cameras are 'switched on' the more they will be tempted to 'switch off' and leave security to the hardware and its operators. As far as customers are concerned, what matters is that they should believe that CCTV brings genuine crime-control benefits. Given the relatively low levels of actual victimisation, especially in shopping centres, the belief in the effectiveness of CCTV may be as important as, if not more important than, its actual contribution to detection or deterrence. It becomes a potent symbol which may in itself raise customer confidence in the shopping environment above the level where misgivings give rise to avoidance behaviour. The current data certainly suggest that customer confidence in CCTV is extremely high.

Finally, although there was little evidence of serious misgivings about the use of CCTV, the potential for abuse clearly exists. This includes covert surveillance of staff and its being used by management to monitor compliance with company procedures rather than to target dishonesty; and misuse by operators directed at staff or customers. There are also fears that video images could be used for purposes other than the security of shoppers, including even blackmail. Although there is some pressure for applying 'codes of conduct', these would not have the force of law; nor are they receiving much publicity. Once again, CCTV is being largely taken on trust.

Security shutters

The case study of the use of security shutters highlighted the tension which arises between the valid desire of retailers to achieve the highest possible degree of physical protection and the need to avoid physical changes which have a negative impact on the appearance and character of a town centre. There was considerable agreement between managers and the public with regard to the effectiveness of shutters and their aesthetic impact. The majority of managers thought that they were effective in preventing crime, but that they had a substantial and detrimental effect on the look of the town centre. The majority of the public thought that shutters were necessary but ugly. Both felt that the perceived need and the presumed effectiveness outweighed any aesthetic reservations.

Implications

It is difficult to deny that retailers have a right to improve the physical defences of their premises; and the evidence from this study confirms that shutters offer effective security. It is also difficult to reject the argument of the planners that they have an obligation (and statutory authority) to protect town-centre environments. But neither, left to their own devices, have the answer to the problems of the town centre: the impregnable 'Fort Knox' town centre is profoundly unattractive, to the detriment of trade and business, and could even be crime-inviting; and the aesthetically perfect town centre, with beautifully proportioned but unprotected shop fronts, would be likely to be blighted by burglary, again to the detriment of trade. Both sides must accept that there is a rational and feasible trade-off somewhere between these two extremes; and there are some encouraging signs.

The Shopfront Security Group has argued cogently that some forms of solid shutters are effective but unacceptable and that aesthetic considerations are important; and that modern designs can be both more effective and more sightly than older designs. And a 1994 circular from the Department of the Environment underlines that crime prevention should be treated as a material consideration when planning applications are considered. These are small but significant indications of the search for the middle ground. This should not be seen as a move towards an unsatisfactory compromise; rather it is a genuine attempt to reconcile competing interests. Finally, the Association of Town Centre Management could claim a major role for itself as a mediator in the process of working out a satisfactory balance between the physical protection afforded by shutters and any detrimental side-effects.

Postscript

This volume has attempted to review major themes in retail security, with a particular emphasis on the safety of shoppers in town centres and shopping malls. There is no simple statement which can be used to summarise the findings in areas as diverse as the fear of crime and avoidance behaviour, the use and regulation of private security guards and the uncritical rise and rise of closed circuit television. Nor is there a simple statement which can be used to summarise the crime and risk management implications for town-centre and shopping-centre managers. There is, however, a strong 'linking logic': it lies in demonstrating the various needs for security in shopping and in pointing to some of the ways in which these needs may be met. As an exercise in applied research, hopefully with real-life implications for improved security risk management in shopping environments, perhaps it is appropriate to let a manager have the last word:

> Security means safety; safety means shoppers; and shoppers mean profits. It's a simple equation.

References

Ahuja, A. (1994) 'Gummer Turns Down Superstore', *The Times*, 5th November.

APEX (1991) *Contract Security Industry 1991: Wages and Conditions Survey*, London: APEX Partnership.

Arlidge, J. (1994) 'Welcome, Big Brother', *The Independent*, 2nd November.

Armstrong, G. and Hobbs, D. (1994) 'Tackled From Behind', in Giulianotti, R., Bonney, N. and Hepworth, M. (eds) *Football, Violence and Social Identity*, London: Routledge, pp. 196–228.

Ashworth, J. (1994) 'City Security Ring Becomes Cast in Stone', *The Times*, 29th November.

Association of Chief Police Officers (1994) 'ACPO Submission to the Home Affairs Select Committee Inquiry Into the Private Security Industry', London: ACPO Crime Committee Sub-Committee on Crime Prevention.

Association of District Councils (1994) 'Evidence to the House of Commons Select Committee on Home Affairs: Inquiry Into the Private Security Industry', London: Association of District Councils.

Association of Metropolitan Authorities (1994) 'Evidence to the House of Commons Select Committee on Home Affairs Inquiry Into the Private Security Industry', London: Association of Metropolitan Authorities.

Association of Town Centre Management (1994) *An Introduction to Town Centre Management*, London: Association of Town Centre Management.

Atkins, S. (1989) *Critical Paths: Designing for Secure Travel*, London: The Design Council.

Atkins, S. (1991) 'The Importance of Passenger Security', Southampton: University of Southampton, Department of Civil Engineering.

Atkins, S., Husain, S. and Storey, A. (1991) *The Influence of Street Lighting on Crime and the Fear of Crime, Crime Prevention Unit Series Paper 28*, London: Home Office.

Audit Commission (1993) *Helping With Enquiries: Tackling Crime Effectively*, London: HMSO.

Audit Commission (1994) *Local Authority Performance Indicators, Volume 3, Police and Fire Services*, London: HMSO.

Bagnall, S. (1995a) 'Sainsbury Unwilling to Step Up Price War', *The Times*, 11th May.

Bagnall, S. (1995b) 'Sainsbury Pours £20 Million Into Courtesy Crusade', *The Times*, 16th June.

Bagnall, S. (1995c) 'Too Many Retailers Woo the Can-Buy, Won't-Buy Shopper', *The Times*, 16th June.

Bamfield, J. (1994) *National Survey of Retail Theft and Security 1994*, Northampton: Nene College, School of Business.

Barker, M., Geraghty, J., Webb, B. and Key, T. (1993) *The Prevention of Street Robbery, Crime Prevention Unit Series Paper 44*, London: Home Office.

Barr, R. and Lawes, H. (1991) *Towards a Better Monsall: Street Lighting as a Factor in Community Safety – The Manchester Experience*, Manchester: University of Manchester (mimeo).

Bassett, P. (1994) 'High Street Sales Fall For the First Time in Two Years', *The Times*, 15th November.

Bassett, P. (1995) 'High Street Sales Show Sharp Fall, Says CBI', *The Times*, 14th February.

Baumer, T. and Rosenbaum, D. (1982) 'Fear of Crime: An Empirical Clarification of a Major Problem', paper presented at the Annual Meeting of the American Psychological Association, Washington, DC, August.

Beck, A. and Willis, A. (1992) *An Evaluation of Store Security and Closed Circuit Television*, Leicester: University of Leicester, Centre for the Study of Public Order.

Beck, A. and Willis, A. (1993a) *The Terrorist Threat to Safe Shopping*, Leicester: University of Leicester, Centre for the Study of Public Order.

Beck, A. and Willis, A. (1993b) 'Fear of Bombings Pushes Shoppers Out of Town', *Financial Times*, 28th July.

Beck, A. and Willis, A. (1994a) 'The Changing Face of Terrorism: Implications for the Retail Sector', in Gill, M. (ed) *Crime at Work: Studies in Security and Crime Prevention*, Leicester: Perpetuity Press, pp. 139–154.

Beck, A. and Willis, A. (1994b) 'Customer and Staff Perceptions of the Role of Closed Circuit Television in Retail Security', in Gill, M. (ed) *Crime at Work: Studies in Security and Crime Prevention*, Leicester: Perpetuity Press, pp. 185–201.

Beck, A. and Willis, A. (1995) *Security Hardware Trial: Volumes 1–4*, Leicester: University of Leicester, Centre for the Study of Public Order.

Beck, A., Gill, M. and Willis, A. (1994) 'Violence in Retailing: Physical and Verbal Victimisation of Staff', in Gill, M. (ed) *Crime at Work: Studies in Security and Crime Prevention*, Leicester: Perpetuity Press, pp. 83–101.

Bell, S. (1992) 'Crime Time in the High Street', *The Sunday Times*, 20th December.

Bellos, A. (1995) 'Obsolete Office Blocks Start New Life as Lofts', *The Guardian*, 10th April.

Bennett, T. (1994) 'Community Policing on the Ground: Developments in Britain', in Rosenbaum, D. (ed) *The Challenge of Community Policing*, London: Sage, pp. 224–246.

Bennetto, J. (1995) 'Cowboy Security Firms Face Vetting', *The Independent*, 8th June.

Benyon, J., Morris, S., Toye, M., Willis, A. and Beck, A. (1995) *Police Forces in the New European Union: A Conspectus*, Leicester: University of Leicester, Centre for the Study of Public Order.

Benyon, J., Willis, A., Beck, A. and Morris, S. (1994) *Police Forces in the European Union: A Summary*, Leicester: University of Leicester, Centre for the Study of Public Order.

Bernoth, A. (1994a) 'Discounters Fall Victim to Their Own Price War', *The Sunday Times*, 31st July.

Bernoth, A. (1994b) 'Wal-Mart Sets Sights on UK', *The Sunday Times*, 13th November.

Bernoth, A. (1994c) 'German Discounter Takes on Sainsbury', *The Sunday Times*, 27th November.

Bernoth, A. (1995a) 'Tesco Ousts Rival as Top Grocer', *The Sunday Times*, 9th April.

Bernoth, A. (1995b) 'Sainsbury Ponders Loyalty Scheme', *The Sunday Times*, 18th June.

Berrington, L. and Ford, R. (1994) 'Woolworths Killer Had Grabbed Cash in Four Robberies', *The Times*, 5th November.

Beyleveld, D. (1979) 'Deterrence Research as a Basis for Deterrence Policies', *Howard Journal*, Vol. 18, No. 3, pp. 135–149.

Blackman, N. (1991) 'Ram Raiding – A Retail Crisis?', *Security Industry*, December, pp. 27–28.

Blair, I. (1994) 'Let the Police Fund Their Own Expansion', *The Times*, 1st October.

Bottoms, A. and Wiles, P. (1994) 'Crime and Insecurity in the City', paper presented at the International Course organised by the International Society of Criminology, Lueven, Belgium, May; forthcoming in Fijnaut, C. (ed) *Proceedings of International Course*.

Box, S., Hale, C. and Andrews, G. (1988) 'Explaining Fear of Crime', *The British Journal of Criminology*, Vol. 28, No. 3, pp. 340–356.

Brearley, N., Francis, P. and Matthews, R. (undated) *Nottingham City Centre Management: Community Safety Action Plan*, Leicester: University of Leicester, Centre for the Study of Public Order.

British Council of Shopping Centres (1987) *Managing the Shopping Environment of the Future*, Reading: Centre for Advanced Land Use Studies.

British Council of Shopping Centres (1993a) *British Council of Shopping Centres: Handbook*, Reading: Centre for Advanced Land Use Studies.

British Council of Shopping Centres (1993b) 'Guidance Note 12 Managing Security in Shopping Centre Car Parks', Reading: Centre for Advanced Land Use Studies.

British Council of Shopping Centres (1993c) 'Guidance Note 14 Use of Closed Circuit Television in Shopping Centres', Reading: Centre for Advanced Land Use Studies.

British Retail Consortium (1995) 'Evidence to the House of Commons Select Committee on Home Affairs: Security Industry – Standards, Certification and Regulation', London: British Retail Consortium.

British Security Industry Association (BSIA) (1994a) 'Regulation of the Security Industry', Worcester: The British Security Industry Association.

British Security Industry Association (BSIA) (1994b) 'Evidence to Home Affairs Committee, October 1994', Worcester: The British Security Industry Association.

Broadbent, D. (1958) *Perception and Communication*, London: Pergamon Press.

Brown, P. (1994) 'Gummer Pledge to Halt Spread of Shopping Malls', *The Guardian*, 13th December.

Brown, P. (1995) 'Gummer Plan to Revive Town Centres', *The Guardian*, 23rd February.

Bulos, M. (1994) 'Neighbourhood Watch', *Local Government Chronicle*, 20th May, pp. 22–23.

Burden, T. and Murphy, L. (1991) *Street Lighting, Community Safety and the Local Environment*, Leeds: Leeds Polytechnic (mimeo).

Burne, J. (1994) 'Caught in the Act', *The Times Magazine*, 16th July.

Burrell, I. and Levy, A. (1995) 'Police Target Gangsters in Local Councils', *The Sunday Times*, 14th May.

Burrows, J. (1980) 'Closed Circuit Television and Crime on the London Underground' in Clarke, R. and Mayhew, P. (eds) *Designing Out Crime*, London: HMSO, pp. 75–83.

Burrows, J. (1993) 'The Impact of Crime on the Retail Business', paper presented to the 15th CALUS Shopping Centre Management Conference, Oxford, 1st–3rd September.

Burrows, J. and Speed, M. (1994) *Retail Crime Costs 1992/93 Survey*, London: British Retail Consortium.

Button, M. and George, B. (1994) 'Why Some Organisations Prefer In-House to Contract Security Staff', in Gill, M. (ed) *Crime at Work: Studies in Security and Crime Prevention*, Leicester: Perpetuity Press, pp. 209–223.

Byrne, C. and Bernoth, A. (1995) 'Irish Store Strike Turns Nasty as Sainsbury Looks On', *The Sunday Times*, 25th June.

Cahill, M. (1994) *The New Social Policy*, Oxford: Blackwell.

Campbell, D. (1994) 'Police Chief Warns of Two Tier System', *The Guardian*, 10th January.

Campbell, D. (1995) 'Spy Cameras Become Part of Landscape', *The Guardian*, 30th January.

Carr, G. (1992) 'Flexible Friend', *Security Management Today*, Vol. 2, No. 4, pp. 20–22.

Casson, J. (1994) 'Evidence to the House of Commons Select Committee on Home Affairs', Kingsbridge, Devon: Securewest (UK).

Causer, D. (1994) 'Bulger – The Full Picture', *Security Industry*, April, pp. 51–52.

CCTV Manufacturers and Distributors Association (1994) 'Mission Statement', New Eltham, London: CCTV Manufacturers and Distributors Association.

Clark, M. (1994) 'Share Prices Suffer as Supermarket War Grows', *The Times*, 2nd December.

Clarke, R. and Hough, M. (1980) *The Effectiveness of Policing*, Farnborough: Gower.

Clarke, R. and Hough, M. (1984) *Crime and Police Effectiveness, Home Office Research Study No. 79*, London: HMSO.

Cohen, N. (1994) 'Tories Let Security Firms Off Lightly', *Independent on Sunday*, 11th December.

Cohen, S. (1983) 'Social Control Talk: Telling Stories About Correctional Change', in Garland, D. and Young, P. (eds) *The Power to Punish*: London: Heinemann, pp. 101–129.

Collett, B. (1995) 'Small Firms Skimping on Security Measures', *The Times*, 20th June.

Cooper, G. (1994) 'Big Brother's Blind Spot', *Independent on Sunday*, 10th July.

Cornish, D. and Clarke, R. (eds) (1986) *The Reasoning Criminal: Rational Choice Perspectives on Offending*, New York: Springer-Verlag.

Cowe, R. (1995a) 'Loyalty Cards Brings Tesco Neck-and-Neck With Rival', *The Guardian*, 12th April.

Cowe, R. (1995b) 'M&S Moves Into Germany and China', *The Guardian*, 28th March.

Crossley, J. and Murray, I. (1993) 'Town Centres Count Cost as Shoppers Opt for Superstores', *The Times*, 8th November.

Davidson, N. and Goodey, J. (1991) *Street Lighting and Crime: The Hull Project*, Hull: University of Hull (mimeo).

Davies, S. (1994) 'They've Got an Eye on You', *The Independent*, 2nd November.

Department of Education (1991) 'Closed Circuit TV Surveillance Systems in Educational Buildings', *Building Bulletin 75*, London: HMSO.

Department of the Environment (1994) 'Planning Out Crime Circular 5/94', London: Department of the Environment.

Department of the Environment – Urban and Economic Development Group (URBED) (1994) *Vital and Viable Town Centres: Meeting the Challenge*, London: HMSO.

Distributive Trades Economic Development Committee (1988) *The Future of the High Street*, London: HMSO.

Dolan, L. and Sivell, G. (1995) 'Supermarkets Shape Up as Food Price Fighters', *The Times*, 10th January.

Donaldsons and Healey & Baker (1994) *Association of Town Centre Management Research Study 1994: The Effectiveness of Town Centre Management*, London: Association of Town Centre Management.

Doran, M. (1992) 'Video Evidence Comes of Age', *Security Management Today*, Vol. 2, No. 4, pp. 24–26.

Drury, I. (1992) 'Car Park Owners Under Pressure to Raise Standards', *Security Industry*, October p.10.

Drury, I. (1993) 'Candid Cameras', *Security Industry*, May, pp. 15–19.

Duce, R. (1995) 'Robbers Cut Women's Hands in Bid For Safe Keys', *The Times*, 18th February.

Dundec Contracts Limited (1994) 'Multi Storey Car Parks and the Shopping Centre', Mitcham, Surrey: Dundec Contracts Limited.

Durham, P. (1995) 'Villains in the Frame', *Police Review*, 20th January, pp. 20–21.

Dutta, R. and Ford, R. (1994) 'Howard to Reject Council Police', *The Times*, 25th August.

Edwards, P. and Tilley, N. (1994) *Closed Circuit Television: Looking Out for You*, London: Home Office.

Ekblom, P. (1986) *The Prevention of Shop Theft: An Approach Through Crime Analysis, Crime Prevention Unit Series Paper 5*, London: Home Office.

Ekblom, P. and Simon, F. (1988) *Crime Prevention and Racial Harassment in Asian-Run Small Shops: The Scope for Prevention, Crime Prevention Unit Series Paper 15*, London: Home Office.

Ellam, D. (1994) 'Guarding Against Hidden Evil', *Birmingham Post*, 5th December.

Erlichman, J. (1995) 'Long Journeys Typify Waste of Out-of-Town Superstores', *The Guardian*, 10th January.

Ezard, J. (1994) 'Ipswich Thought of it First', *The Guardian*, 13th December.

Fennell, E. (1995) 'Lawyers Set Store by Shops', *The Times*, 14th February.

Fishman, R. (1993) *Bourgeois Utopias: The Rise and Fall of Suburbia*, New York: Basic Books.

Ford, Richard. (1994a) 'Fear of Crime Rises Rapidly Despite Tough Tory Words', *The Times*, 21st March.

Ford, Richard. (1994b) 'Police Cut Crime Rate But Rape and Robbery Rise', *The Times*, 20th April.

Ford, Richard. (1994c) 'Police Face Cut in Ancillary Duties', *The Times*, 26th October.

Ford, Richard (1994d) 'Small–Town Focus For Spy Cameras', *The Times*, 19th October.

Ford, Richard (1995a) 'Rid Our Streets of the Beggars and Addicts, Says Straw', *The Times*, 6th September.

Ford, Richard (1995b) 'Home Office Study Urges Sell-Off of 26 Police Tasks', *The Times*, 28th June.

Ford, Richard (1995c) 'Middle-Class Areas Should Pay For Anti-Crime Schemes', *The Times*, 10th May.

Ford, Roger (1994) 'The Liverpool City Centre Installation', *CCTV Today*, Vol. 1, No. 3, pp. 12–13.

Forrester, D., Chatterton, M. and Pease, K. (1988) *The Kirkholt Burglary Prevention Project, Rochdale, Home Office Crime Prevention Unit Series Paper 13*, London: Home Office.

Forum of Private Business (1995) *Crime and Small Business*, Knutsford, Cheshire: Forum of Private Business.

Foster, J. (1994a) 'Anti-Crime Cameras Could Miss the Action', *The Independent*, 6th July.

Foster, J. (1994b) 'Murder Linked to Battle for Fly-Posting Sites', *The Independent*, 4th May.

Frean, A. (1994) 'Shoplifting Insight Tops TV Ratings', *The Times*, 18th February.

Gardner, C. and Sheppard, J. (1989) *Consuming Passion: The Rise of Retail Culture*, London: Unwin Hyman.

General Accident (1994) 'Insurance Discounts For CCTV', *CCTV Today*, Vol. 1, No. 3, p.3.

George, B. and Button, M. (1994) 'The Need for Regulation of the Private Security Industry: A Submission to the House of Commons Home Affairs Select Committee', London: House of Commons.

Gibbons, S. (1994) 'Private Insecurity', *Police Review*, 9th December, pp. 16–17.

Gibbons, S. (1995) 'Buy Your Own Police Scheme Set to Get Backing of Chiefs', *Police Review*, 3rd March, p.5.

Gilchrist, S. (1994) 'M&S Fashions Aggressive Expansion', *The Times*, 9th November.

Gilchrist, S. (1995a) 'Discount Scheme Launched by Tesco', *The Times*, 11th February.

Gilchrist, S. (1995b) 'Service Takes Over From Price as New Retail Battleground', *The Times*, 24th February.

Gilchrist, S. (1995c) 'In For a Penny – In For Seven Billion Pounds', *The Times*, 8th April.

Gilchrist, S. (1995d) 'Shop Till You Drop – Around the Clock', *The Times*, 4th January.

Gill, M. (1994) 'Introducing Crime at Work', in Gill, M. (ed) *Crime at Work: Studies in Security and Crime Prevention*, Leicester: Perpetuity Press, pp. 1–10.

Glasgow Crime Survey Team (1991) *Street Lighting and Crime: The Strathclyde Twin Site Study*, Glasgow: University of Glasgow, Criminology Research Unit.

Glaskin, M. (1995) 'Detector Frisks From a Distance', *The Sunday Times*, 26th February.

Gledhill, R. and Wilkinson, P. (1995) 'Church Sells Giant Shopping Centre to Ease Cash Crisis', *The Times*, 8th February.

Gottfredson, M. (1984) *Victims of Crime: The Dimensions of Risk, Home Office Research Study No. 81*, London: HMSO.

Greenwood, L. (1995) 'Gem Above the Jeweller's Shop', *The Times*, 13th May.

Greig, G. (1994) 'Confessions of a Cured Shopaholic', *The Sunday Times,* 13th November.

Grigsby, J. (1994) 'Shopping For Tenants', *The Times*, 27th October.

Grigsby, J. (1995a) 'The Battle to Save the High Streets', *The Times*, 27th June.

Grigsby, J. (1995b) 'How to Manage the High Street', *The Times*, 27th June.

Groombridge, N. and Murji, K. (1994) 'As Easy as AB and CCTV', *Policing*, Vol. 10, No. 4, pp. 283–290.

Guy, C. (1994) The Retail Development Process, London: Routledge.

Hamilton, K. and Bernoth, A. (1994) 'Sainsbury Joins Tough Guys in Takeover Aisle', *The Sunday Times*, 31st July.

Harlow, J. (1995) 'Car Thieves Put Audi Uber Alles', *The Sunday Times*, 7th April.

Harris, D. (1994) 'Private Companies Cannot Go Unchecked', *The Times*, 16th February.

Harris, S. (1992) 'Shopping For Shutters', *Security Management Today*, Vol. 2, No. 8, pp. 24–25.

Hawkes, N. (1994) 'Drug Cure Offers Breakthrough For Shopping Addicts', *The Times*, 10th November.

Hawkes, N. (1995a) 'The Shopper Always Turns Right', *The Times*, 18th February.

Hawkes, N. (1995b) 'Barclays Opens First Mall on the Internet', *The Times*, 3rd June.

Heal, K. and Laycock, G. (1988) 'The Development of Crime Prevention: Issues and Limitations', in Hope, T. and Shaw, M. (eds) *Communities and Crime Reduction*, London: HMSO, pp. 236–245.

Heal, K., Tarling, R. and Burrows, J. (1985) *Policing Today*, London: HMSO.

Hearnden, K. (1994) *The Use and Management of Closed Circuit Television in Small Businesses: A Research Survey*, Loughborough: Loughborough University of Technology, Centre for Hazard & Risk Management.

Hennessey, S. (1994) 'Long Lens of the Law', *The Independent*, 6th July.

Herbert, D. and Moore, L. (1991) *Street Lighting and Crime: The Cardiff Project*, Swansea: University College of Swansea (mimeo).

Hibberd, M. and Shapland, J. (1993) *Violent Crime in Small Shops*, London: Police Foundation.

Hinde, S. (1995) 'Retail Giants Rout Cut-Price Rivals', *The Sunday Times*, 25th June.

Hobson, R. (1994) 'Keeping an Eye on Security', *The Times*, 16th February.

Hobson, R. (1995) 'New Life For Traditional Shops', *The Times*, 27th June.

Hollinger, R. (1992) *National Retail Security Survey – Final Report*, University of Florida: Department of Sociology.

Hollinger, R. (1993) *National Retail Security Survey*, University of Florida: Department of Sociology.

Home Office (1979) *The Private Security Industry: A Discussion Paper*, London: HMSO.

Home Office (1986) *Standing Conference on Crime Prevention Report of the Working Group on Shop Theft*, London: Home Office.

Home Office (1989) *Standing Conference on Crime Prevention Report of the Working Group on Fear of Crime*, London: Home Office.

Home Office (1993a) *Police Reform: A Police Service for the Twenty-First Century*, London: HMSO, Cm 2281.

Home Office (1993b) 'Disclosure of Criminal Records for Employment Vetting Purposes', London: Home Office.

Home Office (1994a) *Criminal Justice Key Statistics England and Wales 1994*, London: Home Office.

Home Office (1994b) *Criminal Statistics England and Wales 1993*, London: HMSO, Cm 2680.

Home Office (1994c) *Review of Police Core and Ancillary Tasks, Interim Report*, London: Home Office.

Home Office (1994d) 'Memorandum of Evidence: Home Affairs Select Committee Inquiry Into the Private Security Industry (HA93/94–319)', London: Home Office.

Home Office (1995a) *Review of Police Core and Ancillary Tasks*, London: HMSO.

Home Office (1995b) *Identity Cards: A Consultation Document*, London: HMSO, CM 2879.

Honess, T. and Charman, E. (1992) *Closed Circuit Television in Public Places: Its Acceptability and Perceived Effectiveness, Crime Prevention Unit Series Paper 35*, London: Home Office.

Horsnell, M. (1993) 'Stores Forced to Use Vigilante Tactics', *The Times*, 30th June.

Hosking, P. (1995) 'Warehouses Full of Bad News For High Streets', *Independent on Sunday*, 26th March.

Hough, M. and Mayhew, P. (1983) *The British Crime Survey: First Report, Home Office Research Study No. 76*, London: HMSO.

Hough, M. and Mayhew, P. (1985) *Taking Account of Crime: Key Findings From the 1984 British Crime Survey, Home Office Research Study No. 86*, London: HMSO.

Houghton, G. (1992) *Car Theft in England and Wales: The Home Office Car Theft Index, Crime Prevention Unit Series Paper 33*, London: Home Office.

House of Commons (1994) *Environment Committee, Session 1993–94, Fourth Report, Shopping Centres and Their Future, Volume I, Report, together with the Proceedings of the Committee relating to the Report*, London: HMSO.

House of Commons (1995a) *Home Affairs Committee, Session 1994–95, First Report, The Private Security Industry, Volume I, Report, together with the Proceedings of the Committee*, London: HMSO.

House of Commons (1995b) *Home Affairs Committee, Session 1994–95, First Report, The Private Security Industry, Volume II, Minutes of Evidence and Appendices*, London: HMSO.

Information Protection & Management Consultants, Hoskyns Group plc (1994–95) 'CCTV: Data Protection in a Surveillance Society', *Data Protection News*, Issue No. 20, Winter 1994/95, pp. 12–18.

Inspectorate of the Security Industry (1994) 'Memorandum of Evidence to the House of Commons Home Affairs Select Committee: Inquiry Into the Private Security Industry', Worcester: Inspectorate of the Security Industry.

International Professional Security Association (1994) 'Evidence to the House of Commons Home Affairs Committee', Paignton: International Professional Security Association.

Jabez, A. (1995) 'Spy Cameras Capture Thieves in the Drive Against Car Crime', *The Sunday Times*, 7th May.

Jacques, C. (1994) 'Ram Raiding: The History, Incidence and Scope for Prevention', in Gill, M. (ed) *Crime at Work: Studies in Security and Crime Prevention*, Leicester: Perpetuity Press, pp. 42–55.

Jenkins, S. (1994a) 'Remember the Alamodome', *The Times*, 19th November.

Jenkins, S. (1994b) 'Home Office Crime', *The Times*, 28th September.

Johnston, L. (1992) *The Rebirth of Private Policing*, London: Routledge.

Johnston, V., Leitner, M., Shapland, J. and Wiles, P. (1994) 'Crime, Business and Policing on Industrial Estates', in Gill, M. (ed) *Crime at Work: Studies in Security and Crime Prevention*, Leicester: Perpetuity Press, pp. 102–123.

Joint Consultative Committee (1990) *Operational Policing Review*, Surbiton, Surrey: Police Staff Associations.

Jones, T. (1995) 'Fear Drives Women to Phone Deals', *The Times*, 21st January.

Jones, T. and Newburn, T. (1994) 'How Big is the Private Security Industry?', London: Policy Studies Institute.

Joseph, J. (1993) 'Welcome to the Pleasure Dome, At a Price', *The Times*, 8th November.

Joseph, J. (1995) 'Take Your Mouse For a Solitary Stroll Down the High Street of the Future', *The Times*, 3rd June.

Kelling, G. (1986) 'Acquiring a Taste For Order: The Community and the Police', *Crime and Delinquency*, Vol. 33, No. 1, pp. 90–102.

Kelly, R. (1993) 'Something to Watch Over You', *The Times*, 12th May.

Kennedy, D. (1994a) 'Giant That Never Got Off the Ground', *The Times*, 8th February.

Kennedy, D. (1994b) 'Knifeman Stabs 15 in Rampage Through Store', *The Times*, 9th December.

Kinsey, R., Lea, J. and Young, J. (1986) *Losing the Fight Against Crime*, Oxford: Blackwell.

KPMG Peat Marwick (1991) *Counting Out Crime: The Nottingham Crime Audit*, Birmingham: KPMG Peat Marwick.

Langley, J. (1994) 'Smash-and-Grabs at Public Car Parks Rise Seven Times', *The Daily Telegraph*, 14th November.

Laycock, G. (1988) 'Towards the Crime Free Car Park', paper presented to the British Parking Association Safer Car Parks conference, London, 17th March.

Laycock, G. and Austin, C. (1992) 'Crime Prevention in Parking Facilities', *Security Journal*, Vol. 3, pp. 154–159.

Leake, C. (1994) 'Store Giants Cry Foul in Out-of Town Shops Battle', *The Mail on Sunday*, 18th December.

Lean, G. (1995) 'Tories Admit: We Killed Market Towns', *Independent on Sunday*, 19th February.

Leathley, A. and Prynn, J. (1994) 'MPs Demand Revival of High Street Shopping', *The Times*, 2nd November.

Leitner, M., Shapland, J. and Wiles, P. (1994) *Drug Usage and Drugs Prevention: The Views and Habits of the General Public*, London: HMSO.

Leppard, D. (1994a) 'Police End Automatic Response to 999 Calls', *The Sunday Times*, 26th June.

Leppard, D. (1994b) 'Howard Pushes for Identity Cards', *The Sunday Times*, 8th May.

Leppard, D. (1994c) 'Rebel IRA Units Threaten New War', *The Sunday Times*, 20th November.

Lightfoot, L. and Leppard, D. (1995) 'Police to Abandon Football Match Duty', *The Sunday Times*, 19th March.

Liverpool City Centre Partnership (1994) 'Closed Circuit Television in Liverpool City Centre: A Partnership Approach to a Safer City', Liverpool: City Centre Partnership.

Lloyd, C. (1995) 'Shopping Revolution Hits Home', *The Sunday Times*, 25th June.

McCrystal, C. (1995) 'To Let: One Market Town', *Independent on Sunday*, 19th February.

Macdonald, M. (1994) 'High Home Security Raises Risk of Attack', *The Independent*, 4th May.

McKie, D. (1995) 'Shopping For a Cure to the Sickness in the High Street', *The Guardian*, 20th February.

Maguire, M., Morgan, R. and Reiner, R. (eds) (1994) *The Oxford Handbook of Criminology*, Oxford: Clarendon Press.

Marketing Strategies for Industry (1994) *CCTV: UK*, Saltney, Chester: Marketing Strategies for Industry.

Matthews, P. (1994) 'Somebody's Watching You', *The Independent*, 29th August.

Maxfield, M. (1984) *Fear of Crime in England and Wales, Home Office Research Study No. 78*, London: HMSO.

Maxfield, M. (1987) *Explaining Fear of Crime: Evidence From the 1984 British Crime Survey, Home Office Research and Planning Unit Paper No. 43*, London: HMSO.

Mayhew, P. (1994) 'Findings from the International Crime Survey', *Home Office Research and Statistics Department Research Findings No. 8*, London: Home Office.

Mayhew, P., Aye Maung, N. and Mirrlees-Black, C. (1993) *The 1992 British Crime Survey, Home Office Research Study No. 132*, London: HMSO.

Mayhew, P., Elliott, D. and Dowds, L. (1989) *The 1988 British Crime Survey, Home Office Research Study No. 111*, London: HMSO.

Mayhew, P., Mirrlees-Black, C. and Aye Maung, N. (1994) *Trends in Crime: Findings From the 1994 British Crime Survey, Home Office Research and Statistics Department Research Findings No. 14*, London: Home Office.

Midgley, S. (1995) 'Long Lens of the Law is Out of Control", *Independent on Sunday*, 26th February.

Mitchell, A. (1995a) 'Rewards For the Loyal Shopper', *The Times*, 15th February.

Mitchell, A. (1995b) 'Battle of the Brands', *The Times*, 7th June.

Mitchell, G. (1986) *Royal Fine Art Commission: Design in the High Street: Report*, London: Architectural Press.

Moore, S. (1994) 'Will the Real PC Plod Please Stand Up?', *The Guardian*, 5th August.

MORI (1994) *'Living in Britain' Survey*, London: MORI.

Morris, P. and Heal, K. (1981) *Crime Control and the Police, Home Office Research Study No. 67*, London: HMSO.

Morris, S. (1994) 'Crunch Time For Camera-Shy City', *Leicester Mercury*, 1st December.

Morse, D. (1994) 'Lightening the Load', *Security Management Today*, Vol. 4, No. 5, pp. 19–20.

Mortished, C. (1994) 'Chelsfield Raise Stake in Merry Hill to 90%', *The Times*, 13th October.

Mortished, C. (1995) 'MetroCentre Sale Nets Church £75m', *The Times*, 7th July.

Murray, I. (1994a) 'Big Insurers Refuse Policies in Red-Lined Inner Cities', *The Times*, 25th March.

Murray, I. (1994b) 'Security Cameras Zoom in on Crime', *The Times*, 6th July.

Murray, I. (1995) 'Sponsored Police Go On the Beat', *The Times*, 2nd May.

Nair, G., Ditton, J. and Phillips, S. (1993) 'Environmental Improvements and the Fear of Crime', *The British Journal of Criminology*, Vol. 33, No. 4. pp. 555–561.

National Approval Council for Security Systems (1994) 'Evidence to the House of Commons Select Committee on Home Affairs: Government Intervention Into the Private Security Industry', Maidenhead: National Approval Council for Security Systems.

Nuttall, N. (1993) 'Camera Focuses on Fleeing Muggers', *The Times*, 24th February.

O'Brien, L. and Harris, F. (1991) *Retailing: Shopping, Space, Society*, London: David Fulton.

O'Keeffe, D. (1993) 'Making Sense of Absence', *The Times*, 15th November.

O'Leary, J. (1994) 'Patten Launches £14m Crackdown on School Truants', *The Times*, 9th February.

Painter, K. (1988) *Lighting and Crime Prevention: The Edmonton Project*, Middlesex Polytechnic (mimeo).

Painter, K. (1989a) *Lighting and Crime Prevention For Community Safety: The Tower Hamlets Study First Report*, Middlesex Polytechnic (mimeo).

Painter, K. (1989b) *Crime Prevention and Public Lighting with Special Focus on Women and Elderly People,* Middlesex Polytechnic (mimeo).

Painter, K. (1991) *An Evaluation of Public Lighting as a Crime Prevention Strategy with Special Focus on Women and Elderly People,* Middlesex Polytechnic (mimeo).

Partridge, C. (1995) 'Putting Raiders in the Dark', *The Times*, 27th January.

Patel, K. (1994) 'Automatic Eye Foils Mob', *The Times Higher*, 9th December.

Pearman, H. (1995) 'The Crest of a Wave', *The Sunday Times*, 2nd April.

Pearson, G. (1983) *Hooligan: A History of Respectable Fears*, London: Macmillan.

Pepinster, C. (1994) 'Rush to Build Out-of-Town Malls', *Independent on Sunday*, 18th December.

Phillips, S. and Cochrane, R. (1988) *Crime and Nuisance in the Shopping Centre: A Case Study in Crime Prevention, Crime Prevention Unit Series Paper 16*, London: Home Office.

Pierce, A. (1994) 'Oxford St Mugger Beats Up Pregnant Shopper', *The Times*, 7th December.

Police Federation of England and Wales (1994a) 'Evidence to the Home Affairs Committee Inquiry Into the Private Security Industry', Surbiton, Surrey: Police Federation of England and Wales.

Police Federation of England and Wales (1994b) 'Federation Views on Private Security Firms: Get Them Under Control', *Police,* November, pp. 21–22

Police Foundation and Policy Studies Institute (1994) *Independent Committee of Inquiry Into the Role and Responsibilities of the Police* (Chairman, Sir John Cassels), London: Police Foundation and Policy Studies Institute.

Police Superintendents' Association of England and Wales (1994) 'Written Submission to the Home Affairs Committee Enquiring Into the Private Security Industry', Police Station, Fort Hill, Margate, Kent: Police Superintendents' Association of England and Wales.

Poole, R. (1991) *Safer Shopping: The Identification of Opportunities for Crime and Disorder in Covered Shopping Centres*, Birmingham: West Midlands Constabulary.

Poole, R. (1994a) *Safer Shopping II: The Identification of Opportunities for Crime and Disorder in Shopping Malls*, Birmingham: West Midlands Constabulary and London: Home Office Police Research Group.

Poole, R. (1994b) *Operation Columbus: Travels in North America – A Personal Journal*, Birmingham: West Midlands Constabulary and London: Home Office Police Research Group.

Pounder, C. (1995) 'Data Protection in a Surveillance Society', *CCTV Today*, Vol. 2, No. 4, pp. 10–11.

Poyner, B and Webb, B. (1987) *Successful Crime Prevention: Case Studies*, London: The Tavistock Institute of Human Relations.

Preston, C. (1995) 'Someone's Watching', *The Guardian*, 22nd March.

Preston, M. (1995) 'Death of the Salesman?', *The Times*, 1st July.

Property Services Agency (1988) *Closed Circuit Television Systems Handbook*, London: Property Services Agency.

Prynn, J. (1994) 'Out-of-Town Consumer Boom Ends', *The Times*, 8th February.

Ramsay, M. (1989) *Downtown Drinkers: The Perceptions and Fears of the Public in a City Centre, Crime Prevention Unit Series Paper 19*, London: Home Office.

Ramsay, M. (1990) *Lagerland Lost? An Experiment in Keeping Drinkers Off the Street in Central Coventry and Elsewhere, Crime Prevention Unit Series Paper 29*, London: Home Office.

Ramsay, M. (1991) *The Effect of Better Street Lighting on Crime and Fear: A Review, Crime Prevention Unit Series Paper 29*, London: Home Office.

Randall, J. (1994) 'High Noon for Britain's High-Street Retailers', *The Sunday Times*, 4th December.

Reiner, R. (1992) *The Politics of the Police*, Hertfordshire: Harvester Wheatsheaf.

Reinhard, E. (1992) 'Street Crime Goes on Video', *The Times*, 6th November.

Rodwell, R. (1995) 'Sainsbury Sets Out Its Stall in Ulster', *The Times*, 21st June.

Rogers, P. (1994) 'Malls Make Merry in the Days Before Christmas', *Independent on Sunday*, 18th December.

Rosenbaum, D. (1988) 'A Critical Eye on Neighbourhood Watch; Does it Reduce Crime and Fear?', in Hope, T. and Shaw, M. (eds) *Communities and Crime Reduction*, London: HMSO, pp. 126–145.

Rudnick, D. (1993) 'Time to Lock Out the Cowboys', *The Times*, 20th January.

Seaton, M. (1995) 'Shop While You Bop', *The Sunday Times*, 14th May.

Securicor Security Services (1994) 'Evidence to the Home Affairs Committee', Sutton, Surrey: Securicor Group plc.

Shapland, J. and Vagg, J. (1988) *Policing by the Public*, London: Routledge.

Sharpe, S. (1989) *Electronically Recorded Evidence*, London: Fourmat Publishing.

Shearing, C. and Stenning, P. (1983) 'Private Security – Implications for Social Control', *Social Problems*, Vol. 30, No. 5, pp. 493–506.

Sheehy, Sir Patrick (1993) *Inquiry into Police Responsibilities and Rewards: Report*, London: HMSO, Cm. 2280.

Shields, R. (1992a) 'Spaces for the Subject of Consumption', in Shields, R. (ed) *Lifestyle Shopping: The Subject of Consumption*, London: Routledge, pp. 1–20.

Shields, R. (1992b) 'The Individual, Consumption Cultures and the Fate of the Community', in Shields, R. (ed) *Lifestyle Shopping: The Subject of Consumption*, London: Routledge, pp. 99–113.

Shopfront Security Group (1994) *Shopfront Security Campaign Report*, London: British Retail Consortium.

Shrimsley, R. and Darbyshire, N. (1993) 'Public Loses Confidence in Rule of Law', *The Daily Telegraph*, 30th August.

Skogan, W. (1984) *The Fear of Crime*, The Hague: Ministry of Justice, Research and Documentation Centre.

Skogan, W. and Maxfield, M. (1981) *Coping With Crime*, Beverly Hills, California: Sage.

Slapper, G. (1995) 'Handcuffs on the Arm of the Law', *The Times*, 4th April.

Slater, D. (1993) 'Going Shopping: Markets, Crowds and Consumption', in Jenks, C. (ed) *Cultural Reproduction*, London: Routledge, pp. 188–209.

Smith, A. (1994) 'Fibre Web', *Security Management Today*, Vol. 4, No. 5, pp. 27–28.

Smith, D. and Hamilton, K. (1994) 'On the Rack', *The Sunday Times*, 20th November.

South, N. (1988) *Policing for Profit*, London: Sage.

Speed, M., Burrows, J. and Bamfield, J. (1995) *Retail Crime Costs 1993/94 Survey: The Impact of Crime and the Retail Response*, London: British Retail Consortium.

Spillius, A. (1994) 'Invasion of the Category Killers', *The Observer*, 27th February.

Stansell, J. (1994) 'Keeping Watch on Illegal Nightlife', *The Sunday Times*, 30th October.

Sykes, J. (1979) 'Vandal-Resistant Equipment and Detail Design', in The Design Council (ed) *Designing Against Vandalism*, London: Heinemann, pp. 69–89.

Tendler, S. (1994a) 'Customers Pay the Price For Shops' £2bn Loss to Crime', *The Times*, 19th January.

Tendler, S. (1994b) 'Police Keep Helmet to Stand Out From the Crowd', *The Times*, 28th November.

Tendler, S. (1994c) 'Anti-IRA Tactics in City Cut Crime Rate', *The Times*, 4th April.

Tendler, S. (1995a) 'National CID Team Compiles Database', *The Times*, 13th July.

Tendler, S. (1995b) 'Impact of Street Patrols to be Studied', *The Times*, 6th February.

Tendler, S. (1995c) 'Police Fear Budget Cuts Will End Role of Bobby On Beat', *The Times*, 17th May.

Tendler, S. (1995d) 'Police Enrol a Canine Private Eye', *The Times*, 15th May.

Thomas, R. (1995) 'Shoppers Shun Cash For Cards', *The Guardian*, 12th April.

Thompson, H. (1995) 'How to Cope With an Armed Robbery', *The Times*, 25th January.

Tilley, N. (1993a) *Understanding Car Parks, Crime and CCTV: Evaluation Lessons From Safer Cities, Crime Prevention Unit Series Paper 42*, London: Home Office.

Tilley, N. (1993b) *The Prevention of Crime Against Small Businesses: The Safer Cities Experience, Crime Prevention Unit Series Paper 45*, London: Home Office.

Tilley, N. (1995) *Policing and Neighbourhood Watch: Strategic Issues, Crime Prevention Unit Series Paper 60*, London: Home Office.

Touche Ross (1989) *Survey into Retail Shrinkage and Other Stock Losses*, London: Touche Ross.

Touche Ross (1992) *Retail Shrinkage and Other Stock Losses: Results of the Second Retail Survey*, London: Touche Ross.

Toynbee, P. (1994) 'The Channels of Fear', *The Guardian*, 3rd June.

Travis, A. (1993) 'Dixons Chief Urges Official Role For High Street Vigilantes', *The Guardian*, 30th June.

Travis, A. (1994a) 'Thefts Cost Shops Quarter of Profits', *The Guardian*, 19th January.

Travis, A. (1994b) 'Public May Have to Pay for Former Police Services', *The Guardian*, 11th July.

Travis, A. (1994c) 'Letting Empty Flats Over Shops Would Cut Crime, Retailers Told', *The Guardian*, 26th January.

Travis, A. (1995a) 'Labour Survey Estimates Cost of Crime at £20.4 billion a Year', *The Guardian*, 21st February.

Travis, A. (1995b) 'Straw Takes On Addicts and Winos', *The Guardian*, 5th September.

Travis, A. (1995c) 'Ministers Plan Police Record Sales Agency', *The Guardian*, 16th February.

Utley, A. (1993) 'Who's Looking At You Kid?', *The Times Higher*, 30th April.

van Dijk, J. and Mayhew, P. (1993) *Criminal Victimisation in the Industrialised World: Key Findings of the 1989 and 1992 International Crime Surveys*, The Hague, Netherlands: Directorate for Crime Prevention, Ministry of Justice.

Verdict (1994) *Retailing 1998*, London: Verdict Research.

Victor, P. and Skipworth, M. (1993) 'Supermarkets Join Forces to Fight US Cost-Cutter', *The Sunday Times*, 1st August.

Vidal, J. (1994) 'Darkness on the Edge of Town', *The Guardian*, 17th March.

Vincent, T. (undated) 'On the Wagon: Alcohol and Crime Concerns in Our City Centres', Coventry: City Centre Development.

Walker, N. (1991) *Why Punish?*, Oxford: Oxford University Press.

Ward, C. (ed) (1973) *Vandalism*, London: Architectural Press.

Ward, D. (1995) 'Shops Back Plan For Centre to Get Beggars Off Streets', *The Guardian*, 25th February.

Warman, C. (1995) 'Liverpool Plan Awaits Its Fate', *The Times*, 15th February.

Warren, D. (1992) 'Where Shoppers Fear to Tread?', *Security Gazette*, February, pp. 26–27.

Watt, N. (1993) 'Big Brother's Video Cameras Cover Your Every Move', *The Times*, 8th March.

Wavell, S. (1995) 'A Tale of Two Cities', *The Sunday Times*, 11th June.

Webb, B., Brown, B. and Bennett, T. (1992) *Preventing Car Crime in Car Parks, Crime Prevention Unit Series Paper 34*, London: Home Office.

Webb, L. and Laycock, G. (1992) *Tackling Car Crime: The Nature and Extent of the Problem, Crime Prevention Unit Series Paper 32*, London: Home Office.

Weeks, J. (1994) 'A Message From ACPO's New President: We Must Prepare For Change', *Police*, November, p. 14.

West Midlands Police (1994) *Working Party Report: CCTV – Its Interface With the Police*, Birmingham: West Midlands Police, Community Services Department.

Whitaker, A. (1995) 'Protection From the Powerful Superlens', *The Times*, 27th June.

Williams, D., George, B. and MacLennan, E. (1984) *Guarding Against Low Pay, Low Pay Pamphlet No. 29*, London: Low Pay Unit.

Williams, P. and Dickinson, J. (1993) 'Fear of Crime: Read All About It?', *The British Journal of Criminology*, Vol. 33, No. 1, pp. 33–56.

Willis, A. (1992) *Crime Prevention in the Leicester City Challenge Area*, Leicester: University of Leicester, School of Social Work.

Willis, A. (1993) 'Are Retailers Selling Violence Short?', *Security Management Today*, Vol. 3, No, 1, pp. 34–36.

Willis, A. and Beck, A. (1994a) *Public Policing Versus Private Security in the Retail Sector: Memorandum of Evidence to the House of Commons Select Committee on Home Affairs*, Leicester: University of Leicester, Centre for the Study of Public Order.

Willis, A. and Beck, A. (1994b) 'An Analysis of Policing Charters With Special Reference to Risk and Security Management – A Research and Discussion Paper Prepared for the Risk and Security Management Forum', Leicester: University of Leicester, Centre for the Study of Public Order.

Wilson, S. (1979) 'Observations on the Nature of Vandalism', in The Design Council (ed) *Designing Against Vandalism*, London: Heinemann, pp. 19–29.

Wynn Davies, P. (1994) 'Howard Calls for Greater Emphasis on Victims' Needs', *The Independent*, 4th May.

Young, D. (1995) 'Halt, Who Goes There?', *The Times*, 25th January.

Young, J. (1994) 'Simple Formulas That Fail to Answer Genuine Concerns About Crime', *The Guardian*, 8th June.

Young, R. (1994a) 'Tesco Defends Out-of-Town Centres', *The Times*, 2nd November.

Young, R. (1994b) 'Stores Struggle to Stem Tide of Theft', *The Times*, 18th February.

Young, R. (1995) 'Supermarket Checkout Assistants Approach Their Sell-By Date', *The Times*, 6th February.

Zimring, F. and Hawkins, G. (1973) *Deterrence: The Legal Threat in Crime Control*, Chicago: University of Chicago Press.

Index

Crime at Work: *studies in security & crime prevention*

Topics covered include:

robbery, commercial burglary, ram raiding, shoplifting, insurance fraud, violence against staff, crime on industrial estates, cheating in hotel bars, terrorism and the retail sector, the effectiveness of electronic article surveillance, customer and staff perceptions of closed circuit television, security implementation in a computer environment, and the advantages of in-house to contract security staff.

Edited by Martin Gill

This groundbreaking book contains a wealth of information which will be essential reading for all those interested in crime prevention, security, the motivation of different types of offenders, and the effectiveness of various security measures. Each article covers the theme of crime prevention. Papers incorporate the views of offenders, victims, customers and staff.

Until now there has been very little consideration of the extent, impact and patterns of crimes that occur in the workplace. This important text suggests that such an omission is no longer justified. Produced in collaboration with business, the book reflects the growing realisation that effective responses to crime are based on the need to collect and share information.

Crime at Work: studies in security & crime prevention

"This book breaks new ground in many areas and contains a wealth of interesting facts and hard information."

£25.00
ISBN 1 899287 01 9
240 pages
(index included)

Commercial Crime International

1994

Issues in Maritime Crime: mayhem at sea

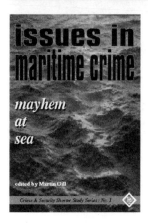

Crime and Security Shorter Studies Series: No. 1

Topics covered include:

fraud, piracy, arson, theft, deception, smuggling and drug trafficking. There is also a focus on containerisation, boat watch, insurance, registration and marking schemes, physical security measures and their potential to prevent offending.

Edited by Martin Gill

This path-finding book offers new insights into aspects of maritime crime and its prevention. Its coverage of both domestic and international issues will appeal to all those interested in crime prevention, security and maritime issues.

Articles have been written by internationally recognised experts on maritime crime. This includes the police, HM Customs and Excise, a private investigator, as well as independent specialists and academic researchers.

Papers refer to real cases offering a fascinating insight into the threat posed by crimes that occur at sea. The information in this text suggests that internationally and domestically the official response to maritime crime has too often been unimaginative, misdirected and partial and has sometimes worked against the interests of crime prevention.

Issues in Maritime Crime: mayhem at sea

**£12.95
ISBN 1 899287 02 7
80 pages
(index included)**

1995

"Any owner who is realistic enough to appreciate that crime is not merely something that happens to other people, would be well advised to study these papers."

Practical Boat Owner

Public Order Policing: *contemporary perspectives on strategy & tactics*

Crime and Security Shorter Studies Series: No. 2

Topics covered include:

theories of crowds, police policy and training practices, developments in strategy and tactics, the policing of political, industrial, festival and urban public order events, the future of policing in a 'post-modern' society.

Mike King and Nigel Brearley

This highly commended book highlights the major 'watersheds' in the policing of political, industrial, festival and urban disorders and contains a wealth of material from interviews with senior police officers. The book is written in a clear and concise style, incorporating an extremely informative glossary of terms. This work will be essential reading for both police practitioners and those studying or interested in the area of contemporary policing.

Public Order Policing: contemporary perspectives on strategy and tactics

"Mike King and Nigel Brearley are to be congratulated on this well documented and compelling analysis of the changing face of British public order policing. This timely and refreshingly accessible book ought to be essential reading for anyone seeking to understand the recent evolution of police crowd control methods, or eager to predict the future direction of police public order strategy and tactics."

£14.95
ISBN 1 899287 03 5
128 pages
(index included)

Dr David Waddington
Sheffield Hallam University

1995

International Journal of Risk, Security and Crime Prevention

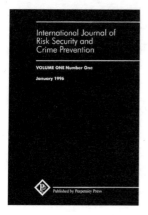

International Journal of
Risk Security and
Crime Prevention

VOLUME ONE Number One

January 1996

Published by Perpetuity Press

This journal facilitates the exchange of expertise and good practice which is essential to effective policy making. It is at the forefront in examining and developing policies and theories enabling readers to be up-to-date, to spot new opport-unities and make more informed decisions. Readers can learn from the findings and recom-mendations of independent research.

Articles already accepted for publication include: the triads and organised crime, regulation of the security industry, preventing arson in schools, the police response to commercial burglary, closed circuit television, computer crime, armed robbery, repeat victimisation and sexual harassment at work.

The Advisory Board

From January 1996
Annual Subscription
Rate (1996):
£130.00 (£145.00
Overseas)

Single issues £40.00
(£45.00 Overseas)
ISSN 1359-1886
280x210mm

Quarterly

The Editorial Advisory Board includes nominees from: the American Society for Industrial Security, the Association of British Insurers, the Association of Security Consultants, the British Bankers' Association, the British Retail Consortium, the British Security Industry Association, the Building Societies Association, the Health and Safety Executive, the Institute of Risk Management, the International Professional Security Association, the Loss Prevention Council, Victim Support and others.

International experts include Professor Joshua Bamfield, Professor John Benyon, John Burrows, Professor David Canter, Dr Marc Cools, Bruce George MP, Professor Mike Levi, Dr Rob Mawby, Professor Joanna Shapland, Professor Nick Tilley, Professor van Dijk and many others. The editors of the journal are Dr Martin Gill and Adrian Beck from the internationally renowned Centre for the Study of Public Order at Leicester University, UK.